WE SHALL NOT BE MOVED

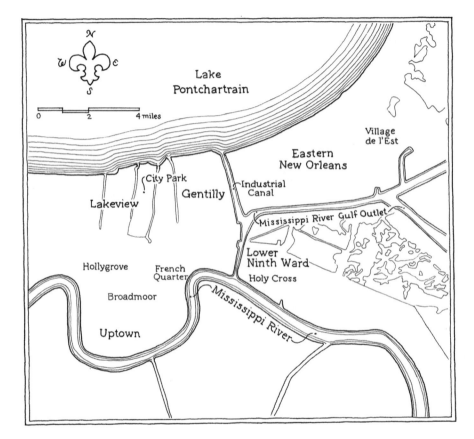

# We Shall Not Be Moved

Rebuilding Home in the Wake of Katrina

**TOM WOOTEN**

Beacon Press, Boston

Beacon Press
25 Beacon Street
Boston, Massachusetts 02108-2892
www.beacon.org

Beacon Press books
are published under the auspices of
the Unitarian Universalist Association of Congregations.

15  14  13  12    8  7  6  5  4  3  2  1

This book is printed on acid-free paper that meets the uncoated paper ANSI/
NISO specifications for permanence as revised in 1992.

Text design and composition by Wilsted & Taylor Publishing Services

"New Orleans Neighborhood Map" printed by permission of Jamie Devol.

Words and music to "Georgia & Blue" by Michael West and Sara Euliss.
Performed by Truckstop Honeymoon. Copyright © 2008 S. Euliss and M. West.
Printed with permission.

Library of Congress Cataloging-in-Publication Data
Wooten, Tom.
We shall not be moved : rebuilding home in the wake of Katrina / Tom Wooten.
    p. cm.
Includes bibliographical references.
ISBN 978-0-8070-4463-6 (alk. paper)
1. Community development—Louisiana—New Orleans. 2. Urban
renewal—Louisiana—New Orleans—Citizen participation. 3. Neighborhood
government—Louisiana—New Orleans. 4. Hurricane Katrina, 2005—
Social aspects. 5. New Orleans (La.)—Social conditions—21st century.
6. New Orleans (La.)—Economic conditions—21st century. I. Title.
HN80.N45W66 2012
307.140976335—dc23                                          2012001273

*To my team and family at Mc. 15*

# CONTENTS

PART III: A RINGING BELL

# FOREWORD

In the context of disasters, the word "recovery" takes on a dizzying array of meanings. It encompasses the physical reconstruction of the built environment. It is an emotional and psychological ordeal undertaken by each survivor. It also applies to institutions—businesses, schools, police and fire departments, houses of worship—that must reopen their doors, resuming and perhaps redefining their work. Recovery in the wake of a disaster means nothing less than the restoration of every aspect of life in the affected place. It presents a profound and deeply fascinating challenge.

*We Shall Not Be Moved* is a story of recovery in New Orleans, and as such, it is a story of neighborhoods. True to life, it tells a tale that is at once inspiring, quirky, and troubling. Inspiring, because the resident leaders it portrays have gone to unprecedented lengths to restore life to their city, and their triumphs speak volumes about the power of community solidarity. Quirky, because New Orleanians are people who throw birthday parties for potholes, celebrate roller-skating duck girls, and seek joy and beauty in all that is unconventional; a recovery led by New Orleanians must by nature be audacious and inventive. Troubling, because the rise of New Orleans neighborhoods has occurred against the backdrop of massive government failures, which no degree of community initiative can overcome.

My stake in this story is personal. I grew up in New Orleans, and like most New Orleanians, I love the city passionately. My childhood home is a raised West Indian cottage on Napoleon Avenue in Broadmoor, one of the neighborhoods profiled in this book. My brother still lives there. It has a wonderful porch shaded by live oak trees and a yard that played host to many a childhood adventure. Broadmoor was and still is a diverse neighborhood—an economic, racial, and cultural crossroads in the heart of the city. As we grew up, my brother and I had both white and black friends, and my parents set few bounds on where we could roam and ride our bikes.

The wider world's call drew me out of New Orleans, but my connection to the city remained strong. In the shock and heartbreak of

Katrina's aftermath, I was left deeply worried for the city's future. Some people in other parts of the country doubted that New Orleans would rebuild. I knew it would, but I wondered whether the spirit and soul of the place would reemerge. In a piece I wrote for *Time* the day after the levees broke, I recalled a collection of New Orleans memoirs by Lillian Hellman titled *Pentimento*. "Pentimento" refers to the texture of old brush strokes on a repainted canvas. The notion that a new image could simultaneously bear the imprint of its predecessor captures an essential aspect of life in New Orleans, where music, food, architecture, and culture have slowly evolved against a rich historical tapestry. A recovery that hurriedly replaced New Orleans' trademark shotgun houses with soulless tract housing, or neglected its vibrant residential neighborhoods to focus on tourism and the French Quarter, would sap the city's essential magic. "Saving New Orleans will require not merely re-creating the French Quarter," I wrote. "It will involve nurturing back to health the genuine and distinctive neighborhoods that serve as an incubator for the city's music and food and funkiness."

In September of 2005, I was offered the vice chairmanship of the newly created Louisiana Recovery Authority (LRA), a state board that would oversee the allocation of recovery funds and coordinate with local officials as rebuilding proceeded. I jumped at the opportunity. The post would let me contribute directly to my state's rebirth, and allow me a hand in rekindling life in New Orleans. I served on the LRA for three years. It was from this vantage point, as a New Orleanian who had played a role in the recovery, that I read with interest the book you now hold in your hands.

*We Shall Not Be Moved* offers a moving portrait of a city's struggle to rebuild. It is not an account of Katrina per se. Several books have already vividly captured the experience of the storm and the days and months thereafter, notably Chris Rose's *One Dead in Attic* and Dave Eggers's *Zeitoun*. Rather, it is a story of the arduous endeavor residents have undertaken in New Orleans since the news crews packed up and the nation's attention moved on. The stories it tells are every bit as gripping and important as tales from the storm itself.

I believe that these stories offer profoundly important insights for our still-young century, a century in which large disasters will remain a fact of life and cities will only continue to grow. New Orleans's neighborhoods show us the vast creative potential latent within urban communities. Under the right circumstances, residents can seize control of their collective destinies, envisioning bright futures for their neighborhoods and then delivering those neighborhoods from the depths of destruction and hopelessness. However, their stories also reveal the limits and pitfalls of a recovery in which, all too often, higher levels of government have left residents to fend for themselves.

The neighborhood mobilization this book narrates is part of a broad decentralizing trend sweeping New Orleans. It is a grand experiment in governance, informed by the decaying institutions that served New Orleans prior to Katrina and motivated by the tremendous destruction and opportunity the flood left in its wake. The city's schools are now almost entirely charters, operated by independent boards that the state holds accountable for their students' academic performance. The New Orleans healthcare system is being overhauled, its historical reliance on large hospitals shifting to a network of community clinics focused on preventive care. That the most successful recovering neighborhoods have become a "fourth tier" of government, below the city administration, is a particularly intriguing and important manifestation of this decentralizing trend.

The neighborhood-driven recovery under way in New Orleans underscores the importance of placing residents first when planning and carrying out the work of recovery or any sort of urban development. One cannot read *We Shall Not Be Moved* without being struck by the vision, optimism, and tenacity of the residents who have taken the lead in the city's neighborhoods. They know their communities better than any outside official or planner, and they have by far the most at stake in the outcome of the rebuilding. Their post-Katrina work confirms what many activists and urban scholars have long argued: that the best kinds of urban development are neighborhood-centric, empowering residents to guide changes to the places they live. Hal Roark, whose flooded house sat a few blocks from my childhood home, is on to something when he says, "We are the world's leading experts on Broadmoor."

New Orleans's neighborhood recovery efforts also offer a vital reminder of the difference between utopian dreaming and actionable planning. The stories Tom Wooten tells show that residents in the city's most successful rebuilding were not simply focused on *what* they wanted but on *how* they would turn their visions into reality. Residents in these neighborhoods have become tremendously savvy, crafting recovery plans that focus on implementation and then following through. In Broadmoor, residents secured a $2 million grant from the Carnegie Foundation to renovate their historical library; founded a school board that operates a 550-student charter school; oversaw a $30 million green renovation of the historical building the school now occupies; founded a successful community development corporation; approved annual parcel fees to fund the residents association; and more. In neighborhoods across the city, such accomplishments became possible through partnerships that residents formed with foundations, corporations, faith communities, and universities.

Post-Katrina New Orleans proves beyond a doubt that through purposeful organizing, planning, and partnering, communities can take charge of their destinies in the wake of disaster. San Francisco, which lives under the constant threat of a devastating earthquake, has taken note of the neighborhood-centric recovery under way in New Orleans. The mayor's office has founded a neighborhood empowerment network to engender the community solidarity and leadership the city will need after a quake. Moreover, as *We Shall Not Be Moved* makes clear, neighborhood-driven development shows tremendous potential outside the realm of disasters. Even as some New Orleans residents run out of recovery work to undertake, their initiative remains as strong as ever. In Hollygrove and Village de l'Est, they are mounting innovative urban agricultural programs. Broadmoor residents, whose mantra is "better than before," are developing an array of neighborhood day care, after-school, and tutoring initiatives to support their charter school. In the Lower Ninth Ward, though much recovery work remains to be done, residents are thinking beyond short-term reconstruction. They aim to bring their neighborhood back in the most energy-efficient and physically resilient way possible. These are powerful examples not only for the survivors of future disasters, but for urban residents everywhere, especially in blighted rust-belt cities like St. Louis and Detroit.

Uplifting stories of community-driven recovery in New Orleans come with an asterisk. For all of the hope present in these pages, for all the promise that neighborhood recovery efforts hold, *We Shall Not Be Moved* remains a collection of cautionary tales. Neighborhood mobilization in New Orleans has taken place against the backdrop of profound government failures. After the faulty federal levees gave way, residents were forced to mobilize because they perceived government institutions to be absent and incompetent. The first of many citywide recovery plans left residents of flooded neighborhoods terrified that their houses would be bulldozed. As the city rebuilt, the allocation and dispersal of recovery funds proceeded painfully slowly. Neighborhood leaders faced mountains of red tape at every turn.

Wooten highlights the toll that these failures took on the leaders and communities he profiles. For the recovery leaders, "going it alone" meant tremendous frustration, burnout, and even premature death. For the neighborhoods, it meant the stagnation of individual rebuilding and community development projects that should have been moving full speed ahead. It is tantalizing to think how much these community efforts could have accomplished with the consistent, willing, and competent partnership of the agencies tasked with rebuilding the city. Neighborhood-driven efforts should exist in partnership with government, not in place of government.

*We Shall Not Be Moved* offers a number of lessons for the coming years, but its greatest contribution lies in the gripping nature of the stories it tells. Wooten has crafted a work of narrative nonfiction, rather than taking an academic approach. This was the right choice. The people driving the city's recovery are New Orleans characters whose stories beg to be told and celebrated. Their accomplishments and courage are every bit as worthy of written commemoration as Dr. John's or Tuti Montana's.

For me, seventy-eight-year-old Phil Harris is the book's defining character. Beginning in November of 2005, Phil hitchhiked daily from an Uptown apartment to his flooded Hollygrove home to gut and repair the property—the very same home in which his wife had been born nearly eight decades before. Through his steady, unfailing effort, Phil embodied the humble determination and resilience that has brought New Orleans back to life. "It was heartbreaking," Phil said of the work, "but we couldn't give up. I just said, 'Well, I've got to get in and do it.'"

Walter Isaacson
Washington, DC
September 15, 2011

## PREFACE

In February 2007, one and a half years after Katrina, much of New Orleans remained pitch black at night. The darkness was striking as I drove into the city for the first time. Like tens of thousands of other college students, I had come to the Gulf Coast as a volunteer. After a long day of gutting houses in Gulfport, Mississippi, I sat crammed in the back of a fifteen-passenger van, itching at the tiny shards of fiberglass insulation embedded in my leg and squinting through the tinted glass. As we sped down Interstate 10 through New Orleans East, we could just make out the ruins: the skeleton of an abandoned amusement park, the darkened hulks of vacant shopping malls, mile after mile of empty houses.

Crossing the Industrial Canal, I-10 climbs high enough to afford views of the entire twenty-mile length of New Orleans. Apart from the illuminated skyline and the lights of a few neighborhoods near the Mississippi River that escaped flooding, we beheld an unfathomably vast black void where the thriving city had once stood. Our destination that night was a work camp downriver in devastated St. Bernard Parish. ("Parish" means "county" in Louisiana parlance.) We arrived to find our hosts set up in an abandoned subdivision, sleeping in the gutted remains of a small apartment complex that still reeked of mold. A bonfire in the driveway shot green flames into the air, eating its way through a stack of pressure-treated wood.

Throughout my time in college—which at that point was nearing its end—I had nursed an interest in disasters and disaster recovery. On a whim during my freshman year, I agreed to help my roommate investigate a massive but poorly documented dam collapse in western India, which had wiped out his mother's city and killed thousands of people in 1979. Our field research left us shocked at the government's heavy-handedness; it had covered up the causes of the dam's failure and rebuilt the city on its own terms. Reconstruction proceeded quickly as a result of the government's involvement, but residents were left feeling bitter and disempowered. I wondered what a grassroots recovery would look like—one in which decisions about how to rebuild lay in the hands of survivors.

New Orleans offered an opportunity to explore my question. Returning to books and classes after my week on the Gulf Coast, I devoured information about the city's recovery. By most accounts, the neighborhood mobilization under way in New Orleans was unlike anything else a modern American city had seen. Government funding for reconstruction was inadequate and mired in red tape, three citywide recovery-planning efforts had sputtered and died, and decision-making power had largely devolved to the level of neighborhood groups. Acting out of necessity, neighborhoods were operating social service agencies; founding community development corporations to build and renovate houses; opening charter schools; fielding police forces; launching marketing campaigns to spur recovery; debating taxation initiatives; and more. In short, they were taking on tasks that were normally the domain of established nonprofits and city government. I was determined to see all of this for myself.

New Orleans draws people in as few places can, and after my return, I fell head over heels in love with the city. I spent the summer of 2007 interviewing neighborhood recovery leaders for my senior thesis in Harvard's undergraduate Social Studies program. I returned for the 2008–09 school year on a fellowship from Harvard's John F. Kennedy School of Government, tasked with expanding my research about neighborhood-based recovery efforts into a book. I spent the year crisscrossing the city's potholed streets on my bicycle—volunteering, attending neighborhood meetings, and collecting stories. Every conversation was captivating. The recovery took survivors on an emotional roller coaster, from the depths of frustration and anger to highs of visionary optimism. They took me with them through their stories. The hundreds of residents with whom I spoke were unfailingly friendly, open, and frank.

I undertook my research as an outsider in a city that highly values racial and geographic legitimacy. I am white and grew up in an affluent Boston suburb, yet I set out to write a book about five neighborhoods in New Orleans, three of which had majority black populations and one of which had a predominant Vietnamese American presence. In social research, a fine line separates collaboration and exploitation. The stories that residents shared with me in voluntary, uncompensated interviews were valuable; handled improperly, my work could be tantamount to intellectual theft—a form of twenty-first-century carpetbagging.

I combated this possibility as best I could by integrating myself into the city. I lived in Broadmoor and worked for the neighborhood association, recruiting volunteers and developing websites. In my interviews, I was straightforward about who I was, where I was from, and what I was doing. I came to count many of this book's characters among my friends and mentors. Done well, I believed that my writing could at least indirectly contribute to the city's recovery, shedding light on the tremendous work residents were undertaking. I loved to write, and I was blessed with the time and funding required to collect and compile stories from across the city—a luxury that most residents unfortunately lacked. When my year of research drew to a close, I stayed put. New Orleans had become home.

Almost five years after my first visit to the city, I have a personal investment in its recovery. I taught writing at a small public charter school in the French Quarter, learning to see the city through the eyes of my fifth- and sixth-grade students. Slowly but surely, I felt the city come back to life, noticing small improvements with every passing week. This rebirth would not have been possible without the vision, grit, and courage of the residents and neighborhood leaders who drove the recovery forward. I am grateful to them for rebuilding New Orleans, and grateful too that so many generously shared the stories and wisdom contained in these pages.

In this book, I narrate recovery efforts in the neighborhoods of Broadmoor, Hollygrove, Lakeview, the Lower Ninth Ward, and Village de l'Est. I tell these stories from residents' perspectives, using their words whenever possible, in order to capture the experience of organizing and rebuilding after the levee failures. I break the book into three parts. Part I introduces each neighborhood through the story of a resident's preparations for the oncoming hurricane. Part II follows each neighborhood's planning and organizing during the first year after the storm. Finally, Part III narrates how these recovery efforts have played out in the years since. Presenting neighborhood recovery narratives in parallel allowed me to highlight telling similarities and contrasts among residents' experiences. Why did Terry Miranda evacuate while Phil Harris elected to remain in his home? How did Village de l'Est residents manage to organize themselves months before Broadmoor residents held their first meeting? I state some lessons explicitly, using residents' voices in chapter 16 and my own voice in chapter 10 and in the epilogue. However, I generally believe narrative to be more engaging and more revealing than exposition, and have proceeded with that in mind. First and foremost, this book is a collection of stories.

# PART I

# A City and a Storm

CHAPTER 1

## "Very Much at Home"

IT WAS LATE AFTERNOON on Sunday, August 29, 2005. Terry Miranda, a white man in his late fifties, craned his neck to peer out the rear windshield as the storm that had sent his city into exile churned on the horizon over the Gulf of Mexico. The storm's first fast-moving outer bands had already set upon the westbound traffic that inched forward on Interstate 10, turning the sky above the cars every hue of gray. Leveling his gaze to the horizon, back toward his home, Terry was struck to see that the distant sky was nearly black.

Katrina was casting a dark, slowly advancing shadow across the earth. Bolts of lightning—far too distant to be accompanied by claps of thunder—leapt through the darkness to the ground. The storm posed the cars on this stretch of highway no serious danger. It would be hours before the worst of its winds and waves would surge ashore, and the traffic was already well to the west of the area forecast to bear the brunt of the damage. Still, a shudder ran through Terry's spine as he turned his attention away from the dark sky.

Beside him, Terry's sister sat at the wheel, clutching it tightly and keeping her eyes fixed on the taillights ahead. The faces Terry beheld in the myriad car windows around them were etched with tension. In his nearly six decades of life in New Orleans, Terry had seen his share of hurricanes, but no other storm had spooked his city this way. At 9:30 a.m., Mayor Ray Nagin had ordered the first mandatory evacuation in New Orleans history.[1] Shortly thereafter, the normally stoic National Weather Service released an uncharacteristically desperate bulletin, warning of "devastating damage" that would leave "at least one half of well-constructed homes" destroyed. Those lucky enough to survive, it warned, would experience "human suffering incredible by modern standards" in its aftermath.[2]

Before the mandatory call to evacuate that Sunday morning, Terry was not sure he was going to leave. For one thing, he had weathered a number of hurricanes at home and was no worse for wear. For another, he did not own a car, never having lived outside of Orleans Parish. He walked to the nearby shops in his neighborhood, a predominantly white and upper-middle-class area of the city known as Lakeview, and until his retirement several years before, he had ridden his bicycle to and from his job investigating cases of fraud at a state food stamp office.

Like all state employees, Terry was pressed into service from time to time as a worker for the Red Cross. Because of his Red Cross experience, Terry would later explain, "When the mayor declared a mandatory evacuation, I knew what a desperate move that was." He did not object when his sister insisted on picking him up.

Terry hoped he would not be away long; he had never moved from New Orleans because he loved the city. Of course, New Orleans contained his entire life: his family, his friends, his house, his possessions, and his memories. But Terry was also in love with the idea of New Orleans; he was a true student of the city. He knew all of its neighborhoods after years of traversing the city by bicycle, and he lapped up its history through books, visits to historical societies, and conversations with old friends on the street. After retiring from the food stamp office, he made several abortive attempts to begin a bicycle tour company, but Terry's entrepreneurial drive did not match his enthusiasm for "narrating New Orleans" to anyone who would listen. More often than not, he gave his tours for free.

"You either get it or you don't, New Orleans," he would tell visitors to the city. "We're backwards. We're not progressive. Some people like that, and some people don't." He would draw visitors' attention back to the Catholic roots of the city's French and Spanish founders. "New Orleans has a different relationship to guilt than this whole country," he would explain. "We weren't founded by the Pilgrims. We expected to live good lives. Eat good food. Drink good, live good—as a part of our lives. We didn't think that was guilty."

By this point in his narration, he often had a twinkle in his eye. New Orleans was a true port city, he would say, a place where races, religions, cuisines, styles of music, and people of every stripe rubbed shoulders and mixed together, effortlessly crumbling barriers that held them steadfastly apart in other areas of the country. The city attracted "peculiar people of all different kinds" and embraced them, their presence often becoming a source of citywide pride. The freewheeling, intermingling, live-and-let-live New Orleans culture, he would point out, had led to one of the city's many miracles. Near the beginning of the twentieth century, in a heady "critical mass" of musical funeral celebrations and traveling vaudeville shows and brothels, New Orleans had given birth to jazz, "this beautiful music that changed the world."

In some respects, Terry was an unlikely champion of his city. His own neighborhood, Lakeview, was not diverse, and in general, its residents strove for suburban bliss rather than the bounteous pandemonium whose virtues Terry extolled. In a city full of overflowing families, Terry never married, and lived alone. In a city steeped in spirituality and saturated with houses of worship, Terry did not attend church. And in a city where work was at best of secondary importance, Terry funneled nearly all of what he described as his "lifelong hyperactivity" into hard work, whether at the food stamp office or doing cleanup and landscaping throughout his neighborhood. Indeed, he acknowledged that his affinity for New Orleans may well have been an accident of birth. "It's all I know," he would tell visitors. The city has "a lot to love and a lot to hate, and I just got used to it. It's like no other city in the world."

Terry thrived in New Orleans, and he was far from solitary. His four siblings also lived in the city, and they would all frequently converge at their mother's house in the Irish Channel for a meal or a relaxing afternoon together. Terry's neighborhood, Lakeview, also embraced him. Many in the community came to know him through his work for the Lakeview Civic Improvement Association—work that won him widespread affection, gratitude, and respect. "I was kind of their manual labor. I didn't want to be on any boards," he said. He spent countless hours cleaning the neighborhood's wide "neutral grounds"—narrow strips of parkland separating opposing traffic on major roads. He would wake up before dawn to set up tents for the annual Lakeview Fest, staying up to strike the tents the same night. He usually begged out of attending the Lakeview Civic Improvement Association's community meetings, with the exception of one the year before at which he had been presented with the association's citizenship award.

The award meant a great deal to Terry, whose affinity for Lakeview and its residents was every bit as strong as his love of the rest of the city. He liked and admired his neighbors, many of them white-collar, well-educated professionals. "Lakeview has easily some of the most talented people in the city of New Orleans," he said. "A lot of doctors, a lot of lawyers, a lot of engineers—smart people, great people. I have absolute faith in those people."

Lakeview encompassed a large area, with approximately 7,000

homes and 17,000 residents, but it was a cohesive community in spite of its size. Much of the neighborhood consisted of 1950s housing, bungalows built on recently drained swampland. Young families purchased new homes under the GI Bill and never left. Decades later, many children who had grown up in Lakeview during the neighborhood's first boom bought houses down the street from their parents and began families of their own. As the years went on, many in the neighborhood would come to marvel at the strength of their community, likening it to Mayberry, the fictional idyllic town in *The Andy Griffith Show*. "People *settled* in Lakeview," Terry said.

The neighborhood's geographic isolation helped it maintain its community cohesion; it was bounded to the south by expansive cemeteries, to the north by Lake Pontchartrain, to the east by a canal and City Park, and to the west by a canal and the Orleans Parish line. It was an island, cordoned off from the outside world. These confines allowed Lakeview's residents to nurture a suburban utopia inside of—and yet apart from—the city of New Orleans.

Community meetings in Lakeview were serious business. The Lakeview Civic Improvement Association—"LCIA," as everyone called it—was the oldest incorporated civic group in Louisiana. Over the years it had come to serve as the neighborhood's de facto government, tasked with helping Lakeview's residents maintain their suburban standard of living in a poor, corrupt, crime-ridden city. Lakeview constituted a substantial portion of the city's residential tax base, and residents were perpetually frustrated that their tax dollars never returned to the neighborhood in the form of adequate city services. Though the neighborhood's houses were well kept and its lawns immaculately manicured, its streets were pothole-ridden, its sidewalks were cracked, and its sewer system was in perpetual disrepair. Most of its children attended parochial schools, as residents tended to distrust the city's public school system. Historically, many had also complained about inadequate police protection.

Residents' frustration came to a head in early 1980s, when the LCIA mounted a push for Lakeview to secede from Orleans Parish and form its own city. The proposal made some progress in the state legislature, but ultimately proved futile when the City of New Orleans, reluctant to let one of its cash cows slip away, refused to sign off on the deal. Instead, Lakeview became the first neighborhood in the state to form its own special tax district. From then on, Lakeview residents paid additional property taxes to support the neighborhood's own police force. Officers were members of the New Orleans Police Department, but patrolled only Lakeview, using equipment and squad cars the neighborhood had purchased.

Now, as Terry sat next to his sister, lulled by the stop-and-go of the traffic on Interstate 10, the thought of Lakeview's special police force gave him comfort. There had been speculation about looting, but the looters would not come to Lakeview, and they would be caught if they did. His house was safe.

☙ ☙ ☙

Four children made their way playfully down Louisiana Avenue Parkway in the Broadmoor neighborhood, skipping and wandering, laughing and tussling under the street's majestic canopy of trees. They were a familiar and usually welcome sight to LaToya Cantrell, but today, their unaccompanied presence made her nervous. LaToya, a black woman in her early thirties with a confident, no-nonsense demeanor, managed a New Orleans educational foundation. Though she did not yet have children of her own, kids were among the foremost beneficiaries of her seemingly boundless energy.

"Y'all know there's a storm comin'," LaToya said as she approached them. This was not a question so much as a statement, delivered in a manner at once stern and reassuring. LaToya could command the full attention of a large, crowded, and angry room at even the most contentious city meetings. It was little surprise that the four pairs of feet came to a halt, the four mouths sealed, and the four sets of eyes looked up at her expectantly. "You all need to go home to your parents. They're telling everyone to leave the city." The four heads nodded, and the children quietly dispersed.

LaToya and her husband, Jason, were almost ready to go. Their preparation had begun the day before, when Jason convinced LaToya to cancel her appearance at a luncheon in her honor at a downtown restaurant. If Katrina sped up, he argued, they would not have much time to leave. They followed a familiar routine that afternoon: packing three changes of clothes, moving valuables to the second floor, assembling important documents to take with them. Their preparation, like that of many families across the city, toed a fine line between the necessary and the obsessive. LaToya laughed when her husband fueled not only their car for the trip, but also the car that would stay parked in their driveway.

For her part, LaToya went to the grocery store to buy food, bottled water, and last-minute extras for the long drive to Houston. A few shoppers entering the store with LaToya were surprised; even that Saturday afternoon, many still did not know of the storm's projected course. "What's going on?" a woman asked, beholding the hordes of grim-faced shoppers and long checkout lines as she entered the store.

Apart from the lines at gas pumps and supermarket checkout counters, the city was quiet. People had canceled weekend plans and stayed in to pack and watch the latest weather updates. Driving back into Broadmoor, LaToya saw few other cars on the road. Among her other jobs and commitments, LaToya had been president of the Broadmoor Improvement Association for a little more than a year, and she hoped quietly to herself that all of the neighborhood's residents had rides out of the city and good places to stay. Surely there were Broadmoor residents who did not, but finding them and helping them at this point would be difficult.

Broadmoor, a triangular neighborhood of seven thousand residents located in a shallow bowl in the center of New Orleans, sat at a literal and figurative crossroads in the city. Three main streets trisected it—Napoleon Avenue, Fontainebleau Drive, and South Broad Street—coming together in the center of the neighborhood. Like many of the city's residential areas, Broadmoor played host to diverse architectural styles, many of them indigenous to New Orleans. The neighborhood had hundreds of "double shotgun" houses—long buildings with two narrow, side-by-side apartments. To the neighborhood's north, these double shotguns slowly gave way to light industry, the interstate, and the expansive Orleans Parish Prison. To the south and west, Broadmoor abutted the old, gentrified Uptown neighborhoods surrounding Tulane University and Audubon Park. To the east, Broadmoor bordered the troubled Hoffman Triangle neighborhood, which had stagnated for decades under disinvestment and had been torn apart in more recent memory by drug-fueled violence.

As a result of its position, Broadmoor's demographics closely mirrored those of Orleans Parish as a whole. Napoleon Avenue, which formed the neighborhood's north–south spine, was lined with large stately homes with high wraparound porches, their yards and swimming pools shaded by tall trees. A block off Napoleon to the east, the houses grew smaller and more dilapidated, many containing two or even four cramped rental units. Families in these predominantly African American blocks struggled. Grandmothers supported children and grandchildren on their meager Social Security checks, having learned the city and its ways well enough to stretch the cash through each month. Often, families owned their houses outright but had very little else. It was a different story a block to the west of Napoleon. Again, the houses grew smaller, but many were garnished with fresh coats of paint and expensive landscaping. This area of Broadmoor was growing increasingly white and well to do, as young professionals and families moved to the neighborhood in a wave of gentrification emanating east from Uptown.

LaToya had lived in Broadmoor since 2000, and she could move with ease through both of the neighborhood's worlds. During the day, she would banter with wizened, toothless old-timers sitting in rocking chairs in the shade of their ramshackle front porches. At night, she might drop in on a house party a few blocks away for high-minded conversation, champagne, and hors d'oeuvres. Between LaToya's job as manager of a New Orleans educational endowment and her husband's white-collar income, the pair could have fully embraced the world of cocktail parties. She chose instead to move onto Louisiana Avenue Parkway, one of the areas of Broadmoor "where the needs were the greatest." She knew what she was signing up for: "Blight, slumlords, drug trafficking, speeding traffic. Just your normal social problems," she recalled. She wanted to help her area of Broadmoor turn around. With families buying houses and property values creeping up in even the poorest areas of Broadmoor, she sensed that there was already movement afloat.

Soon after moving into her white, two-story house on Louisiana Avenue Parkway, LaToya began to organize her neighbors. "All these things started picking up," she explained. "We started cracking down on spotty drug dealers, got stop signs put up where we needed to calm down traffic. We did beautification projects on the parkway. We started getting our trees maintained." LaToya founded the Louisiana Avenue Parkway Association in 2003. As its projects became more ambitious, the group began to revive a sense of community along the street. It spearheaded a Saturday "spring cleaning" event, for which families were encouraged to clean out their basements, closets, and garages. "It was like a big rummage sale on the street," LaToya remembered of the surprisingly festive event. "It was amazing."

The new Louisiana Avenue Parkway Association had set up shop on ground traditionally served by the larger Broadmoor Improvement Association (BIA), which had existed in one form or another since 1930. For the first two years in which LaToya ran the Louisiana Avenue Parkway Association, though, she did not have much contact with the BIA. "They were doing their own thing," she later explained, "which wasn't too much."

Then, the longtime Broadmoor Improvement Association treasurer showed up at her cleanup event. He had not previously met LaToya, but was immediately impressed with both the event and its organizer. The enthusiasm and participation her cleanup generated surprised him. Soon thereafter, the BIA board members asked LaToya to join their ranks. Though LaToya's own organization had already found its legs, she accepted their offer. "It was an opportunity to bridge the gap" between the two associations, she said, to "make sure that there were no different factions" in Broadmoor.

Within a year, she was elected president of the Broadmoor Improvement Association for a term that began in 2005. Her Louisiana Avenue Parkway group continued less formally under new leadership, but LaToya had found her venue. "In order for that area where the needs are the greatest to be cared about," she decided, "it needs to be an issue for the entire community." Organizing a street would not cut it; she needed to organize the whole neighborhood in order to begin to tackle the problems facing Broadmoor's poorest residents.

Now, as she and her husband drove out of the fast-emptying neighborhood and headed off toward family in Houston, LaToya thought with anticipation of all the work that remained unfinished. She had been at it for less than a year, and she was just beginning to scratch the surface, but she was determined.

⚜   ⚜   ⚜

Phil Harris, a black, seventy-eight-year-old man with a gravely voice and a slight paunch, had deep roots in Hollygrove. He and his wife had both been born in the neighborhood at the beginning of the Great Depression. He would often remember with a smile the way the two of them, along with a whole pack of other Hollygrove children, were "all raised up together." Phil and his wife had belonged to the same neighborhood church, St. Peter African Methodist Episcopal, for nearly eight decades.

During his many working years, from the time he joined a segregated Navy in 1945 through his retirement in 1990 from his job as the first black supervisor for Shell Oil, Phil lived and thrived on a few hard-and-fast principles: work hard, respect everyone around you, spend the money you earn wisely, and protect the things that you own. As he looked out the front window of his small home on Olive Street—the house where his wife was born—all Phil could think about was protecting it. "You worked hard for it, and you want to preserve it, keep it in the family," he said.

Over the course of the morning, up and down the street, many of his neighbors piled into their cars and headed out of town. His children pleaded with him to leave, but Phil had stayed in New Orleans for a lot of hurricanes, and this time was not going to be any different. The city had dodged the bullet a number of times. "Usually," he explained, an approaching storm "goes to the mouth of the river and then goes the other way." If the storm did come overhead, Phil reasoned, he would be home to patch leaks and keep his house shipshape.

Furthermore, Phil was keenly aware that the Hollygrove of his memory no longer existed. When he and his wife had raised their children, the area had been full of young, blue-collar African American families. Most of the neighborhood's breadwinners did not have college educations, but New Orleans had plenty of high-wage jobs for able-bodied workers. Its port was booming, and with time, the city became awash in cash from the offshore oil industry. Those were good years in Hollygrove. "Oh, this was a fine neighborhood" Phil recalled with a smile. "It was a lot of fun back here."

Bounded by the parish line and a trio of busy roads—Claiborne Avenue to the south, Airline Highway to the north, and Carrollton Avenue to the east—Hollygrove used to have a safe, self-contained feel. Neighborhood kids roamed about under the watchful eyes of adults, who rarely hesitated to spank youngsters and walk them home (usually to another spanking) if they made trouble. Feelings of trust and familiarity pervaded the neighborhood. "We knew one another; it was like a big family," Phil remembered. "You could leave your house open and go off."

Leaving his house now, even with a locked door, had become a less palatable option over the years. New Orleans had seen its economy and its population decline. White flight from Orleans Parish picked up speed, public schools became starved for funds, infrastructure began to deteriorate, and property values flatlined. As went New Orleans, so went Hollygrove. Its once-cheery streets turned slowly drab. Aging residents shook their heads as they watched paint peel, empty houses grow derelict, and litter accumulate. The young people they encountered seemed to lack direction. There seemed to be no bright future to motivate them.

The crack epidemic had certainly done the neighborhood no favors. As drug use proliferated, corner stores and abandoned buildings became havens for dealing—often to white suburban users who drove into Hollygrove from neighboring Jefferson Parish. Dealers marked their territory with old pairs of sneakers, which they would tie together and toss over telephone lines. Residents complained, but the New Orleans Police Department took little action. As their neighborhood deteriorated before them, old-timers in Hollygrove grew used to sudden, senseless bouts of destruction. Shootings became commonplace, as did house fires. In one instance, a squatter in an abandoned house accidentally set it ablaze while trying to stay warm; in another, a mishap in a meth lab ignited a fire so intense that it jumped a street and incinerated a house on the neighboring block.

On this day, Phil was not worried about fires so much as looting. He did not trust the people who would remain behind in Hollygrove. "A lot of these crooks or these people just wait for a storm to come," he explained. Better for him to stay at home on Olive Street and keep an eye on everything. His wife and grown son, realizing that nothing would convince Phil to leave, decided to remain with him.

⚜   ⚜   ⚜

Pam Dashiell, a black woman in her fifties with short hair and sharp eyes, sat in the Lower Ninth Ward house she rented at the corner of Dauphine and Tupelo streets, taking in the beautiful Saturday morning. She felt thoroughly at home in New Orleans, a city that had drawn her in ever since her childhood days in Boston. According to family lore, her great-grandmother was the daughter of an enslaved black man and a Native American woman. She worked as a nanny for a rich white New Orleans family during the Civil War. "My grandmother would tell stories all day and all night about her mother's adventures here in New Orleans," Pam said. "It really got to me. Everything I could read about New Orleans, I did. And any movie that had New Orleans in it, that's what I was going to see."

As light streamed in through the windows, Pam marveled to herself at yet another idyllic weekend day. Life in the Lower Ninth felt worlds apart from Boston; indeed, it even felt removed from life in the rest of New Orleans. Many who lived in the neighborhood described it to outsiders as being "like the country."

This assertion would strike an Iowa farmer as laughable, but in New Orleans, the distinction made sense. Though the Lower Ninth was as densely populated as most other parts of New Orleans, it lay downriver from the rest of the city, cut off by a waterway known officially as the Inter-Harbor Navigational Canal and informally as the Industrial Canal. It was a world unto itself. Few in the rest of New Orleans crossed into the Lower Ninth Ward with any regularity, and many Lower Ninth residents returned the favor, eating, sleeping, working, and attending school on their side of the canal.

Pam loved the way the Lower Ninth Ward felt self-contained; it retained and attracted particular kinds of people, who were "drawn by the way this place is." The people, in turn, made the place. Ms. Leblanc, an elderly lady who had lived in her house on Tennessee Street for nearly forty years, sat on her porch every morning, telling her neighbors about the newspaper stories she was reading. Steve, a janitor who had grown up in the neighborhood, recounted childhood memories of catching snakes and fishing in the bayou down the street from his house. Ms. Johnson, who lived with her grandchildren in an airy clapboard house on Jourdan Avenue, raised chickens. She was not alone; roosters throughout the Lower Ninth began to crow every morning shortly before dawn.

As Pam walked out the door for Saturday errands, she hoped that the hurricane churning out in the gulf would get her a long weekend. Pam was a subcontractor for Shell Oil, which maintained an extensive array of oil rigs off the Louisiana shore. Twice before that year, threatening hurricanes had forced Shell to shut down production in the gulf and evacuate its offshore workers. As of Friday, though, chatter at the company suggested that this hurricane was not a significant threat. With luck, Pam thought, she might get Monday off from work, but that would be it.

As she rounded a block, Pam looked out at a smattering of derelict houses. Like anyone who lived in the Lower Ninth Ward, she knew that her neighborhood had its problems. On her first visit to the Lower Ninth, during the mid-1980s, she stopped her car to read directions and was approached by four separate drug dealers peddling their wares. Her friend, who lived near the Mississippi levee, told stories of groups of men driving up to the levee at night to quietly dispose of bodies in the river. Some of the neighborhood's pettier criminals were revered. "This was the capital of dogfighting," Pam recalled, "and the cockfighting king of New Orleans lived on Deslonde Street."

The Lower Ninth Ward had another problem: it consisted of two distinct neighborhoods whose residents did not always see eye to eye. A busy commercial thoroughfare called St. Claude Avenue divided the neighborhood of Holy Cross from the neighborhood known, confusingly, as the Lower Ninth Ward. (This distinction worked much the same way as the nomenclature separating New York City's Queens and Brooklyn from the area called "Long Island," even though the two boroughs are on Long Island.) Holy Cross was located south of St. Claude Avenue; it had historical architecture, a large private high school, and a visible, offbeat white minority. The Lower Ninth Ward, north of St. Claude, had newer houses, lower land, and an almost entirely black population. Some did not buy into the distinction between the two neighborhoods, but it was quite real for others. As one resident recalled: "[My mother] would send me to the store, and she would say, . . . 'Don't cross St. Claude.' And I couldn't never understand that until I was older. It was a line that separated the communities."

Problems aside, Holy Cross had been an ideal place for Pam to raise her daughter. A single mother, Pam had moved around the country when her daughter was young. The two lived in Denver, Philadelphia, Tulsa, and in the Marigny neighborhood of New Orleans, but none had been as good a fit as Holy Cross. There, Pam found a community of single parents with children her daughter's age. As Pam later explained, "[We] shared the work and raised our kids together."

Pam also found a group of people, white and black, who were concerned about the community's future. The Holy Cross Neighborhood Association (HCNA) was a small but active group of residents, and Pam became involved with its work soon after moving to the neighborhood. HCNA meetings had their fair share of petty squabbles, with the organization moderating disputes between residents over zoning compliance or garbage removal. But the association also had a more serious task: protecting the neighborhood from a proposed expansion of a lock along the Industrial Canal.

When the U.S. Army Corps of Engineers first proposed an expansion of the lock during the 1980s, the plan called for the demolition of roughly two hundred homes in the Lower Ninth Ward to make room for the new structure. HCNA rose up in arms. Along with members of the Association of Community Organizations for Reform Now (ACORN)—the iconic community organizing group that had a strong presence in the Lower Ninth Ward—HCNA managed to delay the project. The fight was still hot when Pam moved to the neighborhood in 1989, and soon thereafter, she threw herself headfirst into the struggle.[3]

Community work was in Pam's blood. She grew up in Boston's Roxbury neighborhood, home to some of the nation's most egregious cases of disinvestment and misguided urban renewal, but also to some of its most promising nascent community organizing movements. In her twenties, Pam was hired as a youth worker in the nearby Bromley-Heath projects. In one of the first instances of resident management in the country, residents of Bromley-Heath wrested control of the apartments away from the Boston Housing Authority, which had mismanaged and neglected the projects.

"It was stimulating," Pam remembered, because "there was a real push to get community control and to determine [the community's] own destiny." Pam's heart was in the fight; cousins and friends of hers lived in the projects. She watched conditions at the apartment complex improve, and was amazed at how much Bromley-Heath's residents, once organized, were able to accomplish. The tenants association not only maintained the buildings and the grounds, but it also provided extensive community programming, maintained its own security service, and ran a radio station. To Pam, it was a shining example of the potential of organized communities.

So far, Pam's own organized community had managed to keep the Corps of Engineers at bay. Pam was now president of the Holy Cross Neighborhood Association, and kept her finger to the wind with regard to the lock expansion. Though there were frequent rumblings, the project had not gone ahead. Lower Ninth residents would stay on guard and hope that their luck held. For now, there was a more immediate concern.

The day's tasks had kept Pam away from the TV, but it sounded like people in the city were beginning to take the hurricane seriously. Many were planning to evacuate, and Pam was beginning to think that she would too. A worried phone call from her daughter—who never left for hurricanes—sealed the deal. Saturday evening, Pam packed her bags and drove over the Industrial Canal and out of the Lower Ninth Ward.

❧  ❧  ❧

Father Vien The Nguyen, a Vietnamese American priest in his early forties with thinning hair and a short mustache, glanced up at the gray blanket of clouds racing across the sky. The real storm was still hours away, but gusts of wind were already swaying branches and rattling loose windows. He braced himself against a gust as he crossed the large parking lot of the Mary Queen of Vietnam Catholic Church, making his way to the school building at the back of the church campus.

It was shortly after noon on Sunday, August 28, and hundreds of his parishioners had decided to stay for Katrina. Some were too elderly or infirm to brave a long evacuation. Others did not own cars. Most, however, had learned from experience that evacuations were more trouble than they were worth. In September of the year before, Hurricane Ivan had threatened New Orleans. "A lot of people evacuated," Father Vien said, "and the storm didn't hit here. Then they came back and they found that their houses were looted."

Though Ivan had been a supremely frustrating experience, Father Vien nonetheless urged all of his parishioners to get out of Katrina's path. The night before, at a feast for St. Monica—patron of the parish's Catholic Mothers' League—Father Vien had addressed the assembled flock in Vietnamese. "It looks like the real thing," he said. "So, those of you who can leave, leave."

When hundreds of parishioners arrived for the 6 a.m. Mass, Father Vien told the presiding priest, "Don't preach. Just go through Mass quickly, and tell the people to go." The next service was at 7:45, and already, the wind was beginning to whip up. Father Vien stood before his congregation and admonished the assembled crowd to get out of the storm's path. "You felt the wind already as you came to church," he said, "and the distance from where Katrina is to here is about the same as from here to Houston. And yet you can still feel the wind. Imagine what it will be like when it's right on you." His message was the same at the 9:30 Mass. He had planned to cancel the 11:15 Mass, but when the church office fielded call after call from eager parishioners, he relented, allowing his assistant to run a short service.

There could be little doubt that the members of the Mary Queen of Vietnam Parish were among the most enthusiastic churchgoers in the New Orleans archdiocese. The church's longest-standing parishioners had arrived in the United States thirty years before as refugees from the Bui Chu diocese in the Red River Delta of North Vietnam, where Catholic churches had been central to village life. There, priests doubled as community leaders, presiding over the villages that made up their parishes. The church would retain its central importance to the villagers' lives throughout the long exodus that eventually led them to the United States.

With the end of French rule in 1954 and the subsequent partition of the country, the villagers in the Bui Chu diocese joined a mass migration of hundreds of thousands of Catholics from the north to new homes below the 17th Parallel. Their new lives in the south were cut short when the American-backed government in Saigon fell in 1975. As the new communist government opened "reeducation camps" and began widespread retribution against supporters of the old regime, many Catholic transplants from the north joined a wave of emigration from ports along the country's southern coast.

The arrangements were often hasty, the risks high, and the destinations uncertain. Limited space on departing vessels meant that families were sometimes split up. After harrowing voyages, many refugees landed in camps along the South China Sea, spread out in a diaspora stretching from Hong Kong to the Philippines.

Throughout their upheaval and relocation, Catholic refugees held steadfastly to faith and to the connections and structure provided by the Catholic Church. Priests departed with members of their parishes, regularly giving traditional Vietnamese Masses. Catholic officials and nonprofits spearheaded efforts to improve conditions in the camps, and helped to arrange passage to countries in the West. The archbishop of New Orleans, for example, visited the refugee camps and began making arrangements for Vietnamese priests to establish new resettlement communities in the Crescent City.

Refugees who made it to the United States were first housed on military bases. Many were then sponsored by individual families, nonprofit organizations, or religious communities, which helped the refugees transition from the bases to homes of their own. Father Vien was just eleven when he arrived with his mother and siblings at Fort Chafee in Arkansas. After nearly five months in Army quarters, his family moved to southeast Missouri, where a Catholic parish adopted them. Meanwhile, other Vietnamese families arrived in the United States at military bases across the country—from Camp Pendleton in California to Eglin Air Force Base in Florida—and began the slow process of building their lives anew. As Father Vien explained, "The policy was to spread the Vietnamese refugees throughout the country so that they would become absorbed and quickly 'melt' into the mainstream. However, the resettled Vietnamese refugees began to gravitate toward each other geographically and created their own enclaves."

The Archdiocese of New Orleans, under the leadership of the venerable Archbishop Philip Hannan, took a different approach to Vietnamese resettlement. In 1975, after his visit to the refugee camps, Archbishop Hannan arranged for approximately one thousand refugees to take up residence in a set of low-income Section 8 apartments known as Versailles Arms. The Vietnamese American parish over which Father Vien now presided traced its origins to this housing complex. At more than fifteen miles from downtown New Orleans, Versailles Arms lay on the outer periphery of development in the city. This, coincidentally, placed it in a physical milieu similar to that of the river deltas of Vietnam. The apartments abutted a series of waterways, blanketed with water lilies and other greenery, which cut across the low-lying land. A five-minute walk to the north or west ended in rich, overgrown wetlands. Versailles Arms was within the New Orleans city limits, but it was hardly urban.

Not only did the new transplants move to the physical margins of New Orleans, they also took up employment on the margins of the city's workforce. As Father Vien explained, "When people first arrived, they did a lot of manual labor. Mainly shucking oysters and working with shrimp, to remove their heads for packaging. That was the beginning." The hours were long, the pay was low, and benefits and job security were nonexistent. With time, the new arrivals attained more-stable employment. Some got jobs with the Luzianne tea company. Others were hired by New Orleans city agencies, like the Parks and Recreation Department. Still others, after saving and borrowing, managed to buy boats and began lives as fishermen and shrimpers, trawling the waters of the Gulf of Mexico from small ports along the Louisiana coast.

Even as the community struggled to become economically established, its population grew rapidly. Soon after the Vietnamese families moved into Versailles Arms, other newly arrived refugees from across the country began to leave their original placements and resettle near the apartments. Whether to reunite with family members or simply to join the substantial Vietnamese community growing up around the apartments, the new arrivals kept coming. Recently established clusters of Vietnamese families in other parts of New Orleans began to attract refugees as well.

Father Vien and his family joined this wave. In Missouri, the family had felt physically, culturally, and linguistically trapped. "We were really the only Vietnamese family within a thirty-mile radius," Father Vien recalled. "And we had no transportation, and we had no telephone. So we were very isolated. What we had there, that's it." During their time at Fort Chaffee, the family befriended a Vietnamese priest who had since taken up residence in a newly formed Vietnamese community on New Orleans's Westbank, ten miles from Village de l'Est. ("Westbank" and "Eastbank" are the terms used to describe the two sides of the Mississippi River in New Orleans, though they actually lie to the city's south and north, respectively.) When Father Vien's family visited the New Orleans community, they resolved to leave Missouri for good. In New Orleans, Father Vien recalled, "we felt very much at home."

Across the country, newly arrived Vietnamese Catholics quickly established places of worship. At Versailles Arms, impromptu Masses were first held in a community room at the apartment complex, and then in a trailer. Within a few years, the community had saved enough money to construct a small chapel. Then, in 1985, they built Mary Queen of Vietnam Church, a modern structure that could seat one thousand worshipers. Mary Queen of Vietnam Parish, as Father Vien explained, became "both a personal and a territorial parish." It served all Vietnamese American parishioners on the Eastbank, as well as all Catholic residents of Village de l'Est—the neighborhood that surrounded the Versailles Arms.

Commercial development in Village de l'Est progressed at a similarly rapid clip. Vietnamese produce shops, convenience stores, and pharmacies opened along Alcee Fortier Boulevard, catering to the needs of the neighborhood's growing Vietnamese population. Vietnamese restaurants on the Chef Menteur Highway served more non-Vietnamese guests with each passing year. Housing construction, though slow elsewhere in New Orleans, remained steady in the vicinity of Versailles Arms, as families earned enough money to build new houses.

When Father Vien took over as the pastor of Mary Queen of Vietnam Church in 2003, the community stood at a crossroads. Village de l'Est, according to Father Vien, was experiencing a "brain drain." Though the neighborhood's children did not identify as entirely American, they felt increasingly disconnected from their community and Vietnamese culture; they were going away to college and not coming back.

"The young people were the people of liminality," Father Vien explained. "By that I mean, they looked like Vietnamese, but they are not really Vietnamese. Their whole mindset, worldview—all that—was American. And they were more fluent in English than in Vietnamese. So, although they looked like Vietnamese [people], they don't belong fully to the community here. The interiority is American, but because of their looks, they didn't fit in out there. So, they didn't know where they fit. That was a struggle."

Youth in Village de l'Est were not the only ones facing an existential quandary; older generations were also asking themselves tough questions. Many had spent nearly thirty years building new lives and a new community from scratch, and were beginning to look around and ask, "What next?" Father Vien, in a parish newsletter, wrote that the community was entering its third stage of life. Its earliest years had been the "pioneer time," which preceded the "construction time." The community, he wrote, was now completely built, and it was time to embrace a new challenge. "The expression in Vietnamese was *ra kho'i*," he later explained, "meaning to go out into the deep sea."

"The basic necessities are done," he declared. "We need to move out, and somehow we need to move into the mainstream. At the same time, we need to delve deeper into our culture, so that we would still have that anchor." Remaining an isolated enclave was no longer an option. As of the 2000 census, Village de l'Est was home to approximately five thousand Vietnamese residents, but to an even larger number of African Americans. Future progress in the neighborhood, Father Vien believed, would require all of its residents to work together. The Vietnamese community in Village de l'Est would have to turn outward.

This, however, would be a challenge for another day. For now, insular or not, the community's tight-knit nature was its greatest asset. The evacuation had gone smoothly throughout the morning, with neighbors keeping tabs on and encouraging one another to leave. Members of the church choirs formed a large caravan and left the city together. At the thought of his quickly dispersing parishioners, Father Vien took comfort in the community's rigid and thorough organization. The parish was divided into seven wards, each with its own leadership structure. Wards, in turn, were subdivided into "hamlets," which corresponded to streets within the neighborhood. Hamlet captains reported to ward presidents, who in turn reported to Father Vien. Community members would keep an eye on one another even without this system in place, but the leadership structure made it easy for Father Vien to keep track of his entire flock. Even as they scattered about the country, he would be able to remain in touch with all of them.

Communication would be easiest, of course, with those parishioners who had chosen to stay behind. As the wind gusted, Father Vien arrived at the church school in back of the Mary Queen of Vietnam campus. Families were already moving inside, and they greeted him as he entered the building. They carried blankets, flashlights, jugs of water, and bags of food. Many—his assistant included—seemed to greet the storm's pending arrival with a sense of adventure.

# CHAPTER 2

# A Vulnerable City

Iᴛ ᴡᴀs ᴇᴀʀʟʏ ɪɴ the morning on Monday, August 29, 2005. Across the American South, in cousins' kitchens and strangers' dens and motel suites that smelled of air freshener and cigarettes, New Orleanians were waiting with bated breath. Some had stayed up all night listening to coverage of the storm. Others were just waking up, still exhausted after hours in evacuation traffic. The stressful exodus was over, but for many, this part was worse. The drama now unfolded on television. It was a game of hurry up and wait.

Hurricane Katrina, the storm that now captivated millions, had charted a meandering course to the Gulf Coast. It formed in the Atlantic Ocean over the Bahamas on Tuesday, August 23, 2005. By Thursday, August 25, it made landfall over southern Florida as a Category 1 hurricane. After crossing Florida and entering the Gulf of Mexico on August 26, Katrina grew rapidly in size and strength, fed by the gulf's unusually warm waters. As the storm turned north and began to track toward the Louisiana–Mississippi border, its radius grew to more than a hundred miles beyond its perfectly formed eye. By early Sunday, August 28, it showed sustained winds of 160 mph. It had become a Category 5 storm, attaining the most severe rating on the National Weather Service's Saffir-Simpson Hurricane Scale.[1]

Katrina prompted an exodus so vast and swift that it was without precedent in American history. In approximately forty hours, between Saturday, August 27, and Sunday, August 28, 1.2 million Louisiana residents evacuated from parishes in the storm's path. Hundreds of thousands more left their homes in coastal Mississippi.[2] In Orleans Parish, where Mayor Ray Nagin issued a mandatory evacuation order, approximately 400,000 of the city's roughly 480,000 residents heeded his call.[3]

Most of the evacuees left the coast in private vehicles. Inbound lanes on the region's major interstates were reversed in a procedure known as "contraflow," doubling the capacity of roadways to accommodate the outgoing cars. Though traffic progressed at a snail's pace, it kept moving, and slowly but surely those with the will and the means to evacuate made their way out of the city.[4]

⚜   ⚜   ⚜

Evacuees from Orleans Parish left behind a city with a unique array of problems—problems that made it particularly vulnerable to the hurricane that churned ever closer in the gulf. Paramount among these was that most of the city lay below sea level. Surrounded by water on three sides, New Orleans lay in a bowl protected by more than four hundred miles of floodwalls and levees. These structures, made of earth, concrete, or a combination of the two, prevented water from Lake Bourne, Lake Pontchartrain, and the Mississippi River from inundating the city.[5]

Hurricanes posed a serious threat to the New Orleans levee system, because their high winds pushed walls of water in front of them. These "storm surges" could cause sea level to rise drastically, placing a great deal of strain on the city's floodwalls and levees. The levees were designed to withstand the surge of a Category 3 hurricane, but Katrina was a Category 5, and its storm surge promised to be particularly severe. Officials worried aloud about whether the levees would hold; even a single breach, if not quickly repaired, could flood vast swaths of New Orleans.[6]

The city's vulnerable footprint grew out of three storied centuries of development, in which ethnicity, class, and geography became intricately intertwined. The high ground along the natural banks of the Mississippi River—the land least vulnerable to flooding— was the first to be settled. The development spread out on the high land along the river's natural curve throughout the 1800s, and New Orleans became known as the Crescent City. By the early twentieth century, though, settlement was creeping away from the riverbanks and into lower-lying areas. Development spread to the north as residents drained swamps to prevent the spread of yellow fever. The construction of a massive levee along Lake Pontchartrain, coupled with readily available loans under the post–World War II GI Bill, led to a flurry of building in Lakeview and Gentilly during the late 1940s and '50s. During the 1960s, residential development spread to eastern New Orleans, as many middle-class families, both white and black, sought to buy into the suburban American Dream.[7] Substantial residential development in New Orleans was winding down as the 1970s drew to a close, and in 1984, the oil boom that had temporarily buoyed the city's economy went bust. At that point, the city's footprint was established, and its patchwork of neighborhoods looked largely the same as it would in 2005.[8]

Distinctions among neighborhoods developed early in the city's history, and over time, New Orleans neighborhoods evolved powerful identities. The city's earliest development—the area now known as the French Quarter—soon sprung adjoining black and mixed-race blocks in the area that would become the neighborhood of Tremé.[9] Over the passing centuries, most New Orleanians came to identify strongly with their neighborhoods, from members of the city's white gentry living Uptown to poor black people from Hollygrove. By the time the city's residential growth ground to a halt in the late twentieth century, neighborhood identity and personal identity had become closely intertwined.[10]

New Orleans neighborhoods, by most agreed-upon definitions, were much larger than the suburban notion of a neighborhood, which encompasses only a few blocks. On the other hand, they were substantially smaller than officially recognized neighborhoods in other cities. Most New Orleans neighborhoods occupied a "sweet spot" of sorts; they were just small enough to feel contained and intimate, but just large enough to support their own civic associations. As of the 2000 census, their mean population hovered at about six thousand residents; neighborhoods in Chicago averaged twice this size, and Boston's on average were more than four times as large.[11]

There is no counting the exact number of neighborhoods in New Orleans, and it is sometimes difficult to define where one neighborhood ends and the next begins. The New Orleans City Planning Commission, however, came as close as anyone has to accomplishing this impossible task. In 1980, the group identified seventy-three distinct neighborhoods within the city and defined their borders. These neighborhoods ranged in size from a few hundred residents to more than ten thousand and were based as closely as possible on the neighborhood borders and names that residents commonly used and understood.[12]

The neighborhood fabric the City Planning Commission had identified in 1980 remained largely unchanged in 2005. The city's high ground consisted of predominantly white areas, namely the historical neighborhoods located along the banks of the Mississippi and new developments on a narrow strip of infill land along the massive Lake Pontchartrain levees. In between these two slivers of land, in the bowl that constituted the rest of the city, lay a diverse residential checkerboard. Some neighborhoods, like Broadmoor and Holy Cross, were historical, with century-old homes and classic New Orleans architecture. Others, like much of Village de l'Est, were still quite new. Some neighborhoods were poor, like Hollygrove. Others, like Lakeview, were well off. Some areas, like Gentilly, were diverse and relatively integrated, while others remained racially homogenous. For all of their differences, though, Lakeview, Broadmoor, Hollygrove, the Lower Ninth Ward, Village de l'Est, and the dozens of other New Orleans neighborhoods that fell in between the lakefront and the riverfront had one thing in common: all lay below sea level.[13]

⚜ ⚜ ⚜

Topography was not the Crescent City's sole vulnerability. Twenty-eight percent of New Orleans residents lived below the poverty line—more than three times the national average. As Katrina churned toward the city, residents in poverty bore a disproportionate risk. Many of the city's poorest residents did not own cars, and had no way to leave. Others owned cars, but could not afford the steep expense of sleeping in motels, eating in restaurants, and missing work for a week. These residents constituted a sizable portion of the tens of thousands of people who remained behind in Orleans Parish as Katrina approached.[13]

The city's high rate of poverty was, in part, a symptom of a decades-long population shift and economic decline. The Orleans Parish population peaked around 1960, at 627,000 residents. At that time, New Orleans was the largest city in the southeastern United States, and jobs at the city's bustling port and in the offshore oil industry were plentiful.[14] In the subsequent decades, however, jobs moved elsewhere. Downtown New Orleans, once home to some of the nation's largest and most profitable corporations, faced vacancies as companies moved their offices to booming cities like Houston and Atlanta.[15]

Between 1960 and 2000, Orleans Parish lost more than 140,000 people—nearly a quarter of its population.[16] White flight explains part of this trend. Prompted by school desegregation and "blockbusting"—a real estate scare tactic designed to induce white homeowners to sell their properties quickly and cheaply for fear of a coming onslaught of black buyers—middle-class white residents began moving to surrounding suburban parishes. Black families of means began moving as well, some to suburbs in Jefferson Parish, and others to new developments in Gentilly and New Orleans East. Formerly comfortable working-class neighborhoods like Hollygrove, where Phil Harris lived, began to fray around the edges.[17]

With a shrinking corporate sector and a diminishing middle class, Orleans Parish's tax base began to decline. By 2005, city services in New Orleans were among the worst in the nation.[18] Roads and sewers broke down faster than they could be repaired. (In typical New Orleans fashion, residents once famously threw a birthday party for a five-foot-wide pothole on their street. Two city council members attended.)[19] Conditions in public schools were strikingly bad; test scores were low, superintendents averaged only about a year on the job, and administrative corruption was so rampant that the FBI was mounting a top-to-bottom investigation of the school department.[20]

To a degree, New Orleanians of means were insulated from these conditions. Affluent parts of the city—the lakefront, Uptown, the French Quarter—generally received better municipal services than their lower-income counterparts. Moreover, as time passed, the city's middle- and upper-class populations abandoned the public schools nearly completely; both white and black families of means sent their children to a network of private and parochial schools, which grew and flourished as the public schools decayed.[21]

Terry Miranda's neighborhood, Lakeview, arguably went further than any other did to insulate itself from Orleans Parish's decline. Its abortive attempt to secede from the city, which Lakeview residents overwhelmingly supported, indicated just how far residents were willing to go to improve municipal services. Lakeview was also an example of how organized the city's neighborhoods could become. Even without seceding, Lakeview supported many of the workings of a small government. Between the boards of the neighborhood's private schools, its crime-prevention district committee, and its civic association, a number of services typically administered by City Hall instead sat squarely in residents' hands.

⚜ ⚜ ⚜

While Katrina bore New Orleans a particular threat because of the city's low elevation and poor population, another set of threats lurked beneath the surface. In August of 2005, the city, state, and federal governments were unprepared to deal with the consequences—both short- and long-term—of a disastrous hurricane.[22]

The deficiencies started at the top. In the wake of the terror attacks of September 11, 2001, the Bush administration undertook a massive restructuring of the federal agencies dealing with internal security, risk management, and incident response. In November of 2002, twenty-two agencies, ranging from the Animal and Plant Health Inspection Service to the U.S. Coast Guard, were united into the omnibus Department of Homeland Security. Among these groups was the Federal Emergency Management Agency (FEMA), a 2,500-person agency tasked with spearheading and coordinating the federal government's response to disasters.[23]

In 2005, FEMA found itself still adjusting to its new home, and its transition was not going smoothly. Terrorism was the overriding focus at the Department of Homeland Security, and FEMA's disaster-oriented purview put it at odds with the larger department.[24] When it came time to rewrite the federal government's plans for coordinating a response to an "incident of national significance," for example, FEMA was not given the job. Although the agency had spearheaded the creation of the nation's previous set of preparedness plans, the task of writing a new National Response Plan fell instead to the newly formed Transportation Security Administration.[25]

FEMA staffers also watched in dismay as Department of Homeland Security officials redirected their mission and constrained their budget. Previously, FEMA had distributed disaster-preparedness grants to state and local authorities. This task helped the agency to maintain strong working relationships with first responders throughout the country. In 2003, however, this function was shifted to another departmental agency. By 2005, approximately 75 cents of every dollar of federal preparedness funding to states and localities was earmarked for terrorism programs. At the same time, FEMA's operating budget was shrinking.[26]

FEMA's diminished importance took a toll on the agency's morale, and veteran staffers left their jobs. By 2005, only two of the agency's ten regional directors remained; acting directors filled the other eight positions. Approximately 20 percent of the agency's positions were vacant. Few were more dissatisfied with FEMA's position than the agency's director, Michael Brown. Brown took the agency's reins in 2003 and aimed to maintain FEMA's integrity and identity within the new department. Stymied, Brown intended to tender his resignation in September of 2005. As Father Vien The Nguyen attended to his congregation at the school building in Village de l'Est, LaToya Cantrell watched the news anxiously from Texas, and Phil Harris hunkered down with his wife and son in their living room, Katrina had Michael Brown's attention. "Can I quit now?" he asked in a flip e-mail to FEMA's deputy director of public affairs on the morning of the storm's landfall. "Can I come home?"[27]

As the storm raged, FEMA was thus at a low point in its organizational history, neutered relative to its position of just a few years before. Even during its better days, though, the agency had not been prepared to coordinate efficient long-term recovery after a landscape-scale disaster, in which destruction is widespread. Part of this defi-ciency lay in the workings of a law known as the Stafford Act, which dictated the terms on which federal funds could be distributed in a disaster's wake. The law gave FEMA the power to distribute unlimited public assistance funds to municipal governments for rebuilding projects in the wake of disasters. However, it stipulated that municipalities front the money for local recovery projects, and then apply to FEMA for reimbursement. This system worked well in the face of small- and medium-scale disasters, like tornados and minor floods, with which FEMA dealt on a regular basis. In the event of widespread destruction, however, this funding system would prove problematic; having lost their tax bases, and therefore much of their ability to borrow money or issue bonds, leveled towns and cities would have paltry funds with which to break ground on recovery projects.[28]

Unfortunately, as Katrina bore down on New Orleans, government deficiencies in disaster response did not stop at the federal level. At the time, the Louisiana office of Homeland Security and Emergency Preparedness was under investigation for misappropriating as much as $60 million in federal funds. Several officials at the agency were awaiting trial on charges that they had used some of the money to buy cars, clothing, and airline tickets. As a result, the relationship between FEMA employees and state disaster officials was understandably cool; months before, FEMA had demanded that the state return more than $30 million of the money in question. In the event of a substantial hurricane, the stage was not set for a cordial and close working relationship between the two offices.[29]

The city government in New Orleans, though certainly known for its corruption, faced a wider array of problems than those of the state's emergency preparedness office. Mayor Ray Nagin, a former corporate executive who came into office in 2002 on an ambitious platform of weeding out corruption, streamlining city agencies, fixing troubled public schools, and building a new city hall, had found reform more difficult to implement than he'd anticipated.[30] More often than not, he and the city council did not see eye to eye, and his efforts to reform the city's corrupt and intractable bureaucracy had run out of steam. New Orleans lacked an effective governing regime, and was unable to adequately tackle the myriad problems and challenges it faced. In the event of a catastrophe, the city's leaders were not poised to mount a quick or thorough response. The city government would not move with singular purpose in such an event; it would move in fifty different directions at once.[31]

In August of 2005, New Orleans was no better situated politically than it was geographically. If Katrina proved to be the long-feared "Big One," the city, state, and federal governments were ill-prepared to deal with the storm's consequences.

⚜  ⚜  ⚜

As New Orleans evacuees tuned in to storm coverage on Monday morning, the news seemed positive. The worst of their ordeal, by most accounts, was over. The day before, Katrina had been on course to deal their city a direct blow. Its intense Category 5 winds, which were blowing in excess of 150 mph, seemed ready to level much of the city. Then, that night, Katrina changed course. It tracked to the city's east, sparing New Orleans the worst of its winds.

For city residents, this was cause for relief, though not for celebration. Katrina had instead pummeled the Mississippi Gulf Coast. Reports were beginning to trickle in that Katrina's massive storm surge had leveled parts of the towns of Waveland, Bay St. Louis, Pass Christian, Gulfport, and Biloxi, sucking many of their buildings out to sea. The scenes were reportedly postapocalyptic; entire blocks were cleared of houses, with only foundations and plumbing fixtures sticking up from the mud. Buses had overturned, trees had uprooted, and massive radio towers had collapsed. Many of those who had stayed behind were feared dead.

The situation back home in New Orleans, thankfully, was reportedly far less dire. A National Public Radio reporter, keeping tabs on the storm from a downtown New Orleans hotel, called the situation in the city "the best eventuality of the worst possible scenario. They dodged the bullet, but they still got a sound bruising."[32]

"Dodging a bullet" became a catchphrase of sorts for those narrating the storm's aftermath. "We kinda did dodge a bullet," reiterated Colonel Pete Schneider, the next guest on NPR's special coverage of the storm. "We dodged that bullet that we were planning for."[33]

CHAPTER 3

# "Somebody Else's Couch"

Ever so slowly as the day progressed, the story of the city's salvation began to unravel. First came sketchy reports of breaches in the floodwalls that held back the Industrial Canal. There was flooding, apparently, in the Lower Ninth Ward and New Orleans East. Reporters had heard tell of families breaking out of attics with axes to escape rising floodwaters. These reports, however, were coupled with reassurances. The flooding, reporters had been told, was "not widespread" and "contained." Residents watching the drama unfold on TV once again began to hold their breath.

Pam Dashiell, for one, never entirely let down her guard. She, her daughter, and her daughter's boyfriend had spent a restless night at a motel in Vicksburg, Mississippi. The place was a dump; the three of them gave it the ignoble title of "the second-worst motel in the western hemisphere." They spent Monday morning listening to radio reports with the other evacuees at the motel, and hearing firsthand accounts from late evacuees, who were still arriving. A terrible picture began to emerge. Everyone, she later explained, was "listening to the radio. And, you know, a bunch of other evacuees were there. And these reports from . . . people coming in all the time. Truck drivers coming in. And reports of what had happened—reports of bodies floating in Violet and New Orleans East."

News of levee breaches and rising water became more frequent as the day wore on. Commentators who delivered this information did not seem to grasp its potentially dire implications. Because New Orleans lay largely below sea level—a collection of shallow bowls of civilization cradled and protected from the water that surrounded them by levees and floodwalls—a single levee breach could "fill the bowl," inundating much of the city with foot upon foot of saltwater. The flow would cease only when the water level in the bowl reached equilibrium with the sea. For neighborhoods that lay five feet or ten feet below sea level, the results would be catastrophic.

Even as it became clear that New Orleans East and the Lower Ninth Ward were drowning, reports seemed to suggest that the largest and most populous areas of the city had been spared from flooding. Then came news of a two-hundred-foot-long failure of the 17th Street Canal, which abutted the Lakeview neighborhood. Water was filling the city at the rate of a foot an hour.[1]

For Katrina's New Orleans diaspora, life slowly took on the aura of a surreal nightmare. They themselves were safe, but safety did not make up for their feelings of powerlessness as the news grew worse and worse. Terry Miranda, who had evacuated from the Lakeview neighborhood to Lake Charles, Louisiana, with his sister, remembered the moment he heard about the 17th Street Canal. The breach was about ten blocks from his house. "I sat in Lake Charles in somebody else's house, on somebody else's couch, with somebody else's TV and watched it all, you know, be wasted. And at that point I knew I had lost everything."

❧ ❧ ❧

For seventy-eight-year-old Phil Harris, his wife, and son, morning came as a relief. That night, their little house on Olive Street in Hollygrove had shaken mightily in the wind. A cacophony of howling gusts, shuddering walls, jingling cutlery, and thundering sheets of rain kept them awake and praying as the night wore on. Now as the sun shone behind a blanket of clouds, Katrina was a whisper of her former self.

Olive Street, as far as Phil could see out his front windows, seemed to have fared well. Branches were broken and power lines down, but roofs and windows remained intact, and cars sat upright. There was some water in the street, but this was no surprise; heavy rainfall often led to street flooding in low-lying areas like Hollygrove. If past storms were any indication, the water would drain before long.

It was surprising, then, several hours later, when the water instead began to rise. It crept steadily up the driveway, then lapped at the bottom step of their stoop, then climbed the stairs one by one. As it began to seep beneath the door, Phil's wife, Victoria, collected bedding and threw it down to sop up the water and stop its advance. "That water just started comin' and comin' in here," Phil remembered. "My wife started grabbing blankets to put on the floor, and the more she was grabbing blankets, the more water was comin' in."

Soon they were up to their ankles, then up to their knees. They waded desperately though the house, trying to save valuables. As their dining room table began to bob, they took in the increasingly surreal sight. It seemed as if their house—the place where they had lived most of their lives—had been set down in the middle of a pond. And still the water rose.

There was no choice but to climb the rickety stepladder that led to the crawl space of their attic. Through the opening, they watched the water continue to climb until it settled at chest level. The attic grew hotter as the hours wore on, and the enormity of what had occurred began to sink in. Still, Phil and his wife had lived through quite a bit—the Depression, World War II, the civil rights movement—and they were not easily rattled. Later, as he retold the story, Phil was inclined to play down what happened next. "I think we stayed up there in that attic a day and a half or two days or something," he remembered. "Anyway," he continued with a shrug, "we got out."

When it became clear that the water was not going to recede, they began to discuss how they could escape. No one would be coming to the rescue. Phil and his wife, though quite healthy for their advanced age, would not be able to wade and swim many blocks to higher ground. Eventually, they decided that their son would go out in search of a boat, and return for his parents as soon as he found one. He swam out the front door, and came back with a small boat hours later.

"We wanted to get me and my wife on the boat," Phil remembered, "but the boat started sinking. So I told him, I said, 'You take your mother, and you and your mother go out as far as you can.' I said, 'I'm gonna swim, I'm gonna swim to the carport and sit on the carport till you come back.' I said, 'If you can come back, good.' I said, 'If not, don't worry about it. I'll make it out somehow.'"

After depositing his mother on high ground along nearby Carrollton Avenue, Phil's son returned for his father. There was not much to say on the boat ride out, but there was a lot to take in. The streets in Hollygrove, as in most of New Orleans, were laid out on a long grid. As far as Phil could see, salty, oil-slicked water filled the streets, reflecting the now-blue sky. A smell of rot had begun to fill the hot, stagnant air. The city was eerily silent; the only sound came from the ripples the boat made through the water.

They rounded a block. Abruptly, a paved street emerged out of the water, where Phil's wife was waiting for them. From there, they traveled on foot, walking slowly down the wide boulevard. They were thirsty and weakened by hunger, but before too long, they arrived at

Notre Dame Seminary, an imposing, ornate building whose four stories towered above the surrounding flooding. A priest greeted them. Phil, prone to understatement, recalled his first request: "Father, I haven't had anything to eat in a couple of days. I'm kind of hungry." There was not much to eat, but those who remained at the seminary shared clean water and fruit with the tired family.

⚜  ⚜  ⚜

For Father Vien The Nguyen, the first indication that anything was amiss came on the evening of Monday, August 29. Until then, the storm seemed to have progressed as well as he could have hoped.

The night had passed largely without incident. Families staying in the school building remained secure as the wind buffeted its solid concrete walls. The power had gone out at around 4 a.m., but the telephone landlines still worked. In fact, Father Vien had spent much of the storm in the rectory, fielding concerned calls from evacuated parishioners. Time and again, he reassured them that everyone was safe. More than once, he had opened the front door and pressed the receiver up against the screen, asking, "Can you hear it?" as he chuckled over the roar of the wind.

Now, the storm seemed like less of a laughing matter. It was shortly after 5 p.m. when Father Vien returned from a drive to survey the neighborhood. He encountered two of his parishioners staring intently at the ground. As frequently occurred after heavy rains, two to three inches of water blanketed the parking lot. Though not normally a cause for concern, the water had them worried. "Father, it looks like the water is rising!" one of them called out. Father Vien marked the water's level on the walkway leading to the rectory.

Earlier that afternoon, those who spent the night in the school had struck out for home. Father Vien had followed them, surveying the neighborhood from the church's fifteen-passenger van. He had been relieved to see only moderate wind damage to houses and trees. All who had remained behind, he had thought, would be able to sleep in their own beds that night.

Now, this rosy prognosis seemed questionable. The water in the parking lot seemed still, but as the minutes passed, it slowly submerged the mark. Something was wrong. Father Vien still remembered the moment vividly: "I jumped into my car, turned on my radio, and that's when I heard that the levee had breached."

There was not a moment to lose. More than a hundred parishioners had dispersed from the school back to their homes throughout the community. Hundreds more had spent the night in their houses, many of which were only a single story tall. The church and its school building were among the most solid two-story structures in the neighborhood, and could serve as dependable refuges from the rising waters.

With great haste, the men started their vehicles and began to spread word of the levee breaches throughout the neighborhood. Taking advantage of his van's high clearance, Father Vien shuttled family after family back to the church campus. He worked well into the evening, halting only when the waters rose above the vehicle's headlights. The next morning, rescue efforts continued by boat.

By the end of the day on Tuesday, August 30, the church campus played host to more than three hundred evacuees. Quarters were tight and resources were limited, but people quickly set to work to make the best of the situation. They took careful stock of their remaining food and fresh water, instituting a strict system of rationing. A group of parishioners was assigned to cook. Others monitored the news to follow the developing situation, watching TVs powered by a generator. Telephones also continued to function; though the residents were trapped, they were not entirely cut off from the outside world.

Perhaps the most stressful job was caring for the sick and the elderly, whose conditions quickly deteriorated in the stifling heat. Many of the community's frailest residents, unable to brave the evacuation, were among those now trapped at the campus. Some could not walk without assistance. One woman, who had suffered a stroke years earlier, was fed through a tube and depended on a machine to help her breathe. A small gas generator, carefully tended by the woman's family, kept her alive. In the excruciating stillness of the steamy air, minutes and hours passed slowly.

Two days after the waters rose, the ordeal seemed to be nearing its end. Rescuers in a caravan of flat-bottomed boats arrived on the campus, and the parishioners quickly gathered their belongings and began to board the small, open vessels. "I was all packed up and ready to go," Father Vien recalled. When the rescuers saw the stroke victim, however, they did not think they could move her. The woman's husband, still by her side, stood silent and dejected at the news as the excited hubbub of the evacuation continued around them. Telling his assistant to shepherd the people on their long trip to the downtown

Ernest Morial Convention Center, where evacuees were gathering, Father Vien resolved to stay behind with the family.

As the sputter of motorboats faded into silence, Father Vien took stock of the situation at hand. Rescue for his most vulnerable parishioner was still nowhere in sight, but at least the bulk of his flock was now on its way to safety. He and the family settled in for another night at the now-quiet church campus.

Father Vien awoke early the next morning to the sound of a familiar voice calling up to his second-story window in the rectory. It belonged, he recalled, to one of the previous day's evacuees. "Lo and behold—he was on a boat with another person—he told me that they had been brought to Chef Highway and left there. I thought they had gone to the convention center. They were outside, overnight. And it was people who were sick, because I had to carry one or two of them onto the boat! They were on wheelchairs, all of that. Infants, they were out there."

The parishioners were not safe after all. Still, they were one step closer to rescue; Chef Highway stood on high ground and was more accessible than the campus. Rather than struggle to bring the hundreds of evacuees back to the church, the men decided to bring some of the church's amenities to the people. Father Vien issued instructions to the men in the boat: "Bring the propane burner. Bring all the propane. Bring the food. Get a fifty-five-gallon drum and make a makeshift bathroom for the people to use."

Drinking water was also an issue. Father Vien knew that one of the convenience stores along Chef Highway belonged to a member of the church's pastoral council. "I made the decision," he recalled. "I said, 'You have my permission to break into that store. . . . Just break into it, and get whatever drinks you need out from there.'"

As dusk fell on Thursday night, Father Vien remained at the campus. Countless telephone calls had left him with the impression that a medivac helicopter would soon arrive for the stroke victim, but the chopper had not been forthcoming. The life-sustaining generator droned on, and the family continued to wait.

Father Vien had also begun to field phone calls about missing parishioners. After the storm, hamlet captains and ward presidents had accounted for all but two of the more than six thousand members of Mary Queen of Vietnam Parish. The two who were missing, however, could not be found anywhere. Their families and neighbors feared that they remained in their homes.

Friday morning, Father Vien, a policeman who was also a parishioner, and the stroke victim's son set out by boat in search of the
missing residents. As they made their way down the streets-cum-
canals of the flooded neighborhood, they took pictures of the damage. The scenes were heartbreaking, but Father Vien knew that the
pictures would also help to dispel rumors—circulating in the community's new diaspora—that the neighborhood had been completely
destroyed. In fact, few houses in this part of the city had taken on
more than two feet of water. The recovery would be labor-intensive,
but manageable. After a morning's search, they found one of the two
missing residents and headed back for the campus.

Later that day, rescue finally arrived. A boat motored onto the
campus, ready to take the stroke victim and her family. The rescuers brought everyone to the same high land along Chef Highway on
which the bulk of the community's evacuees had spent an unplanned
and uncomfortable night. Happily, the other evacuees had been
picked up before dusk fell on their second day along the highway.

Now, once again, a planned rendezvous did not materialize. A helicopter was supposed to pluck the stroke victim from the highway
and bring her to safety, but it was nowhere to be found. Desperate to
get the woman out of the sun and bring her to medical care, the group
improvised. Upon learning that an ambulance was in the area on another call, they gently loaded the woman into the back of an open
truck and sped off to meet it. The woman's son shaded her with an
umbrella as the other evacuees peered about, relishing the breeze on
their faces. Village de l'Est—their home and the site of their six-day
ordeal—faded into the distance as the truck bounced and sped along
the highway toward safety.

⚜  ⚜  ⚜

The low rumble of a diesel engine broke the unnatural silence that
blanketed the city. It came as a relief; a truck had arrived to take Phil
Harris, his wife, and others who remained stranded at Notre Dame
Seminary to safety. The evacuees climbed aboard, and settled in as
the truck lurched forward. They rolled through nearly empty streets,
peering out at the transformed landscape. It was jarring to see heavily
armed troops standing on the street corners, wiping sweat from their
brows with their long-sleeve camouflage uniforms.

The evacuees were lulled by the sweltering humidity as the truck

accelerated onto the highway and the ride became smooth and regular. Before long, they arrived at a town near Baton Rouge and disem-
barked. "When we got there on the truck," Phil recalled, "they said,
'Well we don't have room to take them.'" The shelter was already
overrun with evacuees. Officials rerouted the truck to Louisiana State
University in Baton Rouge, where it was rumored that cots were still
available. Hours later, though, it was the same story at the university:
"We don't have any room, we can't take them here."

Finally, at a town east of Baton Rouge, they found space. "We
wound up in Denham Springs, Louisiana, in a big, huge gymnasium,"
Phil said. Under the glow of fluorescent lights and the watchful gaze
of doting volunteers, Phil and his wife were shepherded through the
registration process at the shelter, along with hundreds of other newly
arrived evacuees. "Those folks were really nice to us there," he recalled. The shelter's amenities, though basic, came as a welcome relief
after their trying ordeal. Phil found the air conditioning soothing
and the showers mightily refreshing. After a hot meal, he was ready to
sleep; thankfully, he was not too picky about where. "Everybody had
a place to sleep on the floor," he said with a shrug.

⚜   ⚜   ⚜

By midweek, after Katrina's Monday-morning landfall, it was clear
that New Orleans would remain flooded for weeks. Desperate attempts to fill levee breaches by dropping sandbags from helicopters
had been unsuccessful. The city's pumps had lost power, and water
from Lake Pontchartrain and the Gulf of Mexico equilibrated with
the New Orleans "bathtub," settling in at sea level. Eighty percent
of the city's land area was submerged beneath the dirty, oily brine.[2]
The flooding was both deep and extensive, covering an area that
stretched for twenty-two miles from east to west, and fifteen miles
from north to south.[3]

Most of those who remained in the city experienced hellish conditions as they waited to evacuate.[4] The city, state, and federal governments had not been prepared to respond to such a widespread crisis.
At the Louisiana Superdome—the downtown football stadium designated as a "shelter of last resort" prior to the storm—toilets over-
flowed, food and water ran out, and increasingly desperate crowds
of evacuees waited on the stadium's periphery. Stories proliferated of
assaults, robberies, rapes, and shootings taking place in the Super-

dome's dark, cavernous corridors; whether true or apocryphal, they increased the sense of urgency and anxiety as the days passed and help did not materialize.[5]

The situation at the city's convention center was similarly dire. Though designated as an evacuation point after the storm, no authority or infrastructure was in place to support the throngs of evacuees who arrived there. Without food, water, power, or communication with the outside world, individuals and families waited for days in the stifling heat. A news crew reporting on the Thursday after the disaster was horrified to find the bodies of elderly individuals, their faces covered with shirts, still sitting in the chairs where they had died. Some had been diabetics unable to manage their blood sugar; others had simply expired from exhaustion and dehydration.[6]

As the week wore on, the massive effort required to support and rescue the city's remaining population began to take shape. Officials called on Louisiana boat owners to assist with rescue efforts in the city, and a number of sportsmen responded, driving to the city's periphery and then fanning out into its flooded streets in their flat-bed vessels. After an unexplained forty-eight-hour delay, FEMA coordinated with the Department of Transportation to charter the one thousand buses needed to empty the city. More than a hundred helicopters began operations in New Orleans, evacuating patients from overwhelmed hospitals and plucking stranded residents from rooftops. Squabbles between Governor Kathleen Blanco and the Bush administration delayed the deployment of active-duty troops into the city, but by Friday, National Guard troops had fanned out into the city's streets.[7]

Naturally, those in Katrina's vast diaspora were eager to check in with friends, relatives, and neighbors, but this proved to be harder than expected. Mobile-phone users with the New Orleans 504 area code found it impossible to make calls from anywhere in the country, because the telecommunications equipment that routed their calls was under water. Many in the city, especially the poor and elderly, did not have e-mail addresses. Neighbors who saw one another every day on the street had often not thought to swap contact information beyond their home phone numbers. Frustration and missed connections abounded as residents tried in vain to get in touch with one another.

As New Orleans emptied of its remaining population, those who had already evacuated settled in for a long wait. A firm perimeter had been established around the city; until rescue efforts were complete, levees were patched, and the "bathtub" was drained, only essential personnel would be allowed in. For Pam Dashiell and her daughter, this meant driving to St. Louis for an extended stay with a distant acquaintance. Terry Miranda moved in with his elderly uncle in Metairie, a suburb of New Orleans located just across the 17th Street Canal from the flooding and devastation in Lakeview. LaToya Cantrell settled temporarily at her brother-in-law's house in Houston.

No one would be going anywhere fast, and the city's long-term fate was in doubt. "The question now," wrote a *New York Times* columnist, "is whether the jarring aftermath of the storm has fatally wounded New Orleans's reputation in the eyes of the public—residents and business owners who left and those who might consider moving to New Orleans in the coming years."[8]

## PART II

# The Year After

# CHAPTER 4

# "The Whole World Was Gray"

O$_N$ F$_{RIDAY}$, S$_{EPTEMBER}$ 30, 2005, the Sheraton Hotel in downtown New Orleans was a hub of activity in an otherwise-deserted city. Giant debris-removal trucks and National Guard Humvees rumbled past, their occupants gazing out at the shuttered storefronts on Canal Street. The hotel's expansive glass lobby played host to a motley assortment of FEMA contractors, national news crews, and city politicians. A small army of private guards maintained a perimeter around the forty-eight-story concrete tower. Their presence may have reassured the hotel's occupants, but the few locals who encountered them were disconcerted. "Those black ops guys were scary," one resident recalled. "They had the biggest guns I've ever seen."

Inside a hastily converted Sheraton ballroom, Mayor Ray Nagin prepared for yet another press conference. The mayor had regained some of his poise since the most desperate days after the storm, but the tired look in his eyes reflected the enormity of the task at hand. His city had just begun its first tentative steps toward recovery after being completely empty for nearly a month. That week, areas of New Orleans that had not flooded—primarily land on high ground near the Mississippi River—reopened to the public. Residents arrived to find downed limbs, broken windows, and food so rotten that their refrigerators simply had to be thrown away. Those who lived in flooded portions of New Orleans continued to wait for their chance to return.[1]

At the appointed hour, Nagin stepped up to a lectern sporting a simple white sign that read "Bring New Orleans Back!" As cameras flashed, the mayor introduced a seventeen-member commission by the same name. The commissioners joined Nagin onstage as he introduced them. They constituted a diverse group, ranging from multimillionaire developer and Bush fund-raiser Joseph Canizaro to black health activist Barbara Major.[2] Their task was nothing less than to create a comprehensive set of recommendations for the city's recovery and deliver it to the mayor within ninety days.[3]

Nagin understood that the task of planning for recovery was herculean, and he seemed relieved to have companions who could share the burden. "I really didn't know how the commission would react when they got a full briefing on everything we know," he told the assembled media. "After their jaws picked up from dropping, and after they wiped their brow from sweating, they basically all collectively said, 'We can do this.' "[4]

The mayor's announcement of the Bring New Orleans Back (BNOB) Commission did little to assuage uncertainty surrounding the city's recovery. Speculation was rife that New Orleans would come back only as a "boutique city," with a much smaller footprint and a whiter, wealthier population. Indeed, BNOB Commission member James Reiss, chairman of the Business Council of New Orleans, had recently been quoted in the *Wall Street Journal* as saying, "Those who want to see this city rebuilt want to see it done in a completely different way: demographically, geographically and politically. I'm not just speaking for myself here. The way we've been living is not going to happen again, or we're out."[5]

If anything, uncertainty only grew throughout October, as flooded areas of the city opened one zip code at a time for "look and leave" visits. Residents could return to their homes, but had to be gone by nightfall. For many, these first glimpses served only to reinforce nagging fears that had persisted since the levee breaches. The extent of damage often left residents with the distinct impression that they would never move back into their homes.[6]

⚜   ⚜   ⚜

Kathi King, a resident of the Vista Park neighborhood of Gentilly, spent much of October salvaging belongings. Vista Park, as Kathi's husband, KC, explained, had a "solidly middle-class" population. Kathi and KC were both white, but almost two-thirds of Vista Park's residents were African American, reflecting Gentilly's overall diversity.[7] Residents lived predominantly in small, single-story, slab-on-grade brick houses that KC characterized as "the low point of western architecture." With KC working a temporary software job in California, Kathi undertook most of the gutting work on her own. Her bungalow, just hundreds of feet from the London Avenue Canal breach, took eleven feet of water.

Every morning, she drove into Gentilly through the nearly empty roads, pulling to a stop at the dormant traffic lights on the off chance that she would encounter traffic. Before she could enter her house, she pulled on white painter's coveralls, tall rubber boots, thick gloves, goggles, and a respirator to protect against mold spores. The street was caked in silt from the nearby breach, and as she peered out through her goggles, drawing in rubbery breaths of filtered air from the respirator, she beheld a landscape devoid of color. "The whole world was gray, and there was no life," she recalled. "There were no birds, no squirrels, no people."

One morning, a van pulled to a halt on Kathi's block, and people emerged carrying boom microphones and video cameras. "It was Anderson Cooper's news crew," Kathi said. "They were looking for somebody to interview, and seeing as I was probably the only person for miles, they decided to interview me." Removing her goggles, Kathi peered into the camera and began fielding their questions. For twenty minutes, the interview continued. "I was answering their questions matter-of-factly," Kathi later explained, "and what they were trying to do was make me cry."

Eventually, they got to her. "They kept asking me, 'Why are you here? Why are you here?'" Kathi explained. "I had to think about it, you know? Why am I here? There's nothing here for me." That night, Kathi tuned to CNN and watched as her tearful response was broadcast across the nation. "Because I have to say good-bye," she had eventually replied. "I have to say good-bye to this place. And it's very hard to say good-bye."

⚜ ⚜ ⚜

Kathi and her husband, like hundreds of thousands of other residents of flooded New Orleans neighborhoods, would ultimately return home.[8] For months after the storm, however, that was hardly a foregone conclusion.

On January 11, 2006, New Orleanians woke up to a startling headline. "4 Months to Decide" read the front page of the *Times-Picayune*. "Nagin Panel Says Hardest Hit Areas Must Prove Viability." The BNOB Commission's urban planning committee had just issued its Action Plan for New Orleans.

The action plan divided all of New Orleans into Immediate Opportunity Areas and Neighborhood Planning Areas. Immediate Opportunity Areas were sectors of the city that had not badly flooded, which were ready for immediate rehabilitation and further development. Neighborhood Planning Areas, on the other hand, constituted the many parts of the city that had taken on substantial floodwaters. BNOB's urban planning committee recommended that residents of these areas undertake four months of planning, and then decide how to proceed with their rebuilding and recovery efforts. Until this planning period was complete, the committee recommended, the city should not issue building permits in flooded areas.[9]

The capstone of this BNOB report was a map, reproduced on the front page of the *Times-Picayune*, which drew six green dashed circles around flooded areas of the city. The urban planning committee designated these as "areas for future parkland." One of the circles enveloped the Fillmore, Burbank Gardens, and Vista Park neighborhoods of Gentilly, where Kathi and her husband lived. Another encompassed much of the Lower Ninth Ward. A third sat over all of Broadmoor. The remaining circles surrounded two neighborhoods in New Orleans East, and a mixed residential and industrial area that included parts of the Desire and St. Roch neighborhoods.[10]

Later, commission members argued that the circles represented an innocuous suggestion. Commissioners said that they simply intended to point out that flooded areas of the city could mitigate for inevitably reduced populations with new "parks and open space." The circles, they said, represented areas that could benefit from such a strategy. Residents, led by the press, interpreted the map and its accompanying report differently. The *Times-Picayune* printed a version of the map with dashed circles replaced by solid green dots, warning that residents could "face the prospect of having to sell out to a new and powerful redevelopment authority."[11]

Intentions aside, the BNOB urban planning committee's report and accompanying press coverage created a firestorm of public outcry.[12] Across the city, trust in the mayor and city institutions was low; the report did nothing to assuage residents' concerns. "I was hysterical," recalled Broadmoor resident Virginia Saussy. "I didn't know what I was going to do. . . . I was like, this is *not* going to happen. They're going to tear our houses down!" People across the city, already reeling from the failure of federal levees and bungled relief efforts, increasingly viewed the city government with distrust and resentment as well.

Sensing political disaster, Mayor Nagin quickly distanced himself from the BNOB Commission's work. While he did not dismiss the report outright, he called it "controversial" and reminded residents that it constituted only "a recommendation."[13] In the months that followed, the proposed building moratorium did not materialize. In his rhetoric, Nagin stressed that no particular neighborhood would be singled out for demolition, but stood by his commission's call for neighborhood planning. Soon, proving "viability" became a catch-phrase across New Orleans, as residents scrambled to organize and craft alternate visions for their neighborhoods' futures.[14] Other city-wide planning efforts would follow the BNOB Commission's report, but from this moment on, recovery-planning power shifted decisively to neighborhoods.

An array of remarkable community leaders emerged in the wake of the BNOB report. Some had been active in their neighborhoods prior to Katrina; many others simply sensed that if they did not step up, no one else would. Recovery planning was just one of a host of challenges these leaders faced. Many of their neighbors were hesitant to reinvest in their homes, fearful that their communities would re-main deserted, leaving them alone in a sea of blight. This threatened to become a self-fulfilling prophecy unless many residents were per-suaded to "take the plunge" and return home. Moreover, even if they wanted to, tens of thousands of residents simply lacked the means to reinvest in their flooded houses. Widespread recovery would require not only convincing residents to return, but enabling them to do so. If residents wanted their neighborhoods to recover, they were on their own to make it happen.

# CHAPTER 5

## Village de l'Est: "Back on the Map"

IT WAS LATE SEPTEMBER of 2005, and once again, Father Vien sat behind the wheel, watching the mile markers tick away on the interstate as he drove between cities. It had been a difficult four weeks since Katrina's landfall. His parishioners were spread out across the American South, staying in shelters or with friends and family, waiting for the city to reopen. Father Vien had made it his business to visit them all. It seemed as though every morning he awoke in a different city: Atlanta; Houston, San Antonio, Austin, and Dallas; Fort Chaffee, Arkansas; Baton Rouge and Lafayette, Louisiana. Now, he was on his way back to Houston, for what he hoped would be his final meeting in exile.

Wherever he went, Father Vien sought to reassure his parishioners and lay the groundwork for the community's return. Until recently, though, a more urgent motivation had spurred his travels. One of his parishioners, an elderly woman, remained missing for weeks after the storm. Though her family believed that she had evacuated, they had not heard from her and could not find her. After visiting the family in Houston, Father Vien inquired at a number of potential evacuation sites, to no avail.

Eventually, at the family's urging, he returned to the woman's apartment in the Versailles Arms complex with a police chaplain and a policeman parishioner. There, the men found the worst: the woman lay in her hammock, dead from dehydration. As far as anyone could surmise, she had not answered the knocks on her door after the storm, fearing looters. Though the community had pulled together and shown remarkable resilience during the storm, members had let down one of their own. The image of the woman, waiting alone in her hammock as the days passed, weighed heavily on Father Vien.

Mayor Nagin's office had recently announced that many flooded zip codes—including Village de l'Est's—would be opened for limited visitation starting on Wednesday, October 5. A dusk-to-dawn curfew would remain in effect, but families would be allowed to return to their neighborhoods during daylight hours to assess damage and begin repairs to their homes. This was the moment for which Father Vien and the rest of the community had been preparing. At every evacuation site he visited, he set up teams of parishioners to coordinate the community's return. With the mayor's announcement, it was time for residents to converge and hash out their final plan for a coordinated recovery effort in Village de l'Est.

After Father Vien and other community leaders arrived in Houston on Sunday, October 2, they set to work laying plans and dividing tasks. Who had access to tools and generators? How would they get drinking water? Who would cook? They decided that Father Vien would locate a staging area—a place outside of the curfew zone where community members could sleep, cook meals, and recharge after long days of working on their houses. After making some phone calls, he secured several locations along the unflooded West Bank of the Mississippi, including his childhood home. Before long, he and the others departed for New Orleans. Soon, Father Vien recalled, "People were pouring in."

When asked years later if many of his parishioners had been hesitant to return to Village de l'Est, Father Vien replied that it had been only "a very small number," adding that the general sentiment was that people wanted to return as fast as possible. Many, he added, snuck back to their homes before they were officially allowed into the neighborhood. He chalked up this enthusiasm to the strong affinity community members had developed for the church, for one another, and for Village de l'Est.

According to one of Father Vien's longtime friends, the community's overwhelming desire to quickly return also had a great deal to do with the priest's proactive leadership. "He went to wherever the parishioners were, and I think that's the image that he put into his parishioners' minds," she recalled. "That's why they look up to him. Because he didn't wait for them to reach out to him—he reached out to them."

By the night of Tuesday, October 4, after the delivery of a truckload of supplies, the community's West Bank staging area was ready for business. A team cooked dinner for the assembled community members, and the group awoke early the next morning to be ready for their drive across the river and into New Orleans East.

"It's just so devastating just to see it," recalled one woman, describing the drive. "It's just stale and quiet. You don't hear anything. You don't hear a bird chirping, you don't hear anything at all." The pungent smells were equally disconcerting. "Even just driving," she said, "you roll down the window and it definitely smells really strange. So driving in, it's just shocking. . . . The further east you went, it was just kind of like, 'Oh my goodness, what *happened?*'"

In spite of the devastation, Father Vien said, community members approached the reentry with a degree of calm and optimism. "People here are very interesting," he said. "They went either first to the church and then to their homes, or first to their homes and then to the church." The church building itself needed a lot of work, and parishioners wasted no time. As Father Vien later explained, "The church lost a strip of the tin roof that was about six feet wide and eighty feet long. That part of the roof collapsed on to the floor and the pews. The floor tiles in that portion of the church buckled due to the water. We patched up the roof with plywood boards and covered it with blue tarp. There was mold throughout the church. However, we did the best we could to clean up and endured what we could not."

Almost as soon as the reentry began, parishioners were asking Father Vien when Masses would be held again. "One man came up and said, 'Father, can you have a Mass for us? We really miss the Vietnamese Mass.'"

Father Vien was at first skeptical. "Do you think we have enough people for Mass?" he asked.

The answer was unequivocal: "Yeah. There are a lot of us who returned to Metairie or Slidell, but [it was] only today that we [could] return here."

His mind made up, Father Vien instructed the interlocutor to paint two pieces of plywood with the announcement: "Mass at 10 a.m. Sunday." The two men tied the signs on either side of the church gate. Four days later, using a generator to power the sound equipment, Father Vien celebrated Mass for three hundred people.

⚜   ⚜   ⚜

On Saturday, November 19, just over a month after their return to Village de l'Est, members of the Vietnamese community in New Orleans East received a startling piece of news. "Rebuilding Should Begin on Higher Ground, Group Says," read the headline in the *Times-Picayune.* The article went on to explain that a Washington-based think tank known as the Urban Land Institute had released a series of recommendations to the Bring New Orleans Back Commission. Among these, the ULI suggested that New Orleans substantially shrink its footprint. Severely flooded areas of the city, the article noted, "could have the potential for mass buyouts and future green space." The article tallied the areas of the city that might be shrunk out of existence. First on the list was New Orleans East.[1]

Trang Tu, an urban planner and consultant for nonprofits, immediately called Father Vien to discuss this troubling new development. The two were old friends, having met during the 1990s while working for an organization that served Vietnamese refugees. To date, Trang's volunteer work in Village de l'Est had mostly involved interpreting and other forms of direct assistance to returning homeowners. Now that the very existence of New Orleans East was threatened, though, it seemed that Trang's planning background would be pressed into service.

She and Father Vien began discussing ways to counter the Urban Land Institute's recommendations. They were stunned that its work was being done without any input from residents. Commissioners, most of whom had never set foot in the neighborhood, were now bandying about its fate. The process was utterly divorced from the community. It was "not nearly as accessible as it could have been, had they intended it to be," Trang recalled.

The BNOB Commission would have its next meeting the following Monday afternoon, November 21—just two days away. In light of this, Father Vien and Trang hatched a plan. They would gather as many residents as they could and drive them to the downtown conference room at the Sheraton Hotel where the meeting would take place. The Vietnamese community's arrival at a BNOB meeting threw the commission a curveball. As one commission member later wrote, "Almost no citizenry attended the meetings (at the time there could not have been more than 35,000 people living in New Orleans). . . . Attendees were almost all FEMA contractors (or wanna-be contractors) and the heads of a few non-profits, and representatives of a few national activist groups."

As one Village de l'Est resident recalled, "I remember that [the commissioners] were so surprised to look up and see, like, two hundred people" from the Vietnamese community filing into the room. "Surprised" may have been an understatement. "They overwhelmed the BNOB meeting," a commission member wrote. "For hundreds of residents from the Vietnamese community to show up at a meeting where they could not even fit in the room, was quite a signal sent to the BNOB. Before then, I do not think that many on the BNOB even knew there was a Vietnamese community in New Orleans and those that did, certainly had no idea as to their organizational strength."

In a moment captured in the documentary film *A Village Called Versailles*, Father Vien rises to the microphone. "There are 95 percent of my people at least that I know are anxious to come home," he says. "When we first saw this Urban Land Institute report, we were *shocked*. We were never invited to the table. We have a right to be part of a community-driven process." Stunned, the commissioners listen in silence. "I'm speaking here not only for my parish," Father Vien continues. "I believe I speak for the people of New Orleans East as well on this matter."[2]

A succession of residents follow Father Vien to the microphone. One woman later remembered, "We basically just said that we're back, we're building. You cannot make us into green space. And then, after that, we changed their minds."

In fact, although the community remembers the meeting as a turning point, the BNOB commissioners made no official decision that night about the community's fate. Father Vien and Trang knew that a great deal of work remained before the city would fully embrace the neighborhood's return. Still, they were off to a good start. The commission, which that weekend had been only vaguely aware of the community's existence, was now on notice that a very determined group of residents from far eastern New Orleans was doggedly committed to its neighborhood's survival.

⚜  ⚜  ⚜

"You'd think that the seniors would be hesitant," mused Cam Tran, a middle-aged former school teacher whose round face usually bore a kind smile. Coming back to the flooded city was an ordeal for anyone, let alone for septuagenarians. Village de l'Est's seniors, however, had survived decades of war and two great periods of exodus. "To them," Cam explained, "this is such a minor thing."

Cam's own adjustment to the recovery was progressing more slowly. It was late December of 2006, a month after the community's protest at the BNOB meeting. Cam had been living in the smaller half of a cramped Village de l'Est duplex for three short months, having come from her home in Colorado to help her husband's family rebuild. She spent her days crammed in a space with her in-laws and assorted guests; as many as ten people lived in the hastily renovated apartment at any time. "We were just sleeping using FEMA cots," Cam recalled. "We would pretty much just find space."

Relative to other community members, Cam realized, she had nothing to complain about. "What really hit me was to see the commitment of some people that were staying at the church. Because those people who were staying at the church, they did not have any water. They did not have electricity. There was *nothing*. Nothing was working in the city," she said. "But they were committed."

Many residents would look back fondly on the close spirit of cooperation and the communal atmosphere of the months after the storm. Father Vien, a consummate optimist, went so far as to say, "It was fun! Everyone was very close together."

Cam, for one, greatly enjoyed the meals that she and her family shared with their neighbors. As weeks passed, word began to spread around the neighborhood that the house had become a communal kitchen of sorts. Her mother-in-law, Cam said, "was designated as the cook. She cooked for everyone during that time. And so, people know that there's a house that they can go in to get some food." Grateful neighbors began to refer to the cramped duplex as "the house of love."

"Eventually, there were other ladies who came and started to help [my mother in-law] cook," Cam recalled. "And they started cooking larger portions, for people who wanted to have warm food to eat." The meals proved especially popular with older residents, who could not stomach the hot food being distributed by the Red Cross. Red Cross meals, Cam said, were "too Americanized for some of these people. They couldn't eat it. So then, whenever they wanted to, they just came to the house."

As residents returned to the neighborhood, they contended with a host of challenges, from finding honest contractors to enrolling their children in school. Their problems were compounded, in many cases, by a language barrier. Though older Vietnamese American residents of Village de l'Est had been able to navigate the city prior to Katrina without speaking English, the language was unavoidable when contending with the onslaught of aid workers, insurance forms, and vital news bulletins that characterized the recovery. As a result, Cam said, "I started out doing a lot of translating work, more social work kind of work." Residents, she said, needed help "filling out applications with FEMA, getting health care, and things like that."

Cam also kept abreast of aid initiatives in the city, and told community members about opportunities. She informed them of food, clothing, and gift card giveaways, and made bulk-supply runs for the neighborhood. Different organizations were passing out food, Cam said. "So we would go pick [people] up and bring back. And there was this place in Mississippi that was giving out chicken. . . . We would drive over there and get it back." Each day's work proved different, and with time, Cam fell into the rhythm, growing used to her home away from home.

⚜ ⚜ ⚜

On February 3, 2006, the crisp night air was ablaze with color. Yellow and pink strobe lights threw their flashes against a luminous blue-white blanket, and fireworks traced orange streaks across the sky before bursting into glittering, golden showers. Much of the color emanated from a floodlit stage, from which a wall of sound also issued forth. A Vietnamese American pop act was performing an upbeat song, twisting in unison in tightly choreographed dance moves as singers belted out an English chorus punctuated by verses in Vietnamese. The smells of frying seafood, steaming vegetables, and boiling *pho* broth wafted from a ring of tents surrounding the platform. The crowd, a sea of thousands of faces that packed the expansive parking lot at Mary Queen of Vietnam Church, was drinking it all in. This was Tet, the lunar New Year, and cause for serious celebration.

Trang Tu was too busy to listen to the music. Periodically, however, she managed to step out of the tent where the results of the community's design charrette were on display. The charrette, a two-and-a-half-day event in which residents and planners collaborated to create designs for the community's recovery, had taken place in November of 2005. Now, months later, its results were ready for public display.

The organizers could not have picked a better night. The crowd was radiant; children darted right and left, spraying one another and hapless bystanders with Silly String. Grandmothers sat in lawn chairs facing the stage, smiling as they nodded along to the music. Newcomers followed their noses to the grills, coming away with heaping Styrofoam containers of steaming food.

Trang's tent welcomed a steady stream of visitors. They oohed and aahed at the large, color renderings of revived commercial space in the neighborhood, complete with Vietnamese-style façades. They complimented the plans for a new senior center. It was wonderful, they said, that the community's planning had come so far.

The charrette that produced these renderings had been brief, but it was only a small piece of a much larger campaign. Planning in Village de l'Est, as Trang later explained, was as much "an advocacy tool" as it was a means to envision the community's future. "Because, literally, it's the community putting itself back on the map," she said.

Timing was an important piece of the puzzle, too. Father Vien and other community leaders decided that the neighborhood should unveil its initial redevelopment plans at the beginning of Tet. The move would be partly symbolic, associating the community's rebirth with the start of a new year. More important, displaying the redevelopment plans during the Tet festivities would provide the perfect excuse to invite politicians and city officials to Village de l'Est, showing them that the community had already sprung back to life.

This approach worked well. Over the course of the evening, Trang greeted a steady trickle of city bigwigs, many of whom seemed shocked as they entered the tent. The long, fifteen-mile drive to Village de l'Est from downtown passed through a dark corridor of bungalows, condominiums, and strip malls, most of which lay untouched five months after the flood. To emerge from this dark and lonely passage into the Tet carnival was a sensory overload. The officials nodded, their mouths slightly agape, as Trang and other volunteers showed them the products of the community's planning. If any of them doubted whether Village de l'Est would recover, those doubts had evaporated by the time the evening wound to a close.

City officials entered the tent amid a rush of community members, many of whom had taken part in the charrette and the weeks of preparation that preceded it. For many residents, the planning process felt deeply empowering. The community's power structure had traditionally centered on its priests, with decision making vested squarely in their hands. Now, "for the first time," Trang said, "the community really started doing community engagement. It was community-driven planning, as opposed to the Fathers making decisions."

Community engagement had begun weeks before the charrette with two focus groups, one consisting of dozens of business owners and another of more than seventy seniors. Each group was tasked with creating a list of priorities for the incoming planning team to address. Trang remembered that both groups—the seniors especially—were surprised that their opinions carried so much weight. They rose to the occasion, laying out a rich and diverse collection of suggestions for commercial redevelopment and senior housing in the neighborhood.

The business owners agreed that the community could capitalize on its Vietnamese identity to strengthen its commercial life. By pulling in traffic from the nearby highway and becoming a unique and desirable Vietnamese destination in New Orleans, they could build a broad non-Vietnamese customer base to supplement the business they already received from local residents. Facade improvements and traditional Vietnamese architecture could turn the community's strip malls into a "Viet Village," helping to realize this transformation.

The seniors agreed that if the community were to build them a retirement home, it would have to be different from its typical American counterparts. Many of the seniors were prodigious gardeners, and insisted that the facility maintain open space for them to grow their plants throughout the year. The facility's staff, of course, would have to speak Vietnamese, and its food would need to be traditional Vietnamese cuisine. Trang, realizing that "talking jargon would not be meaningful," printed a number of pictures of existing senior centers, which the seniors referenced as they hashed out their preferences for the center's design.

With this preparatory work complete, the community was ready to host the architects and planners. In the five weeks leading up to the charrette, Trang said, "I just relied on as many contacts as I could think of." Other community members had connections to local architects, and invited them, as well. Father Vien knew two architects in Vietnam who were well-versed in that country's traditional design, and arranged for them to fly to the United States for the charrette. All told, several dozen architects and planners were on hand for the planning blitz.

On the first night of the charrette, hosted in what Trang later described as a "jury-rigged" classroom in the church's school building, community members briefed the architects on the groundwork they had laid for the charrette. They stressed that the community's priorities were paramount; not only did residents want to see *their* version of a restored community emerge, but politicians would also be far more swayed by a plan based on the entire neighborhood's preferences. "For you to be able to say this is based on input from hundreds of people," Trang later explained, "it will be so much more compelling."

The planners split into four teams and set to work, creating plans for traditional Vietnamese façades on local businesses, drawing schematics for the proposed senior center, and tackling smaller projects along the way. The process remained open to the community. As the planners worked, Trang recalled, community members continually asked "implementation-oriented" questions. As the drawings emerged, they sparked excited discussions among residents about how the community would turn these plans into reality. After decades of displacements and new starts, Trang said, residents were used to a collectively self-reliant orientation. "Doing it yourself," she said, was "built into the psyche of this particular community."

Indeed, as the charrette drew to a close and the team presented its plans, discussion had already turned to other projects that the community could undertake. Schools in Village de l'Est had not reopened, and residents began to discuss the possibility of opening their own. A community health center, some mentioned, would save residents the long drive to hospitals and doctors' offices. One person suggested that the neighborhood could found a community development corporation to put all of these ideas and more into action. It was clear that after Tet, the community would have a great deal of work to do. Moreover, an unforeseen challenge waited in the wings.

⚜   ⚜   ⚜

Once the floodwater was drained and the bodies collected, residents of the Gulf Coast began contending with the trash Katrina had left behind. The storm created so much refuse that, if pressed into one-yard cubes, it would stretch around Earth.[3] Before long, people were grappling with exactly where to put it all. Within two months of the levee breaches, a mile-long stretch of parkland along West End Boulevard in Lakeview had been piled two stories high with mud, broken tree limbs, and refrigerators. The city towed thousands of flooded-out cars to a temporary graveyard under the elevated interstate. Downriver, in Plaquemines Parish, the Army Corps of Engineers fed the remnants of storm-battered houses into a fearsome shredder known as "the Annihilator."[4]

These, however, were temporary solutions. Sooner or later, all of

Katrina's garbage would have to find a final resting place. Mississippi and Louisiana landfills north of New Orleans ultimately claimed most of the refuse, but some would remain in the city. In February of 2006, Mayor Nagin quietly issued a six-month permit for a landfill that would abut the Bayou Sauvage National Wildlife Refuge, just down Chef Highway from Village de l'Est.

The community's ire grew as the dump began to fill. The landfill was "just taking any sort of debris," recalled Mai Dang, a recent George Washington University graduate and transplant to the neighborhood who became the community's head organizer against the dump. "Whatever was coming out of a house: car batteries, paint cans, sheetrock, anything. When rainwater hits sheetrock, it actually emits hydrogen sulfide, which is that rotten smell. So that causes a lot of respiratory problems." What's more, Mai said, the landfill "didn't follow EPA standards. It didn't use a synthetic liner, it was placed in wetlands, it's directly next to the Bayou Sauvage Wildlife Preserve, and then it's also next to a waterway that actually runs directly through this community."

Mai, Father Vien, and other community leaders organized several protests at the church, inviting local media to cover the events and lining up community speakers to address the crowds. "You had young voices, old voices. Everything was in two languages," Mai said. "The diversity of voices speaking out against the landfill gave the movement a great deal of credibility and made it more powerful."

As the months wore on, the campaign began to focus on a firm goal. In August of 2006, the landfill's first six-month permit was due to expire, and community members were determined to ensure that Mayor Nagin did not issue an extension. With the deadline approaching, they prepared to mount a direct-action campaign against the landfill, planning to form a physical line of protesters that the dump trucks could not cross. "We actually had community members who were prepared to get arrested," Mai recalled. "They were mostly elders, too. They had their medicine and everything."

Father Vien recalled that there was such enthusiasm for the idea that he had to dissuade a few elderly residents with questionable immigration statuses from participating. When the day of the protest arrived, community members formed human chains across the road leading to the landfill. Captains—assigned their leadership roles prior to that day—wore armbands and directed their neighbors. "And they rotated," Father Vien explained. "So every group was out to block for two hours. And then, [they] moved to another location where there would be water and food and shade for another group to come in."

The protests paid off. On August 15, over the vehement objections of the company that operated the landfill, Mayor Nagin announced that he would not extend its permit. Thousands of tons of debris had already been dumped at the site, but the last truckload had been delivered. Once again, residents would be able to turn their attention to rebuilding.

CHAPTER 6

# Hollygrove: "To Re-create a Neighborhood"

I⊤ was early November of 2005, and Phil Harris missed Hollygrove. For months, he and his wife had been playing hopscotch around the country. From a shelter in Denham Springs, Louisiana, the two had first moved into their daughter-in-law's small apartment, which had been crammed with fifteen people after the storm. Then, their granddaughter flew them to California for two months. From there, they moved in with a different family in Georgia, by which point New Orleans had reopened. Phil nursed a hankering to return.

"After we began to get ourselves together," he said, "I came back. . . . I left my wife in Georgia. I said that I would go back home and see what's going on. And boy, this place was a mess." Olive Street was rotting, with every surface caked in a brown muck that smelled of feces, chemicals, and oil. Grass, trees, and bushes were dead. Inside Phil's house, furniture was upended, mold crept up the walls, and the refrigerator let off a foul odor of spoiled food. "It was disgusting," Phil recalled. "Boy, it was heartbreaking. But, we couldn't give up. I just said, 'Well, I've got to get in and do it.'"

Phil's extended family owned an Uptown apartment that had not flooded, and he moved in there. He worked on his house during the day and returned to the apartment at night. "During that time," he said, "I didn't have no transportation. People were hitchhiking and doing the best they could. I didn't have an automobile because my automobile was flooded out. People would say, 'Well where are you going?' And I would say, 'I'm going back on Olive Street.' And they would say, 'C'mon, come with me, I'll take you back there.' And they'd drop you off and you'd start walking again. Well then, not long, somebody pick you up and drop you off at City Avenue. Well okay, they drop you off, and somebody will come along. . . . People was helping one another. Because didn't nobody have anything hardly."

During the day, Phil set to work "gutting" his house—a dirty business that needed to be done in any flooded building before it could be rebuilt. He hauled soiled furniture and destroyed appliances to the curb. He tore up carpets. He broke moldy, crumbling drywall down from the walls. He ripped out all of the house's wiring. With the building stripped to its studs, he had workers apply chlorine and another chemical cocktail to the exposed wood, killing any remaining mold spores.

The work was hot and physically exhausting, but even at seventy-eight, Phil got it done, counting himself lucky when friends and volunteers came by to lend him a hand. Eventually, he received a small white trailer provided by the Federal Emergency Management Agency. "FEMA trailers," as they were known, would become ubiquitous in residential areas damaged by Hurricane Katrina and the subsequent flooding. With the trailer, he and his wife were able to move back to their property as work on their house continued. They fell asleep every night on a dark street; many of the houses around them remained untouched.

⚜   ⚜   ⚜

Meanwhile, Carol Dotson, another Hollygrove resident, was also returning to New Orleans. A short black woman with tremendous energy and expressive features, she was not one to sit idly by as the recovery got under way. On December 1, 2005, she moved into an impromptu trailer park on the grounds of Xavier University, her alma mater, whose campus sat just across the wide lanes of Carrollton Avenue from Hollygrove. Carol had worked in Xavier's public relations department prior to the storm, and she hoped to return there when the university reopened. For now, she had found work reading traffic reports for a local radio station. Her house on Fig Street had taken more than five feet of water, but she was looking forward to the work of fixing it up and bringing back her neighborhood.

Before Katrina, Carol had been involved with a neighborhood association called the Carrollton Coalition. The group, which consisted of residents from the Hollygrove, Gert Town, and Fontainebleau neighborhoods, had mobilized in response to a large Army Corps of Engineers drainage project that began in 2000. The project created underground piping to pump water from low-lying areas into a canal in Hollygrove, and it required tearing up some Hollygrove streets. As Carol remembered, "It was just a disruption of the neighborhood for three years." Now, although a much bigger disruption had occurred, the Carrollton Coalition was nowhere in sight.

Hoping to organize a group of her own, Carol began talking with her friends, family, and neighbors from Hollygrove, many of whom remained scattered across the country. After living most of her life in the neighborhood, her connections were extensive. As she later explained, "Everybody doesn't *all* know each other in Hollygrove, but you know most of the folks there. You either went to school with them, you know somebody in their family, you're related to them. I've got cousins in Hollygrove on both sides of the family. So, you know, there's a connection through there."

She had long felt the need for a residents' association to serve just Hollygrove. Working with her friends, Carol scrambled to organize a neighborhood meeting, securing space at a nearby church. After many phone calls and lots of word-of-mouth advertising, more than thirty residents showed up. There was not much of a formal agenda. As Carol said, "I think our first goal really was to find out where everybody was and what [their] plans were."

The meeting, by all accounts, was a success. Those who attended found it encouraging to learn that other Hollygrove residents were interested in coming back to the neighborhood. The residents resolved to have more-frequent meetings, hoping that they would become a clearinghouse for their many unanswered questions and a locus of organization that would begin to bring Hollygrove back from the dead.

⚜   ⚜   ⚜

Kevin Brown was one of the Hollygrove residents who attended Carol's meeting. He was among the neighborhood's few white homeowners, and his path to the community had been an interesting one. "In '63, my dad, a Presbyterian minister, came to New Orleans and went to register to vote," Kevin said. "He had to take a literacy test. When he asked why he had to take a literacy test—'What does reading have to do with voting?'—he was told, 'It's to keep the *n*'s out.' And he said that was what turned it for him. If there's that blatant institutional racism at a government level, and it's so broad that they'd tell newcomers to the town about it, then something is really wrong."

That day, Kevin's father knew that his calling was in New Orleans. He had come to the Crescent City to work at a Presbyterian church, but he found himself called to a broader urban ministry. In 1967, he founded Trinity Christian Community (TCC), a mission based primarily out of the Irish Channel neighborhood. The organization's undertakings were numerous and diverse: integrated youth baseball leagues in city parks, a coffee house and ministry for hippies, a garage to teach mechanical skills.

Eventually, Kevin went away to college and then settled in Chicago, becoming a successful adolescent psychotherapist. He authored several books, hosted two radio shows, and started a family. Life in Chicago went well, but Kevin began to feel inklings of boredom just as his father planned to retire from the helm of TCC. Kevin decided he wanted the job. "We moved out of the nice suburb, sold one of our cars, and my pay got cut in half, and we moved into the inner city," he said.

Before Kevin's father retired, TCC had moved its headquarters to Hollygrove, and its operations were spread thin. When Kevin took the reins, he said, "It was time to retrench, time to refocus, time to think about what we did. And to focus on one thing and do it well for a while." Drawing on his work with teens, Kevin transformed TCC into an organization that served neighborhood youth.

By 2005, seven years after Kevin moved to New Orleans, TCC was running a thriving youth program. It partnered with AmeriCorps—a national service program funded in part by the federal government— to place tutors in some of the city's underperforming public schools. After school, the shouts and laughter of eighty Hollygrove children emanated from TCC's playground and echoed in the hallways of its nondescript, two-story, concrete-block building on Joliet Street.

TCC was explicit about its religious mission. As Kevin said, "What we do is faith-based community development. . . . A lot of the stuff that normal community development organizations do, we do, but we do it for a different reason, and we do it with a different end in mind. My end is community transformation, but what I want to see is a bunch of Christian leaders transform the community."

Katrina brought TCC's youth work to a halt. Its building took on more than six feet of floodwater. Its ten staff members were scattered. The kids with whom TCC worked were gone, because their neighborhood had been destroyed. Public schools across the city were closed. Kevin and his family had moved temporarily to Gonzales, Louisiana, because their house in Hollygrove had flooded. From Gonzales, Kevin began the arduous process of reinventing, yet again, the organization his father had started nearly forty years before.

TCC was in a conundrum. On the one hand, Kevin's passion, and TCC's strength, lay in school-based and after-school youth programming, but this work would be impossible until Hollygrove's recovery substantially progressed. As Kevin considered his options, he resolved that "sitting around and waiting for [the] mission to return" was not an option. If TCC hoped to one day resume its youth work in Hollygrove, its immediate task was clear. "If you don't have a house to live in, you don't have any kids," Kevin explained. "We had to re-create a neighborhood so that we'd have kids to work with so we could get back to our mission."

At the time, TCC faced the forfeiture of the AmeriCorps volunteers it had secured to tutor in the public schools. But then the Louisiana Service Commission, which coordinated AmeriCorps workers throughout the state, approached Kevin with a proposition. Would he be willing to recruit two hundred people into AmeriCorps positions, and put them to work on recovery projects? As Kevin later explained, "If you'd have been here at the time you would have understood how crazy this was—there was nobody here, and the housing stock was decimated."

Kevin knew that he, his wife, and the one other TCC staff member whom they had located after the storm would not be able to recruit and deploy two hundred volunteers. One hundred volunteers, on the other hand, might be within reach. The Louisiana Service Commission agreed to the lower number, and the three got to work. "We hustled," Kevin said. "We got on Craigslist. We called everybody around the country who we knew. I was on the phone from seven a.m., [when] I'd start calling the East Coast, to ten p.m., to be calling the West Coast."

The trio pulled it off, recruiting ninety-seven AmeriCorps volunteers. Meanwhile, seven of TCC's ten staff members returned. When the city reopened in October, Kevin and a volunteer team went to work on TCC's building, converting it from a youth center into a volunteer housing space. The downstairs was ruined, Kevin explained, but with the help of a volunteer electrician and the creative use of extension chords, "we were able to jury-rig the upstairs." Meanwhile, an organization called the Samaritan's Purse donated a few trailers, adding to TCC's housing capacity.

TCC would deploy most of its AmeriCorps workers with organizations across the city, keeping only ten for itself. Those ten would serve as coordinators, leading larger groups of short-term volunteers in house-gutting work and other recovery projects throughout Hollygrove. All of the volunteers would eat and sleep in TCC's hastily converted building.

TCC's latest transformation was staggering, but the circumstances left little other choice. The organization would live or die with its neighborhood.

❖  ❖  ❖

By May of 2006, nine months after the storm, Hollygrove's recovery was well under way. Teams of volunteers, led by TCC's AmeriCorps workers, gutted house after flooded house. Hollygrove Neighbors meetings drew ever-larger crowds, and the organization held elections and drew up formal bylaws. Perhaps most promisingly, a coalition of residents and volunteer architects had begun laying the groundwork for a homegrown neighborhood recovery plan.

Spurred by the call for neighborhoods to "prove their viability" in the wake of the Bring New Orleans Back Commission's January report, Hollygrove Neighbors and TCC had partnered with the New Orleans planning nonprofit City Works to craft a vision for Hollygrove's future. In a series of meetings over the four intervening months, residents laid out their priorities: restoring desirable retail shops on Carrollton Avenue, revitalizing the neighborhood's housing stock, reopening the shuttered Dunbar Elementary School. They were in the midst of planning a complete inventory of Hollygrove properties when a new citywide planning effort took the wind out of their sails.

In April of 2006, seeking to create a recovery plan more politically palatable than the mayor's BNOB effort, the city council hired the planning firm Lambert Advisory LLC to facilitate recovery planning across flooded areas of the city. Lambert Advisory would in turn subcontract with other urban-planning firms to run planning efforts for each of the city's flooded neighborhoods. Broadmoor resident and reporter David Winkler-Schmidt, writing for New Orleans's alternative weekly newspaper *Gambit*, stated that the plan's "underlying premise was diametrically opposed to the mayor's authorized BNOB report." He continued, "The BNOB said it was inevitable that some neighborhoods would be consolidated, whereas the City Council considered every neighborhood's 'viability' a given."[1]

As Winkler-Schmidt reported, the planners hired by the city council were surprised at how far neighborhood groups had progressed with planning on their own. He quoted Paul Lambert, the planner in charge of the new effort, who had expected his teams to have to start from scratch. "When we first started, we thought we would go to all the neighborhood groups, and we did that," Lambert said. "But we found that a lot of planning was already going on. So we've adjusted our process and now we're sitting in with many of the planning meetings. . . . We're doing that all over the city."[2]

Lambert, it seems, wanted his teams to integrate themselves into the grassroots efforts already underway across the city. Unfortunately, not all of his planners handled themselves with aplomb. A number of neighborhood leaders reported friction with the newly arrived teams. In Hollygrove, the situation grew ugly.

The first encounter between Hollygrove residents and the planning team was innocuous enough. In late May, residents filed into an auditorium at Xavier University to meet Gerald Billes, the architect whose firm would spearhead the Lambert planning process in Hollygrove. They informed Billes of their prior work. One man, a volunteer with TCC, e-mailed him after the meeting. After explaining the neighborhood's grassroots planning work in greater depth, he invited Billes to the resident planning group's next scheduled meeting, in hopes that the work they had done so far could be folded into the city's new effort. Residents across Hollygrove were shocked at the response he received. Billes dismissed residents' planning efforts as unprofessional and unrepresentative of broad public opinion in the neighborhood. He suggested that any further work on the group's part would run counter to the neighborhood's best interests, and implicitly derided the group's accomplishments to date.[3]

"I don't believe it. I honestly don't believe it," Kevin Brown later fumed. Residents, heeding the BNOB Commission's call, had gone above and beyond the call of duty and begun an open and inclusive planning process for their neighborhood. Nonetheless, after four months of hard work, Billes and his team were shoving them dismissively to the side.

Residents were especially miffed at Billes' suggestion that their work was unprofessional. "We had the American Institute of Architects with us, Steve Villavaso, I mean he's famous all over the world," Kevin later explained, recalling the partnerships that he and other residents had forged. "We had a bunch of really sharp people with us. All of these people helping us plan out the neighborhood." The experience left residents with a bad taste in their mouths. " 'You guys are not professional planners, get your nose out of my business, get out of here,' " Kevin recalled, paraphrasing the attitude of the planning teams hired by the city. "If that's the attitude of city government, what's the point?"

The Lambert plan, like the BNOB plan before it, went on to die a quiet death. Though meetings were held, reports filed, and plans for each of the city's flooded neighborhoods posted online, the Lambert plan failed to galvanize residents or politicians around a shared course of action. Meanwhile, Hollygrove residents increasingly concerned themselves with the nuts and bolts of renovating flooded houses and encouraging their neighbors to return.

⚜  ⚜  ⚜

In the fall of 2006, eleven-year-old Dorian Johnson began a new school year. His family had recently moved back to Hollygrove. Every morning, Dorian would bid his dog, Precious, farewell in his family's modest home, then board a school bus near the 17th Street Canal for another day of fifth grade at Benjamin Banneker Elementary. As the bus lurched down the potholed street, the view out the window remained grim. "When we moved back," Dorian recalled, "we were the first people on our block for a long time." The derelict streetscape wore on Dorian's psyche. There was "nobody," he said. "No friends, [extended] family, nothing. Just us."

Life after the storm did not feel normal, but it was beginning to fall into a routine. "I didn't used to go outside," Dorian recalled. "I used to just go to school." After a brief hiatus, crime was returning to the city, and Hollygrove's streets bore a disproportionate burden. Dorian's mom was reluctant to let him out. The family's house, one of the first in the neighborhood renovated after the storm, felt to Dorian like it had lost some of its former charm. "It was like, basically the same, but they took out some windows," Dorian said. "There was this shortcut through my brother's room to the washroom that we used to always run through, and that wasn't there anymore."

More than anything else, Dorian simply felt lonely. He was not the only one. Other kids who began moving back to the neighborhood a year after the storm also began dealing with the shattered childhoods they had left behind. Growing up in Hollygrove had not been easy before the flood; now it had become even harder. Support networks of friends and neighbors remained displaced. Many kids fell behind academically during their long evacuations, and faced further adjustments when their former schools in New Orleans did not reopen. TCC, because of its focus on house gutting and rebuilding, was no longer offering its after-school programs and tutoring. For the time being, kids in Hollygrove would have to be remarkably self-reliant.

Shekiel LeBlanc, who was two years older than Dorian and had grown up several blocks away, had it particularly hard. Barely a teen-ager, he endured a year of Katrina-induced exile without his parents or siblings. His mother was incarcerated. "It was hard," he recalled. "They split my brothers and sisters up. My younger brother and younger sister, they lived with their dad. My other little sister, she went with my mom's friend." The storm left Shekiel's splintered family scattered across several states. Shekiel evacuated with his aunt to Houston, and then moved with her to Atlanta. They returned to Hollygrove for the start of the 2006–2007 school year.

"Trailers, trailers, trailers, trailers," Shekiel remembered. "All the houses were messed up, it was just trailers everywhere." As he watched families repopulate his block, Shekiel looked forward to the day when his mother would join the ranks of the returned. Without her, and without many of his former friends, the slowly recovering neighborhood continued to feel forlorn.

# CHAPTER 7

# Lakeview: "Don't Get in Our Way"

O<small>N</small> O<small>CTOBER</small> 1, 2005, Terry Miranda and thousands of other Lakeview residents remained displaced. Bari Landry, however, was on the move. Fresh off a five-hour drive from Houston, she was determined to get back to her cordoned-off neighborhood. "I bought a pair of combat boots from Perret's [Army and Outdoor Store] in Kenner, and snuck past the National Guard," she recalled. Blond and petite, she would have looked peculiar in her new footwear if not for the intense resolve that lent purpose to her stride and burned in her eyes. She was returning to her Lakeview bungalow, a home she had owned for nearly twenty years. There she had raised two sons as a single mother, befriended nearly every neighbor on her block, and risen to a respected position on the board of the Lakeview Civic Improvement Association (LCIA). If anyone was coming back to Lakeview, Bari was bound to be one of the first.

She still remembered the rising panic she had felt as the major networks began broadcasting live footage of a two-hundred-foot breach in the 17th Street Canal. For days, she would later recall, the news dispatches from Lakeview had been dire. "Originally, all of the reports from the national media said all is lost. It's up to all of the roofs. There's nothing left." With these reports, Bari felt an emptiness that transcended the loss of her worldly possessions. Her life was in Lakeview.

"You go all over and there are neighborhoods where you don't know the guy next door," she explained. In Lakeview, by contrast, neighborly connections were numerous and meaningful. A sixty-year-old rosebush in her backyard, Bari recalled, was "given to the previous owner by the lady who lived next door." Because of her connections in the neighborhood, Bari felt that "there was too much there to give up." Bari's fellow LCIA board members felt much the same way. On the day after Katrina, they had been scattered across the country, from Houston to Florida to the Carolinas. "Literally," Bari said, "I don't think the water had stopped coming in through the levee when we were trying to get in touch with each other."

Within days, the board had arranged regular conference calls, and set about gathering as much information as possible about Lakeview's predicament. One board member, a longtime Lakeview resident named Freddy Yoder, was the president and chief operating officer of a large New Orleans–based contracting business known as Durr Heavy Construction. Durr had worked closely with the Army Corps of Engineers on past projects, and Freddy began consulting with the corps over the phone as soon as the levees breached. Milking his connections, he managed to return to the otherwise cordoned-off city, and began relaying firsthand information about Lakeview's condition to the rest of the board.

Board members, in turn, worked around the clock to give residents regular updates. Within three days of the storm, they had posted a new post-Katrina LCIA website. Soon thereafter, they created an e-mail listserv that quickly grew to include thousands of members. These venues soon became information clearinghouses, providing updates from highly placed sources. As Bari later explained, the LCIA leveraged its considerable political clout to keep residents in the know. "We would have conference calls, and we would get the city council member, the state representative, we had the lieutenant governor on the line one time from Baton Rouge. 'Give us the update, give us what's going on, when can we get into Lakeview, what resources are coming?'"

The early updates were not encouraging. All of Lakeview was indeed severely flooded. For several blocks around the breach of the 17th Street Canal, the water's force had knocked houses off their foundations. National Guard troops motored up and down the streets in boats, their wakes lapping against shingled roofs that jutted out of the otherwise-stagnant water. It took weeks for the breach to be closed and the water to drain. Nearly all of the neighborhood's more than seven thousand houses would have to be gutted or demolished.

The loss was overwhelming, but the unspoken consensus on the LCIA board was that there was no time to grieve. "You just didn't have the opportunity," Bari said, "because there were people downtown with more power than you just saying, 'Tear everything down.'"

Moving quickly, Freddy Yoder secured a contract for his firm to spearhead cleanup work in Lakeview. "Within two weeks," he recalled with pride, "I had signed contracts with Phillips and Jordan, who was the national recovery contractor. . . . Part of the terms of the contract I signed was that my company would have the ability and the right to clean up Lakeview. . . . I pushed so hard for that particular contract, because I wanted to have a personal involvement in the cleanup."

Clearing the streets was one matter, but convincing residents to return and rebuild would be another. Sneaking past the roadblocks, Bari Landry was one of the first residents to reenter the neighborhood. Crossing the Orleans Parish line and rolling down Lakeview's deserted streets, Bari encountered the awful tableau of sights, sounds, and smells that greeted hurricane survivors across the Gulf South. With animals dead, residents gone, and mud muffling any sound, an unnatural silence blanketed the city. A fine layer of gray silt covered every surface, robbing the blocks of their familiar color. Inside her house, a lifetime's possessions lay strewn across the floor, mold and oil coated the walls, and food left in the refrigerator had grown indescribably vile. It would have been easy to conclude, as many early visitors did, that rebuilding a life in the city was impossible.

Incredibly, Bari instead found herself heartened by the visit; the damage was not as great as she had feared. "You can rebuild a smaller, traditional New Orleans house a lot faster than a modern-built house," Bari later explained. Her eighty-two-year-old bungalow stood on three-foot piers that lessened the flooding. Rather than reaching the roof, the water had stopped halfway up the windows. Moreover, the old hard-plaster walls could simply be scrubbed clean, unlike newer permeable drywall, which sucked up oil, chemicals, and mold.

"You didn't give yourself time to mourn," Bari recalled. "You just had to get [working] as quickly as possible." She hired a Bobcat front-end loader to clear debris from her yard. "I had pieces of debris everywhere," she said. "I had awnings, I had a pink flamingo from my neighbor's house in my backyard—people's trash cans from six blocks away." The Bobcat cleared everything, leaving only the bare topsoil. Then, she and her boys emptied the house, carrying broken appliances to the curb and throwing everything else out the windows. Five days later, the Bobcat operator returned to shovel the remains of their life out onto the street. "After I'm sitting in the house with the bare walls," she said, "*then* I could cry about it."

Over the following weeks, Bari washed her vinyl siding, hung plants on her front porch, and began the difficult work of refinishing her interior. It was not long before her work drew notice. Bari found herself juggling engagements with "every media outlet in the country." NBC, ABC, CBS, Fox, CNN, NPR, and the *Christian Sci-*

*ence Monitor* all lined up for interviews. She enjoyed the spotlight,
but was far more heartened by the attention she received from within
Lakeview.

"I heard brakes squeal one day. I looked out and this four-wheel
drive [was] just screeching to a halt in front of my house," she recalled. It was a neighbor, incredulous to see a house that looked "normal" in the sea of destruction. Soon, more neighbors arrived. "The
guy across the street didn't even want to come back and look at the
house," Bari recalled. "His wife came, and she went home and told
him, 'Bari's back, she looks like she's got half the house fixed already,
she's moving in.' He came back."

In late October, Lakeview remained almost completely empty.
The 70124 zip code had reopened for "look and leave" visits—Bari no
longer had to sneak past soldiers to access her house—but a curfew
remained in place. The neighborhood's fate was an open question.
Bari would later shudder when she recalled a front-page article in the
*Times-Picayune.* Joe Canizaro, developer and chairman of the mayor's
Bring New Orleans Back Commission, was quoted saying that "his
vision for Lakeview [was] acre-sized lots with plantation-style homes,
palmetto trees, and tennis courts." In the months following Katrina,
it seemed entirely possible that Lakeview's housing stock could be
demolished to make way for such a vision.

Indeed, with particularly severe flood damage and a solidly
upper-middle-class demographic that could afford to "wait and see,"
Lakeview faced the danger of a massive collective-action problem.
Convincing residents to reinvest in their homes would require proving to them that their neighbors planned to do the same. No one
wanted to move into a house surrounded by empty lots and blight—
or even worse, a house that would simply be bulldozed at the behest of
a citywide recovery scheme. With the city government in chaos and
the neighborhood's population scattered across dozens of states, the
LCIA board members faced a tremendous challenge as they began
early efforts to prove Lakeview's viability. Their first major attempt
would come at a large rally, scheduled for the second-to-last weekend
of October in the parking lot at St. Dominic's Church.

⚜   ⚜   ⚜

The morning of Saturday, October 23, 2005, was warm and sunny.
Bari Landry surveyed the asphalt swath as residents began to arrive.

The preparations had been hasty—ten flooded-out cars were towed off the parking lot shortly before the meeting was scheduled to begin— but now everything was in place. Drago's, a nearby seafood restaurant that escaped flooding, had donated 2,500 lunches for what most anticipated would be a large crowd. Nearly twenty people would be addressing the gathering, from the police superintendent to officials from utility companies. There still was not any electricity in Lakeview, so Bari had brought her home generator to power the meeting's sound equipment.

Most of those arriving at the meeting had driven in from outside of New Orleans. Some were staying just across the 17th Street Canal in Jefferson Parish; others came in from Baton Rouge or out of state. Tears and hugs abounded as friends and neighbors saw one another for the first time since the storm. Little was certain in Katrina's aftermath, but the mere presence of familiar faces was reassuring. As the crowd swelled and the parking lot filled toward its periphery, many hoped that the meeting would begin to answer the many questions that would determine whether, when, and how they would rebuild their homes.

The topics covered at the meeting were wide-ranging. Peppi Bruneau, the neighborhood's state representative, urged homeowners to call for a class-action lawsuit against house insurance companies that failed to compensate homeowners for flood damage. A representative from Entergy, the local energy utility, elicited groans when he estimated that it could take as long as eight months to restore power to all of the homes in Lakeview. A tense moment ensued when a speaker rose and introduced himself as a worker for the Army Corps of Engineers. As Bari later recounted, "I thought they would eat him alive until he explained that he was from the debris collection and he was a Lakeview resident. He felt our pain."

More important than the speakers, though, was the meeting's staggering turnout. The Drago's restaurant table ran out of food, leaving long lines of disappointed and hungry residents. Bari later estimated that three thousand people were in attendance. For those who were unsure whether their neighbors would return, the turnout came as a truly welcome surprise. As one resident reported, "We thought about not coming back at all. And my husband was very adamant about not coming back. He was like, 'There's no way. We're not going to deal with this again. We're not going to have to worry about flooding or losing everything.' . . . I was surprised at how many people had turned out. . . . And I was like, 'We're coming back. We're gonna do this. I don't know how, but we're gonna do this.'"

The meeting's high turnout was also important, according to Bari, because it sent a clear message to the city that Lakeview was on the mend. Looking back on the months following Katrina, she recalled that Lakeview's future had been in question. She and other LCIA board members had close connections to many of the BNOB Commission members. "They might have a relationship with this businessman, this banker, this educator," she later explained, "and call them up and say, 'Hey, you're on this committee, what's up?'" From these contacts, she continued, "we got the idea that they were trying to write us off."

The rally's turnout, Bari later asserted, nipped any thought of abandoning Lakeview in the bud. The meeting sent the message that "we're messed up, but you don't kill us that easily. . . . There [are] too many people who care too much about this neighborhood. It's gonna be back."

⚜ ⚜ ⚜

Freddy Yoder was a bear of a man, with a deep voice and a commanding presence. Three decades in Lakeview had instilled Freddy with the firm conviction that there was nowhere else in the world like his neighborhood, and over the years, he had become one of the community's most prominent leaders. During the 1980s, he was a vocal proponent of Lakeview's secessionist movement. Since then, he had remained active in the LCIA, serving as the organization's president and then as one of its board members.

Now, after Katrina, Freddy found himself thrust into the limelight, trying to explain to the rest of the world what made Lakeview so special. Whether talking to reporters or representing the neighborhood during the public comment periods of early citywide planning meetings, Freddy found himself repeatedly making the case that Lakeview *had* to come back.

"I know everybody loves their home and most people love the neighborhoods they live in," he would say, "but people in Lakeview *love* Lakeview. They don't want to live any place else. . . . I've described it publicly as being almost like an Indian reservation. You know, that's kind of the way it is. I've got four generations [of family] within a two-block area of my house. That's like an Indian reservation. And that's what *life* is all about. That's what young people . . . should be excited about and striving for."

On January 11, 2006, the Bring New Orleans Back Commission released its report. Freddy joined hundreds of other New Orleanians in a cramped ballroom at the downtown Sheraton Hotel to hear the commission's presentation. He watched as a representative from the planning firm Wallace Roberts and Todd gave a PowerPoint presentation titled "Action Plan for New Orleans: The New American City." Few were impressed with the commission's recommendations for an expanded network of parks and a new light-rail system. Freddy was quoted in the next day's *Washington Post* complaining, "Give me a break. We don't need a light-rail system. We're in the mud."[1]

"I was very disillusioned with what I heard," Freddy recalled. "The plan was more visionary than it was nuts and bolts. It was more conceptual than it was actually something that the people could use for the recovery. It was talking about the way things were going to be in the future and the great things that they were going to stress and try improve on. And in the meantime, everyone was trying to dig themselves out . . . and put their lives back together."

The presentation ended with the BNOB commission's controversial recommendations for neighborhood reconstruction. Freddy balked at the suggestion that flooded areas heed a four-month moratorium on rebuilding while they decided on their fate. When the meeting opened for public comment, he joined the rush to the microphone. "Our neighborhood is ready to come home," he said. "We want to be able to go down to City Hall and get a permit now. We have the means to help ourselves. So don't get in our way."

Indeed, Freddy had already done a great deal to spur Lakeview's recovery. His company, Durr Heavy Construction, had cleared mud from the streets, removed downed trees, and hauled away debris. Thanks in part to Durr's work, Lakeview residents could now safely get to their flooded homes. Many had already taken advantage of this access, beginning the difficult task of gutting their properties. Lakeview residents, Freddy believed, could draw on their personal resources and community connections to bring their neighborhood back to life. The BNOB meeting made it clear that Lakeview would be receiving little help from higher levels of government. "After the meeting," he later explained, "it became obvious to me that if we were going to recover, it was going to be the people in the field, on the ground. It was going to be from the people in their communities rebuilding and taking action on their own."

To this end, Freddy decided to call a meeting of his own. Shortly after the release of the BNOB report, the president of the LCIA and three former presidents converged at Freddy's office, with the goal of plotting a path forward for their neighborhood. How could Lakeview "prove its viability" without frittering away four valuable months of its recovery?

The BNOB recommendations suggested that teams of urban planners be assigned to each of the city's neighborhoods by February. As the meeting in Freddy's office progressed, those present quickly reached a consensus that Lakeview could not afford to wait for an outside team to chaperone the neighborhood through a planning process. They did not want Lakeview to be pigeonholed by outside constraints, nor did they want outsiders influencing residents' preferences for their neighborhood's recovery. Lakeview, they decided, needed to embark on its own planning process.

This would be challenging. The planning would have to balance and constructively channel the opinions of thousands of affected residents. Its resultant plan would need to be seen as legitimate both by residents and by the city government. The plan would also have to be realistic, building toward an achievable vision for the neighborhood's future. Parks and bike paths and light rail sounded nice, but most Lakeview residents had been perfectly content with their neighborhood prior to the storm; to many, utopian visions seemed like a waste of time given the concrete problems the neighborhood now faced.

Lakeview resident and former LCIA president Martin Landrieu was present at Freddy's meeting. A short but solidly built man, Martin attacked problems with a no-nonsense vigor that endeared him to his neighbors and coworkers. Though he hailed from the state's most prominent political family—his father, Moon, had been mayor of New Orleans; his sister Mary was one of Louisiana's U.S. senators; and his brother Mitch was the state's lieutenant governor—he eschewed the refinement and restraint of the political world. He was perfectly comfortable sporting several days' worth of stubble, and usually was not shy about voicing his opinions. "Planning is crap," he said. "What you really need is the cleaning up of houses. Everybody's thinking, 'Where are the hammers and nails?'"

Planning and implementation, Martin asserted, "shouldn't wait for each other." As Freddy's meeting wound down, a strategy emerged. Lakeview would undertake a planning process, but much of it would focus on tackling the most immediate obstacles to the neighborhood's recovery. Planning committees would overlap and interact with implementation committees, so that short-term problems could be immediately addressed even as longer-term plans were in the works.

To maintain the legitimacy of the process in the city's eyes, and to coordinate Lakeview's planning with that of neighboring communities, the group resolved to reach out to the presidents of residents' associations in the six neighborhoods that bordered Lakeview. Lakeview and these other six neighborhoods together constituted City Planning District 5—a division created before Katrina by the City Planning Commission. Creating a unified district recovery plan, those present reasoned, would grant it credibility. Besides, one of those present at the meeting recalled, "There's strength in numbers." Lakeview, they resolved, would prove its viability, and not waste any time in the process.

⚜ ⚜ ⚜

Four months later, on a Friday evening in April of 2006, the members of the District 5 neighborhood recovery steering committee assembled for yet another capstone meeting at the end of another exhausting week. Roughly a dozen people filtered into the room, collapsing into chairs as they greeted one another. This Friday routine was becoming familiar, and the attendees were getting to know one another well. Though the plurality hailed from Lakeview, which was larger than all of the other six neighborhoods in District 5 combined, representatives from the other neighborhoods were present as well. Everyone in the room had taken on a superhuman workload, and the committee members commiserated about the past week's roadblocks and difficulties as they rummaged for pens and notepads, waiting for the meeting to begin.

Martin Landrieu, the former LCIA president, chaired the steering committee. It had been nearly three months since Freddy Yoder called the small meeting that first gave rise to the District 5 group, and a great deal had occurred since. In February, neighborhood presidents from Lakewood, Lake Vista, Lake Shore, City Park, Country Club Gardens, and Parkview had signed on to undertake a grassroots, district-wide planning process. They formally constituted the District 5 steering committee. Then, Martin, Freddy Yoder, Bari Landry, and others had used their LCIA connections to recruit leaders for the numerous committees and subcommittees the planning effort would spawn. In March, the District 5 group had officially opened its planning process with a meeting at the large First Baptist Church, which four hundred people attended. After the meeting, committee heads worked the crowd, shaking hands and recruiting new members to help them with their work.

Now, in April, the District 5 group was a juggernaut, with eight primary committees and seventy-two subcommittees laying the groundwork for the recovery of nearly every facet of neighborhood life, from police coverage to playgrounds. Freddy Yoder chaired the infrastructure committee—tasked with helping to restore roads, utilities, and city services in the flooded neighborhoods—which alone had more than twenty-five subcommittees. He and his fellow committee heads toiled throughout the week, juggling countless phone calls and subcommittee meetings as they came to grips with the challenges on their respective fronts of the recovery war. The Friday meetings, as Freddy later explained, provided a chance to climb out of the trenches and compare notes. "Each of us brought back our own areas of ideas and expertise from our subcommittees of what needed to be incorporated into the plan," he said. "When we met on Friday, the goal was to bring all of these concepts together."

The planning being undertaken by the District 5 group was proactive. As Martin called the meeting to order and committee chairs began to give their reports, it was readily apparent that the committees were implementing as much as they were planning. The approach was intentional; Martin had asserted that the committees and subcommittees of District 5 should "plan for it and do it at the same time." A written plan was of only limited use; if committee members saw a clear path forward to solve a problem facing the neighborhood, they had a green light to pursue that solution.

Freddy Yoder's infrastructure committee adopted this proactive stance by resurrecting a block captain program. Years before the storm, the LCIA had tried to recruit leaders for each of the neighborhood's four hundred city blocks as part of a crime-watch initiative. "We were never successful," Freddy said. It was a different story in Katrina's wake. When residents came back to the flooded neighborhood, he said, "They wanted to help . . . people were very anxious to try to do what they could." It was not long before the infrastructure committee had recruited a captain for every block in the neighborhood.

Freddy tasked the block captains with keeping an inventory of physical problems in the vicinity of their homes. Many had not yet returned to their neighborhoods but took stock of problems on their blocks when they drove in to work on their houses. They cataloged junked cars, clogged drains, fallen trees, severed telephone wires, inoperable gas lines, broken power transformers, missing street signs, potholes, and any other physical problem close to their homes. Then, they reported each of these problems to the relevant infrastructure subcommittee.

As Freddy discussed his committee's work for the week, he read through the litany of problems it was addressing. Each of the roughly two dozen infrastructure subcommittees had a very particular purpose. One dealt exclusively with the New Orleans Sewerage and Water Board to restore running water to every block in the neighborhood. Another focused only on contending with stagnant, algae-filled swimming pools on abandoned lots, which posed a downing hazard to children and bred mosquitoes at an alarming rate. With such narrow purviews, each of the subcommittees grew efficient at cataloging complaints and following up on them. Often, the subcommittees worked with utility providers and city agencies to address problems. As Freddy later explained, "There was a conduit established between the committee head and whoever the key organization was. It might have been the regional planning authority, it might have been the permit department, it might have been the gas department. . . . We established networks of how to work with these people to get our mission done."

Infrastructure was just one of the seven committees that made up the District 5 group. The others dealt with community engagement, green space, urban planning, finance, crime prevention, and interneighborhood relations. Each committee confronted unique challenges. Brad Fortier, a Lakeview resident in his early thirties who chaired the finance committee, recalled his introduction to the committee's work: "My background is in finance, so I thought I could help. I quickly learned that they really didn't need anyone who was good with money, they needed someone who was good at *finding* money." Brad and his committee were writing grant applications and fund-raising—tasks to which he was a relative newcomer.

Other committee heads were delving into uncharted territory as well. In addition to chairing the District 5 steering committee, Martin Landrieu took leadership of District 5's neighborhood planning team. A lawyer by training, Martin had no formal experience with planning, but dove headfirst into the task nonetheless. Much of his committee's work dealt with zoning, envisioning alterations to the district's residential and commercial fabric that would improve its neighborhoods and spur their recovery.

As one committee member said, "We thought that we were going to have to rewrite the zoning regulations for Lakeview because . . . there was going to be a change in the way houses were going to need to be built because of the storm." Many new buildings—constructed above Katrina's high-water mark—would be substantially taller than pre-Katrina zoning would have allowed. Other changes would be needed as well; lots in Lakeview would get larger, as residents bought out neighbors who were not planning to return. Larger lots could in turn necessitate changes in the required distance between houses and the street. The planning would be technical and involved.

Luckily, the numerous District 5 committees had some assistance. Early on in their planning process, the District 5 organization had partnered with the University of New Orleans, which would provide professors with whom committee members could consult. As Freddy said, "We knew that we needed some real academic help in how all of this stuff comes together. Because we were from all different walks of life, you know, we had contractors, we had attorneys, we had real estate agents, we had all of these typical people . . . trying to do extraordinary things and write a recovery plan."

Students and professors from UNO partnered with District 5 committees and subcommittees as consultants, helping them put their ideas into action. While the UNO representatives helped create the structure of the emerging plan, however, the plan's content came from residents themselves. The resident-run committees and subcommittees were responsible for writing the plan, taking their cues from community-wide meetings. As Freddy later explained, "We had meetings in each of the different neighborhoods to pick everyone's brain to find out, 'What do you want us to do? What's important to you?'"

As Martin called this Friday night meeting to a close, he watched as the committee chairs continued to hover, conferring with one another and laying plans for the week ahead. He felt a quiet sense of satisfaction. Lakeview had a very long way to go, but its future lay in the best possible hands.

⚜  ⚜  ⚜

Connie Uddo had the compact athletic build of a former tennis pro, and always tackled new challenges with gusto. In March of 2006, however, she found herself ready to give up. She and her family had returned to Lakeview in January, when most of the neighborhood remained deserted. They lived in the upper two stories of a triplex, so their apartment and possessions remained intact. "I didn't really want to go back [yet]," Connie later explained. "I was kind of out-voted. . . . My kids and husband just felt like after moving four times in six months, that they just didn't care as long as they were home." Connie had gone along with the move, but now her reservations were beginning to boil over. "My car got broken into," she said. "I remember going to my husband and saying 'I can't do this.' It's one thing to live in this bombed-out kind of nuclear-disaster kind of environment with nobody around, kind of facing that every day, but then to put fear on top of it" was too much.

Looking back on the situation more than a year later, Connie could see clearly how the pieces began to fit together. "I know there's no accidents with God, I've learned that," she said. Connie prayed, read the Bible, and happened upon a verse in 2 Chronicles that struck her. "Be strong and courageous. Do not be afraid or discouraged of the king of Assyria and the vast army with him, for there is a greater power with us than with him," it read.

"I really looked at it, thought about it, meditated on it, prayed on it, wrote it up, took ownership of it," Connie recalled, "and said, 'Okay, I got the message, you want me to stay and face it. Show me how.'" Soon thereafter, Connie met a woman named Denise Thornton.

Denise, who kept her straight red hair in a short bob, lived in Lakewood, a small, affluent neighborhood that sat adjacent to Lakeview to the southwest. Her husband, the manager of the Superdome, was coordinating the effort to repair the stadium. Like Connie and her family, Denise and her husband had been among the first people back in their neighborhood. Denise found herself listless and depressed after moving back. For months, she and her husband camped out in their upstairs rooms, cooking on a portable electric stove while they renovated their downstairs. Then, one day, she had an idea.

Many of her neighbors were driving into the neighborhood to work on their homes, but had no place to get water, cool off, or use the bathroom. The renovation on Denise's property was going well;

she realized that her house was one of the few places for blocks in any direction that had air conditioning, running water, and comfortable places to sit. She decided to open her house as a resource center for her neighbors. The thought of letting strangers into her home did not seriously deter her. "You've got nothing to lose!" she later exclaimed.

Denise's open house was a hit, and it did not take long for word to spread in Lakewood that the brick two-story building on Bellaire Drive was the place to go to cool off, hear encouragement, and trade information after long, hot hours of gutting. With the steady flow of foot traffic through her living room, Denise kept abreast of the neighborhood's evolving needs.

Nearly everyone she met was starved for information. When would the new flood maps come out? How did the process of applying for a FEMA trailer work? Which roofing companies were reliable? What were the best wood treatments for mold? Before long, her living room had become an information clearinghouse. She kept lists of trustworthy contractors, helped her neighbors with paperwork, and traded tips about everything from power washing to electrical wiring. Her downstairs became a recovery office of sorts; she sent and received faxes on behalf of Lakewood residents, allowed them use of her Internet connection, and gave them free printing.

With a grant from one of the owners of the New Orleans Hornets basketball team—a friend of her husband's through his stadium work—Denise also purchased lawn mowers, weed whackers, and power washers to lend out in the neighborhood. Now that it was growing quickly and receiving money, Denise's new enterprise needed a name. When one grateful resident told Denise that her house had become "a beacon of hope" in the neighborhood, the name stuck. Denise had a banner printed that read "Beacon of Hope Resource Center," and hung it over her porch.

Denise recalled that when the two met, Connie's request was simple. "I want what you have," Connie said. "Show me how you do it." Denise proposed that the two spend a week working together out of Denise's house in Lakewood. Connie could shadow her, learn the ropes of running a home-based resource center, and then open a second Beacon out of her own home in Lakeview. "The only way to survive here," Denise said, "and to battle this depression, is to start helping people. Once you start helping people, you get focused off of your own problems, you get so darn busy, and at the end of the day you're ten feet off the ground."

By late spring in 2006, members of the District 5 recovery council in Lakeview began to catch word of the Beacons. Residents were talking enthusiastically about the help they had received from the centers, and about how they were spurring recovery in the areas where they operated. Freddy Yoder, whose infrastructure committee had helped restore utilities to Lakeview and clean up the neighborhood, saw a chance to pass the torch. "I looked at the model [Denise] had put together," Freddy said. "It became obvious to me that that could become the model for a lot of other things. That model could be used throughout the city for recovery."

Brad Fortier, the chair of District 5's finance committee, was also excited about the Beacons. He and his committee members had applied for grant after grant to fund the neighborhood's recovery, but they had been consistently denied. "I wasn't having much success helping the neighborhood," he said. The neighborhood was "generally perceived to be too affluent to get any governmental support and any kind of nonprofit support," he said. In the Beacon of Hope model, though, Brad saw a narrative that potential funders would love. "It's what the nonprofits want to see," he said. "It's got the feel-good aspect. It's neighbors helping neighbors."

Of course, if the Beacons were to partner with Lakeview's other recovery efforts, Denise and Connie would have to come on board. Freddy took it upon himself to recruit them. "I went to Denise [and] introduced myself to her," Freddy said. He presented a proposal to expand the number of Beacons in Lakeview. "I laid out an organizational structure for her of how we could grow the Beacons," he said. "I took that Lakeview area right there on that map and I divided it up into six major quadrants."

Each area, he proposed, could have its own Beacon of Hope Resource Center. The Beacons would be centers for neighborhood organizing around recovery. In addition to providing their usual array of services, the centers could recruit residents to coordinate volunteer teams, mow unkempt lawns, and help needy neighbors rebuild. "I was convinced," Freddy said, "that the recovery [was] going to take place from and by the people." Denise embraced the idea of expanding her organization, and gave Freddy a place on the Beacon's newly formed board.

With the agreement cemented, Brad Fortier began a push to secure funding for the new initiative. His wife worked for the United Way, and he had been waiting for a chance to make a pitch to the organization. "I wasn't going to go to them through Lakeview Civic Improvement Association or the District 5 planning group, because funders had been reluctant to give money to Lakeview-branded efforts," he said. "But when I heard about the Beacon of Hope, and this little mom-and-pop organization that had sprouted up, I felt that was a story I could tell, and so that's when I went to them and we got them engaged."

The United Way agreed to fund the Beacons. It had been tentative at first, Brad said, but warmed up to the idea as the months passed. By August of 2006, Connie, Freddy, and other Lakeview residents had recruited six new Beacon administrators and found six locations from which to base the new centers. Five of the Beacons would be run from private houses; the sixth would be run on the campus of an Episcopal church in the neighborhood. On Friday, August 25, Lakeview celebrated a simultaneous ribbon cutting for the six new centers.

⚜  ⚜  ⚜

By the fall of 2006, Terry Miranda had his morning routine down pat. It began with a short bike ride across the 17th Street Canal from a small house in Metairie to the St. Paul's Beacon of Hope Center. Most mornings, Connie Uddo was there to greet him. "We are his local coffee shop and newspaper every morning," she explained with a smile.

Terry was living with his uncle, an eighty-five-year-old veteran who had spent four years in a Japanese internment camp and served two tours in Korea. "He needed someone to stay with him and I needed someone to stay with, so it worked out well," Terry said.

Because he had a secure place to live, Terry decided to take his time as he renovated his house. "I just started getting contractors, which was insane. Try getting an electrician when one hundred thousand people are looking for electricians. . . . I decided that I wasn't going to drive myself crazy. So I just took one at a time. Needed a roof. So it took me a couple of weeks to get three bids, I took the middle bid. I used the Beacon of Hope. . . . To be on the list, you have to be insured and incorporated and have three references. So I started using the Beacon of Hope people, the contractors. So the guy came out and put a roof on for $5,600. I was happy with it." He went through a similar process for the next steps in his reconstruction.

Like many New Orleanians, Terry was able to rebuild his house because of the federally funded recovery program called The Road

Home, which provided grants to residents in flooded neighborhoods who either had no flood insurance or were underinsured. Terry had fallen into the former category, and had received a $105,000 grant—the maximum allowable amount for residents without flood insurance. Residents who had purchased flood insurance were eligible for grants of up to $150,000, if their insurance payouts did not cover the cost of their repairs.

Terry's experience with The Road Home was atypical in that it had been fairly easy. When the program was announced, he had called the appropriate 1-800 number, submitted his application, and gained relatively quick approval for funding. Other homeowners, however, found their applications inexplicably mired in red tape. More than a year after the program was unveiled, only 22,000 of the program's 140,000 applicants had received their checks, and the program was projecting a $2.9 billion shortfall.[2]

Terry also benefitted from Lakeview's high prestorm property values. Grants were calculated, in part, based on a property's prestorm value. Many criticized this policy, pointing out that housing repairs cost the same, regardless of the neighborhood in which a flooded house was located.

As he worked slowly on his own house, Terry worked closely with his neighbors to rebuild. "I'm retired; I had time," he said of his initial decision. "I was not going to sit. When I was going to come back, I was going to do something. And what I did was, as my neighbors came back, if my neighbors decided to come back, and needed help, I went from neighbor to neighbor to neighbor to neighbor to help 'em." His neighbors returned the favor. "We each had strong points and weak points that worked very well together," he said. One neighbor installed doors, trim, and appliances in Terry's house. Another decorated the interior once it was finished. He and his neighbors hired the same contractors, "which is why we didn't get ripped off," he recalled. Terry found the cooperation empowering.

As for the work, he said, "I found I could destroy anything." By his own estimate, he gutted twenty houses. He was quick to point out that self-interest partially motivated his generous acts. "It doesn't do me any good to come back if nobody else is here. So I'm getting something out of it. I'm getting a neighborhood." Sometimes, neighbors who were intimidated by the process of rebuilding decided that, with Terry's help, they could do it. The work usually left Terry sweaty and exhausted. After hours of gutting, painting, or hauling furniture, he would often return to the St. Paul's Beacon of Hope in the mid-afternoon to cool off, chat, and finish the newspaper.

The St. Paul's Beacon of Hope was the largest, best equipped, and most active of the Beacon locations in the Lake area. Some residents called it the "Super Beacon." It was based out of a large house on the campus of St. Paul's Episcopal Church, adjacent to the shops that constituted Lakeview's town center on Harrison Avenue. It had a wide covered porch with rocking chairs, tall windows, and a bright, refreshing, airy feel. Upstairs were volunteer housing and office space. Downstairs was a reception area with plush couches, a kitchen, a free-access computer, and a friendly receptionist named Merri Kay, who was always available to lend a hand, an ear, or a shoulder to cry on to the constant stream of residents who came through the door.

The St. Paul's center was a joint venture between the church and the Beacons of Hope. After running a successful Beacon out of her house, Connie Uddo received church funding to open and run the larger recovery center. Unlike Beacons in private homes, the center had regular hours, staff members, and an array of special resources and services, ranging from public washing machines to free weekly legal consults. The center had become a "one-stop shop" for a whole host of recovery needs, and served hundreds of returning residents every week.

The Beacons of Hope grew quickly adept at filling residents' unmet needs. As time passed, the Beacons also began an outreach campaign to contact residents who had not returned to the neighborhood. This was a sensitive task; in many cases, unreturned residents were not taking sufficient care of their properties. Lawns grew high; moldy furniture festered; mice and rats made their nests in nooks and crannies of houses that were not tightly boarded. Beacon administrators reaching out to the residents who owned these properties had to weigh the difficult situations the owners faced against the needs of the community. Their goal, in the end, was always to coax absent residents to take responsibility for their properties, and move toward deciding whether to return to Lakeview. The first challenge, though, was finding them.

Resident outreach began "in the summer of 2006," Connie said, when "nobody was doing anything. People were not around. And part of the Beacon, part of that one-on-one thing, is that you start finding your neighbors. . . . It just starts up by word of mouth."

When Beacon administrators contacted absent residents, they received a variety of responses. One administrator explained that when she called residents with unmaintained lots, "sometimes they'll get defensive right away, and I say, 'I'm not calling to fuss at you, I'm calling you to offer you some help. I've got a list of people that you can contact to get your lot or your lawn cut.'"

Others asked for guidance about whether and how they could ever return to the neighborhood. Connie often found herself playing counselor. "Where's your heart?" she would ask. "How are you feeling? If we showed you how you could come back and gave you resources and gave you a helping hand, do you think you would like to?"

"If they said yes," Connie explained, "or if they were on the fence, we would say, 'Why don't you let us [mow] your yard and why don't you meet us there if you can and then we'll walk around your property and identify the issues that maybe [are] making you think you can't come back.' And so many times after doing that . . . people turn their heads where at the end of that day they were coming back when they [thought] there was no way they could come back."

Not every resident came to this conclusion. For some, returning to Lakeview was too difficult a proposition. "I think you have to be very sensitive to where they are," Connie said. "It's a process. You can't push. Now we do push to get them *in* . . . a decision-making process. And you have to respect where they are. I mean point blank some people say, 'You know, look, we have young children . . . we don't think we can live there.' We have to respect that, because we have to put ourselves in their shoes."

The neighborhood's substantial prestorm population of elderly residents posed a particularly difficult challenge for Beacon administrators. Often the children of elderly residents took possession of their parents' property after the storm, only to neglect it as they waited for property values to rise or renovation funds to materialize. When elderly residents retained control of their properties, they faced a particularly daunting task. Physical limitations, lack of access to long-term credit, and familial pressure to move into assisted living all conspired to keep many of the neighborhood's elderly from rebuilding. For the Beacons, helping with displaced seniors presented a delicate tightrope walk. "You can't push an eighty-year-old who's in a nursing home to come back," Connie explained. "But if you have an elderly person calling you from a nursing home saying, 'I don't want to die here, I want to die in my home, what can you do to help me?' we're going to do everything we can to get that elderly [person] back."

As Lakeview slowly continued to recover, the Beacons of Hope began to broaden their focus from rebuilding outreach and assistance. A Beacon administrator named Rita held weekly meetings in her dining room that proved wildly popular with her neighbors. Often, she would invite administrators from City Hall, utility companies, or the Army Corps of Engineers to provide updates on specific aspects of the city's recovery. Residents also took the time to catch up with and get to know one another. Many marveled at how much the storm had done to bring them together, crediting Rita with having helped turn their neighbors from strangers into friends. Lakeview had a long way to go, but seeing their shared commitment made the residents more optimistic about its future.

Terry, for one, shared this optimism. As he biked down Lakeview's streets at the end of a hard day's work, he was encouraged to see renovations under way on block after block. "There's tremendous loyalty here for a lot of people," he explained. He knew that Lakeview would never be the same—the neighborhood in which he had grown up was "gone forever," he said—but he had faith that the next chapter in the neighborhood's story would be as rich as the previous one had been. "New Orleans history will be divided pre-Katrina and post-Katrina," he said, but Lakeview's post-Katrina story would be one of rebirth.

# CHAPTER 8

## Broadmoor: "This Is No Ordinary Plan"

FATHER JERRY KRAMER WALKED down an improvised aisle, careful not to trip on the extension chords that crisscrossed the bare floorboards. Around him, piled high to the exposed rafters, were stacks of relief supplies. There were gallon jugs of bleach, cans of food, boxes of blankets and clothing. Before Katrina, the space had been Annunciation Church's meeting hall, used for church dinners, Sunday coffee, and vestry meetings. Now, its gutted remains served as the warehouse for a hastily organized and quickly expanding relief operation.

Outside in the parking lot, the line was already growing. It was a chilly morning in late December, and though the church would not open for another half hour, several dozen people were pacing about the blacktop, their hands shoved deep into jacket pockets to ward off the cold. Broadmoor, the triangular neighborhood in the center of New Orleans that Annunciation Church called home, remained largely empty. Most residents, including Broadmoor Improvement Association president LaToya Cantrell, had yet to return. Annunciation was an oasis. If today turned out anything like the day before, the line would be far longer by 10 a.m., when supply distribution would begin. Word was spreading fast about the relief operation at the little church on Claiborne Avenue.

So far, Father Jerry's tenure had been a brief but eventful chapter in the history of this small parish. Founded in 1844, its full name was the Free Church of the Annunciation, so called because it had been one of the first churches in the city to abolish pew rent. From its egalitarian roots, the church grew a small but loyal following of parishioners. It moved several times during its first century of existence, coming to rest in a yellow brick building on a shaded block on Broadmoor's southern periphery—the building at which Father Jerry arrived in the beginning of 2005.

Father Jerry and his wife came to New Orleans from Tanzania, where the two had worked as missionaries. He made quite an impression on his parishioners and church leadership when he arrived. He did not fit the predictable mold of a reserved, pious minister. "The bishop likes me because I drive a truck, I always carry a loaded gun, and I spit tobacco," he later explained with a laugh. "You think that's funny? I have a loaded .38 with me at all times."

Father Jerry was appalled by what he found in New Orleans. "Before Katrina, New Orleans was worse than East Africa," he recalled. "We had better roads, schools, and hospitals, and it was safer in East Africa than here." At Annunciation, Father Jerry found a small, sleepy congregation. Most of the church's operating budget came from rent drawn from a downtown high-rise it owned, and from Father Jerry's perspective, the secure stream of money bred a culture of complacency at the church. His African missionary work had accustomed him to active and outward-looking ministry, and he felt compelled to continue this work in New Orleans. Inspiring his congregation to embrace this approach, it had seemed, would be a long struggle.

Then, in August of that year, Katrina changed everything. Parishioners were scattered around the country and the church building was badly flooded. As quickly as he could, Father Jerry rounded up his staff and joined relief efforts being coordinated through the Episcopal Diocese in New Orleans. "Our mandate was to go where no one else was," he said. He drove a newly purchased RV into Lakeview as soon as it reopened, following the Humvee tracks through the mud and setting up a temporary relief center on the flooded campus of St. Paul's Episcopal Church.

After the Red Cross arrived in Lakeview, Father Jerry and the others moved on to Broadmoor, setting up shop in the parking lot at their own church. At that point, Father Jerry said, there was "no nothing" in the neighborhood. The houses looked bombed out, and the streets were largely empty. No one at Annunciation had heard a peep from the Broadmoor Improvement Association, though they did not really expect to. As Father Jerry recalled, "The only involvement that we had with the neighborhood [before the storm] was fighting with the neighborhood about zoning issues. We had no relationship with Broadmoor whatsoever."

October had been a month of organized chaos as Annunciation's relief operation came together. "We were begging, borrowing, stealing" to get the needed supplies, Father Jerry said. Noel, the church's groundskeeper, shuttled daily between Baton Rouge and New Orleans, maxing out credit cards to stuff his Jeep with supplies. For larger supply runs, Father Jerry dispatched a parishioner in the RV. Bleach—used for disinfecting floors and cleaning flooded possessions—was in such high demand that the church would give away hundreds of gallons per hour. Other items, like tanks of potable water, had to be delivered by truck. A shipment of fresh water cost $6,000 to deliver and lasted for less than a week.

Throughout November, Annunciation's relief operation grew more regularized and better resourced. This was due, in large part, to funding from larger churches across the nation. These churches, Father Jerry explained, "follow a very interesting pattern. They will shoot you a little up-front money, just to keep you alive, and then they wait. . . . Then they just go around quietly and investigate. . . . They find the grassroots frontline trench workers who are getting the job done, and they resource the hell out of them."

Such was the story at Annunciation, which received substantial support from the United Methodists and the Salvation Army. "They have the best relief operation out there," Father Jerry said, "because all they did was give us what we needed." Every Monday, trucks of relief supplies pulled up to the church, and Annunciation's staff members stood ready to shuttle crates and boxes into the hastily converted warehouse. "We would pack it to the rafters," Father Jerry recalled. Of late, the warehouse had been emptying out by Thursday.

Father Jerry walked out the door and began working his way down the line, exchanging greetings, laughing at jokes, dispensing hugs, and prompting residents who looked the most distressed to join him in quiet prayer. When the operation opened its doors, the line moved quickly, and people were soon dispersing from the parking lot, their arms filled with cartons of bleach and boxes of food. Tomorrow, Father Jerry knew, the line would be even longer.

⚜ ⚜ ⚜

As Annunciation Church distributed relief supplies to returning residents, the Broadmoor Improvement Association was nowhere to be seen. For four months after the storm, BIA board members were scattered across the country. The BIA's president, LaToya Cantrell, was still stuck in Houston with her husband. She did her best to keep up with developments in New Orleans, but her hands were tied. "Up to January," she recalled, "it was just finding people, I mean, you're displaced, you don't know where anybody is, you're e-mailing."

Then, on January 11, 2006, the Bring New Orleans Back Commission released its recommendations. "All hell broke loose when we saw that green dot over Broadmoor," LaToya recalled. She began fielding calls from worried residents almost immediately after the BNOB commission's plan was released. Many Broadmoor residents still remember exactly where they were when they first learned of the green dot. Virginia Saussy, who had already moved back into to the upstairs of her large house on Napoleon Avenue, was at work. She had not read the paper that morning, but friends called her and gave her the news. As she later remembered, "I was hysterical. I didn't know what I was going to do."

Virginia joined the growing list of residents who were calling the Broadmoor Improvement Association's president. "I pulled LaToya Cantrell's cell-phone number out," Virginia said. "I said, 'This is Virginia Saussy, I'm really upset, and I'm planning a rally.'" The vice president of a major New Orleans jewelry company and a cofounder of the successful all-female Mardi Gras troupe Krewe of Muses, Virginia had an entrepreneurial flair colored by moments of creative inspiration. When struck by the idea of a rally, she ran with it, making up the details on the fly. She decided on the event's time and location—4 p.m. the following Saturday on Napoleon Avenue's wide neutral ground—after a neighbor called her to ask when the rally would take place.

Virginia picked the weekend date so that still-displaced Broadmoorians could drive back into the city, and scheduled the rally just in time for the evening news cycle. She called Renee Gill Pratt, Broadmoor's city council representative, who said, "It's not legal to use the neutral ground, so I don't know anything about it, but I'll be there." Then, Virginia systematically worked to contact everyone she knew in the neighborhood, a difficult task given that home phone numbers were useless. Word of the rally nonetheless spread.

In the four days between the release of the BNOB Commission's report and the rally, Virginia also put her marketing training to work. Broadmoor needed a slogan—something catchy that would become the neighborhood's answer to the green dot. She e-mailed LaToya some ideas. "No Parking in Broadmoor" was one, but it did not make the cut. Eventually, she settled on the simple phrase "Broadmoor Lives." The slogan came in response to the BNOB Commission's implicit assertion that flooded neighborhoods had yet to come back to life. Recalled Virginia: "I said, 'Screw that. Broadmoor lives right now.' If they're not driving around and seeing the amount of debris that shows people are gutting, they don't even know what they're thinking about!"

Virginia knew that people at the rally would have to see the slogan in order to fully internalize it, so she had a fifteen-foot-wide banner made. The banner proclaimed "Broadmoor Lives" in bold green, appropriating the color of the green dot but turning it on its head. Virginia hung the banner from her front porch, in plain view of where the rally would take place.

Meanwhile, the eleven-member board of the Broadmoor Improvement Association was discussing its own response to the green dot. LaToya had scheduled a neighborhood-wide meeting for Wednesday evening of the next week, which Virginia's impromptu rally seemed to upstage. Rather than treating the rally as a competing event, though, LaToya and the board resolved to use it as a venue to advertise their meeting and sign up BIA members. Virginia's rally could be a good first step for the neighborhood; LaToya and others hoped to capitalize on its momentum and channel it constructively.

Board members also realized that a strong BIA presence at Virginia's rally would be critical to maintaining the association's relevance to Broadmoor. In her old neighborhood, Virginia had overthrown an entrenched residents association after growing dissatisfied with its hostile stance toward local businesses. As Virginia recalled, "LaToya was smart, because she realized that I really, seriously would have started another organization."

Saturday came, the news trucks pulled up, and residents began to arrive on the neutral ground en masse—many from out of town. One resident later remarked, "We were surprised that there were that many people there. Because . . . before the storm, neighborhood involvement was about twenty-five people." An anti–green dot petition that was circulated at the rally garnered more than three hundred signatures. Though paltry in comparison to Broadmoor's seven thousand prestorm residents, the tally was impressive in the context of a still-abandoned city.

Displaying her flair for the dramatic, Virginia climbed atop a car to address the crowd. A well-known local barber, who had temporarily reopened his shop in a tent, held her feet in place so she did not slip. As Virginia later explained with a smile, "I just screamed out, 'I live in that house, and it looks better after Katrina than it did three years ago when we found it. How dare the city question whether our neighborhood is alive. We're not going to let the city tell us what we're going to do with our property.' "

⚜   ⚜   ⚜

Days after the release of the Bring New Orleans Back Commission's recommendations, Broadmoor resident Hal Roark was not doing well. For months, he had camped out at an acquaintance's empty house, trying to come to grips with the flooded properties he owned across the city. Most days, he found himself alone; many of his friends had not returned to New Orleans, and his wife and daughter had only recently returned from staying with family in Chattanooga, Tennessee. Hal always had plenty of work to do: gutting, long and often angry phone calls with insurance companies, trips to City Hall for appropriate permits. But whenever he slowed down a bit to think, he would notice his death grip on the steering wheel or his quavering handwriting and realize that the stress was taking a serious toll.

Hal, like many other transplants to New Orleans, realized only after Katrina just how emotionally and financially invested he had become in the city. Born in Rhode Island, he had moved to New Orleans to participate in a community service program shortly after attending college at Yale. He fell in love with his surroundings and never left. Always looking for a new project, Hal had taught high school, received a master of social work degree from Tulane, and cofounded several companies and nonprofits. Of late, with a family to support, he had begun to invest in rental properties, and was going into business with a self-published series of "how-to" books focused on the fair and profitable operation of Section 8 housing. Only now did his once-profitable real estate business seem foolish; all but one of his rental properties had flooded.

Hal's own house—a five-thousand-square-foot, three-story gem with a wide elevated porch and ornate trim—was located in Broadmoor. "Before Katrina," he later explained, "I used to tell people that I loved my house but I tolerated my neighborhood." Surveying the rest of Hal's block from his front porch told part of the story; a smattering of less impressive double-shotgun-style homes surrounded his house. Some were rentals, including one that Hal owned himself, and others were fairly dilapidated. For the most part, Hal's friends lived outside of Broadmoor.

Nevertheless, Hal took the green dot over his neighborhood personally. Worn down after months of work, he had been preparing for the day when he and his family could move back home. Both Hal's own house and the rental property he owned down the street had been flooded severely, but he worked around the clock to make them livable. He had recently finished repairs to the rental, and a group of Tulane students had signed a lease on the house. The next day, he finally allowed himself a break, only to sit down in front of the paper and read about the BNOB Commission's recommendations.

Katrina had robbed Hal of any sense of control over his life, but through hard work on his properties over the intervening months, he had felt himself slowly coming back into his own. Under the green dot, he was back at square one. Only after two days of "shock and bereavement," he said, did he gain a renewed sense of direction.

Used to a frenetic pace, Hal found himself in an unusual position. He was sitting still, reading and pondering, poring over the BNOB report. "The urban planning committee identified all of these values," he later explained, "and I couldn't figure out how the values they articulated corresponded with the plan they had produced." He began to make a spreadsheet, taking stock of the values listed by the report, noting their page numbers, and then finding examples of contradictions to these values in the plan.

The report, for example, called for recovery policy to be based on rationality and scientific reason; Hal, on the other hand, viewed the green dots as "policy recommendations based on private interests, and not the greater public good." The report called for neighborhood self-determination, but to Hal, it smacked of "outsider control and determination." As he worked, he began to formulate an idea.

Hal had not been involved with the Broadmoor Improvement Association (BIA) prior to Katrina, and he had never met LaToya Cantrell, but days after the green dot's announcement, he sent her an e-mail. The BIA was planning a Wednesday night meeting, he learned, and it was probably going to be big. No public buildings had reopened in Broadmoor, so LaToya was renting a tent that could hold hundreds of people. The city was abuzz with talk of the need for neighborhoods to "prove their viability," and at this meeting, residents would begin to decide exactly what proving viability would mean for Broadmoor.

Hal told LaToya about his brainstorming, and proposed that the community vote on the values contained in the BNOB report. As the two talked, the idea clearly formed. Rather than vehemently protesting the Bring New Orleans Back plan, Broadmoor residents could band together to "beat the city at its own game," as Hal put it. They could take each of the values articulated by the BNOB plan, and then create their own plan for Broadmoor that actually lived up to those values. The BIA could pull enough residents into the process that the neighborhood would "prove its viability," demonstrating that people were indeed intent upon returning to their homes.

LaToya liked the idea. It seemed that Broadmoor residents would be well served by taking the neighborhood's fate into their own hands; the city government was certainly doing Broadmoor no favors. She invited Hal to present his idea to the neighborhood.

In preparation for the meeting, LaToya also created two committees that would spearhead the neighborhood's recovery work. One, cochaired by Virginia Saussy and Kelli Wright, a local realtor, would focus on spurring and tracking the neighborhood's repopulation. The other, cochaired by Hal and Mark Maurice, a local attorney, would focus on the neighborhood's physical revitalization. Each committee's purview was vast, and their missions were intertwined; residents could not return without renovated buildings and restored infrastructure, but these repairs would occur only if residents recommitted themselves to the neighborhood. The neighborhood's fate depended on residents taking the plunge.

The meeting would be LaToya's one shot to mobilize the neighborhood around the Broadmoor Improvement Association, and it had to go well. The BIA, LaToya knew, would have to "set the tone in the very beginning by being extremely organized . . . and results-driven in our approach." Residents would also need to know that they would have a direct stake in the BIA's work moving forward. If the meeting fell apart, the BIA could lose its mantle of leadership in the neighborhood. If that happened, residents might lose confidence and decide not to return to Broadmoor.

As the appointed hour approached on Wednesday night, a crowd of more than five hundred residents gathered at the tent. They huddled against the cold, congregating around the rented electric heaters, and spilling outside when the tent reached capacity. Many were anxious; they had little idea what would become of their neighborhood. "When we had that meeting in January in the tent," one woman recalled, "we didn't know *what* was going to happen about *anything*."

LaToya began the meeting promptly, and progressed quickly through the agenda. First, she introduced the new chairs of the repopulation and revitalization committees, urging the assembled residents to join their ranks. Then, Hal stood to address the crowd, and spoke frankly. "There is no guarantee of success," he said, "but our best shot at survival will be for us to come together and produce our own plan."

Father Jerry Kramer was standing in the audience. After months of silence from the BIA, he was surprised to see that they had put together such a big event; the green dot, it seemed, had everyone spooked. Father Jerry had never met Hal, but Hal's speech stuck with him. "I'm at the rally," he recalled, "and like it's a friggin' freezing cold night with the tiki torches. And all that I hear is this voice of someone who's just like, 'We're coming back and to hell with the city.' I don't know who this is, but it's making a lot of sense to me."

Other residents bought into Hal's idea too. The BIA, they agreed by consensus, would facilitate a resident-driven planning process for the neighborhood. Before the meeting adjourned, the assembled residents took a poll with a simple question: "Do you plan to return to your home?" More than 90 percent answered yes.

As residents stood to leave, the new committee chairs hurriedly collected contact information and signed up new members. Conversation turned to the specifics of the planning process; a few people began to create impromptu e-mail lists for planning subcommittees. The general feeling was upbeat and reassured. As one woman recalled, "I went to the meeting, and I saw neighbors and I saw organization and I saw caring and I saw smart people working. Then I thought, 'Okay, well I'd *like* to live here now. Now it seems like, wow, this is a *special* place to live.'"

Hal, for one, felt at once exhilarated and relieved. Speaking with his wife that night, he said, "For the first time in a long time, I feel like there's something in my life that I have some semblance of control over."

⚜   ⚜   ⚜

After Father Jerry Kramer attended the BIA's meeting in the big tent, he vowed to stay involved with the neighborhood. He was impressed with the organization and determination he saw, and hoped to get to know people in the neighborhood better. When the BIA organized residents to distribute flyers to every home in the neighborhood, Father Jerry invited the flyer team back to the church's trailer for lunch.

Two things struck him that day, he said. First, those who came to the church for lunch were effusive in their thanks. "Thank you," Father Jerry paraphrased. "We have no place to sit in air conditioning—or heat, at the time—and with power, and visit with friends we haven't seen since the storm. Thank you.

"The number-two thing that I heard from all 180 people [was] . . . 'We never knew what these buildings were. We didn't even know you were a church.'" As Father Jerry explained, "That was the seminal moment. I knew intuitively that for the recovery, for this church to be viable, that we had to be intimately involved with the neighborhood, which we never were before. . . . I used to do church consulting work [and] my relevancy test was very simple. 'If your church went away, would anybody miss you, other than your members?' And we failed it miserably. Nobody in Broadmoor would have missed this church for any reason whatsoever. None. We were an island."

Soon after hosting neighborhood volunteers for lunch, Father Jerry extended an offer to LaToya Cantrell and the rest of the BIA. Knowing that they were without a space to meet and work, he implored them to move into the church's trailer, pledging to give them half of the space for as long as they needed. "We'll give you everything you want and need," he said. "Anything you want, we'll find for you. Just move in." LaToya took him up on his request.

Planning had been moving quickly in Broadmoor after the big meeting in the tent, with three or four meetings taking place every week. LaToya, whose flooded house was not yet renovated, moved into a downtown hotel to facilitate the planning process full time. Like LaToya, most Broadmoorians had not yet returned to their homes, but many made a point of driving back into the neighborhood to attend the meetings. The committee cochairs worked furiously to keep one step ahead of developments, compiling their notes from previous meetings while preparing agendas for subsequent ones.

In the first week of planning, Hal Roark advocated for the neighborhood to be divided into three roughly equal geographic sections, so that smaller and more-intimate planning meetings could take place among neighbors in each area. The subsections, as LaToya later explained, were "naturally defined." Three main roads transected Broadmoor and met at its center, which created the geographic boundaries for the subsections. The subsections were divided by more than just geography, however. Though a great deal of racial and socioeconomic diversity existed within each subgroup, the neighborhood's southwestern subsection had been gentrifying, its northern subsection was predominantly working class, and many families in its southeastern subsection were impoverished.

LaToya saw the merits of the idea to subdivide Broadmoor during the planning process, but also perceived risks. She later explained that because of demographic differences, "factions" already existed among the subgroups. "This was not an opportunity for a certain section to feel like they were much stronger, or like they needed to be saved versus another section."

If the neighborhood was to be subdivided, she later explained, "There was a way we'd have to handle that. It wasn't just have a meeting in a subdivision, because that's not building community." The subsection meetings could proceed, she decided, but only if all of the subsections regularly "came back as a community" to decide on a path forward for the entire neighborhood. This process—subgroup meetings followed by neighborhood-wide meetings in which subgroup plans were synthesized and voted upon—became Broadmoor's standard planning procedure.

Residents involved with the planning process quickly became well versed in the jargon used to designate each subsection. The subsections were given letters, with A referring to Broadmoor's working-class northern section, B to its impoverished eastern section, and C to its gentrifying western section. Sentences like "She's from up in A" or "B had a great meeting last night" became commonplace.

It soon became clear that the subsections were a helpful innovation. Early on in the planning process, LaToya noticed a tendency for white middle-class residents and poor black residents to articulate their needs and priorities in markedly different ways. For example, discussion at early subgroup meetings in Subsection B revolved around reducing crime, as a crime wave was sweeping through that part of the neighborhood. By contrast, residents in Section C were eagerly discussing plans for bike paths. With all of the residents in one room at the same time, she reflected, there was a danger they would "talk past one another."

"There's some tension there," LaToya noted, "and you have to make sure that people feel like they have a vested interest, that they are a part of these talks. And if you don't do that, things can go to the far left real fast. Real fast. And that would have shut down everything that this neighborhood was doing."

The job of reconciling differences in priorities and outlook among the subsections fell to planning facilitators—residents who had signed up for the job of attending every meeting to guide discussion and take notes on what the residents had to say. JC Carroll was one such resident. An architect who had been active in the BIA even before the storm, JC was a member of the urban planning subcommittee of the revitalization committee. "There were a lot of arguments" at these meetings, he said. "It's hard to get that many people to agree on stuff."

As time passed, though, consensus began to emerge—in part as a result of creative problem-solving by the facilitators. As residents of Subsection C eagerly discussed bike paths in their meetings, for example, and residents of Subsection B continued to worry about crime in theirs, the BIA facilitators realized that a common theme underlay both priorities: residents across Broadmoor wanted to feel safe on the neighborhood's streets. At the next neighborhood-wide meeting, the facilitators proposed a "safe streets" initiative, which included plans both for a neighborhood crime watch and for bike paths. The proposal was overwhelmingly approved.

Safety was just one of hundreds of issues addressed as residents discussed how to put their flooded neighborhood back together. Subgroup meetings had themes such as Security and Housing, or Education and Culture. Hal often facilitated these meetings, writing residents' ideas on an easel, resolving disputes, and keeping everyone on task. When residents expressed particular interest in one facet of the discussion, Hal encouraged them to form a committee to better address the issue. As a result, Hal's revitalization committee quickly sprouted a number of subcommittees, which focused on issues including urban planning, flood mitigation, housing, education, legal affairs, economic development, transportation, and emergency preparedness. A few subcommittees were short-lived—Hal would later recall the brief existence of Broadmoor's monorail committee with a chuckle—but many found firm footing and began to take on significant amounts of work.

Indeed, as residents continued to plan, they grew surprised at the breadth of issues they needed to address. As JC Carroll said, "We started realizing, 'You know, revitalization covers so many things!'" Restoring Broadmoor would mean much more than fixing houses and sprucing up yards; Katrina had disrupted every facet of life in the neighborhood, and each would have to recover in its own way.

Compounding the difficulty was the fact that many aspects of neighborhood life were interdependent. Everywhere residents turned, they encountered "chicken and egg" problems. The school could not reopen without students, but families with school-aged children could not return if their children had no school to attend. The best way to reduce looting and property crime was to repopulate vacant blocks, but residents would not move back to blocks they perceived to be unsafe. The city would patch potholes and fix streetlights in fast-repopulating areas, but the need for these repairs were themselves a disincentive to Broadmoor's repopulation. Where to begin?

⚜  ⚜  ⚜

It was late February when LaToya Cantrell first caught wind that Harvard was in town. The university's John F. Kennedy School of Government, she learned, was looking to forge a partnership with a neighborhood in New Orleans, and Broadmoor was on the short list. Word spread quickly among returned residents, who had been taking time off for a week of muted Mardi Gras festivities after more than a month of full-time planning. No one quite knew what to make of the prospect. JC Carroll recalled, "We were kind of intimidated, a little bit, we didn't know what to expect—Harvard guys coming down and whatever. I mean, we're just a bunch of Joes."

Whomever Broadmoor residents pictured when they imagined "Harvard guys" arriving in their neighborhood, they probably did not expect Doug Ahlers. Doug was not a professor, and he avoided many of the trappings of academia. He did not have a PhD, but he did have a tattoo. For many years, he had worked in the computer industry, founding an Internet e-commerce and advertising firm that served Fortune 500 companies at a time when most people had not thought of using the Internet to sell anything. After cashing out his stake in the company for tens of millions of dollars, Doug went on to serve on corporate and university boards, participate in international elections monitoring, and open the now-famous Muriel's restaurant on Jackson Square in New Orleans. He had only recently arrived at the Kennedy School as a senior fellow, intending to write a book about the Internet's role in changing political power dynamics across the globe. Katrina hit soon thereafter.

Doug's ties to New Orleans ran much deeper than the link to his French Quarter restaurant. Over the years, he had fallen deeply in love with the city, with all of its quirks. He joined a prominent Mardi Gras krewe, threw lavish masquerade parties, and became well-versed in the ghost stories involving some of the city's centuries-old buildings. Doug, unlike other Harvard faculty members who had lived for years in Boston, felt a profound and immediate stake in the

Crescent City's survival. Until New Orleans got back on its feet, his book could wait.

Doug was determined to find a role for the Kennedy School in New Orleans. "As the largest natural disaster in U.S. history," Doug later wrote in a newsletter to alumni, "Katrina raised serious policy questions about how effective disaster recovery management is conducted. Clearly, there was a leadership role in New Orleans for the Kennedy School."

Convincing busy faculty members to sign on to his nascent project initially proved challenging, but with persistence, a clear vision of the school's role in New Orleans began to emerge. "Most other universities, volunteer groups, and NGOs were approaching the problem of recovery by pursuing a single issue (such as housing, economic development, or education)," he later explained in an e-mail, "but since these problems are interdependent within a disaster zone, we believed that the only viable solution was to work with a community across all of their issues, across time. We decided to work with a single neighborhood . . . in order to focus our attention and resources."

Doug wanted the Kennedy School to partner with a neighborhood whose demographics closely matched those of the city as a whole, so that lessons learned from the partnership could be applied across New Orleans. While Broadmoor was on his list, Doug was also considering Gentilly, a large and diverse portion of the city with 47,000 prestorm residents. As one Broadmoor resident said, "We had to sell ourselves to the Kennedy School, because they were looking into Gentilly as well."

Most of the pressure to make a good impression, however, lay on Doug. "I got grilled," he recalled with a chuckle. LaToya had planned out the whole meeting. First she met with him privately, and then she introduced him to the BIA board. "We had a little lunch for Doug," she said, "and he told us what his thoughts were and what he was trying to do." Some of the questions he faced were pointed. Was Harvard going to try to boss the neighborhood around? Would it pick up and leave in six months after completing its study?

Doug fielded the questions as best he could. The Kennedy School, he explained, was interested in learning about how a group of residents could spearhead their neighborhood's recovery. Residents themselves *had* to be in charge, and they had to do the hard work. The Kennedy School was not offering money, nor could it carry out any particular piece of work for the neighborhood. What it could do, though, was consult with the residents as they navigated the murky political waters that the storm had left in its wake. It could also send students to support residents as they crafted their recovery plan. Out of this partnership, the Kennedy School would get a front-row seat from which to study the city's recovery; it would stick around for the long haul.

There were smiles and handshakes all around. For Doug, this meeting sealed the deal. With Broadmoor residents this organized, the Kennedy School had found itself an ideal partner. Soon enough, Doug found himself back in his car.

It was not until years later that he told the story of what happened next. He decided to drive around Broadmoor's streets to get a better sense of the neighborhood. Only then did the enormity of the task at hand sink in. A pit developed in his stomach as he drove through block after empty block. Even six months after Katrina, houses sat seemingly untouched; a smudged brown line across their exteriors marked the height at which water had sat for weeks. It was hard to imagine that the neighborhood would ever recover. Doug kept the thought to himself, but he was privately terrified. "This neighborhood is not coming back," he said to himself. "What have I gotten Harvard into?"

⚜ ⚜ ⚜

Months later, as the days grew longer and more oppressively hot, Broadmoor found itself in the midst of what Father Jerry Kramer termed "our crisis moment with Harvard."

The neighborhood's many planning committees had assembled a preliminary version of a recovery plan for Broadmoor, and then distributed the draft for feedback. After Doug Ahlers read the document, his reaction was frank. "The feedback was, an urban plan is not butterflies and high schools and rainbows," Father Jerry remembered. "You have to show *wood, bricks, nails*. Nth-degree detail. Not what you want, but *how* you are going to do it."

The relationship had not been rocky until that point; in fact, it was off to a great start. Swallowing his initial reservations, Doug had thrown himself into the neighborhood's planning work. Just three weeks after his first meeting in Broadmoor, he assembled two teams of students, one from Harvard Business School and another from the Kennedy School, to come to the neighborhood during their nonoverlapping spring breaks. After consulting with LaToya and Broad-moor's committee heads, Doug gave the first team of students a very specific task: create a template for Broadmoor's plan.

Broadmoor's committees had been generating ideas for the neigh-borhood's recovery, but the residents struggled with synthesizing and presenting their ideas. The template would help them to start down that path. It would have no specific content—residents would have to generate that themselves—but it would provide a framework upon which residents could build.

Hal remembered being skeptical of the first team when the stu-dents arrived. After setting up shop in the double-wide trailer at Annunciation Church, the students remained hunched over their computers for days. "The five of them just sat there with their lap-tops," Hal later remembered, "and I was privately telling LaToya, 'I don't think we're going to get *anything*. I don't know what they're doing.'" LaToya apparently replied, "I don't know, don't hold your breath."

When the week was over, however, LaToya, Hal, and the other residents were floored by the work the students produced. Residents had already decided upon the categories Broadmoor's plan would ad-dress, from flood mitigation to housing programs to education. The students, in turn, assembled a substantial collection of plans from other communities that addressed the same issues. "We got like doz-ens of these [plans]," said Hal. "It ended up being this document that just goes in order of the things we said we wanted." With this tem-plate in hand, residents had a framework on which they could base their own plans.

The second team to arrive was larger, consisting of twenty-three students and staff members. This team split up, sending small groups of students to work with many of the neighborhood's individual plan-ning committees. "They were there as research and support teams," Doug later explained. "The students would work during the day—researching best practices, writing up sets of options, documenting the notes from the meeting with residents from the night before. Then, in the evening, the Broadmoor committees would meet and work through the issues with the support of the Harvard teams."

The neighborhood's evacuation committee, for example, had asked its students to research neighborhood-based evacuation plans, searching for models on which Broadmoor could base its own evac-uation preparation. The next day, the students searched in vain for such a model, returning to the committee that evening to report that only state and municipal governments undertook coordinated evacuations; Broadmoor's neighborhood-based evacuation plan would be breaking new ground. Over the subsequent days, the students and community members worked together to create an evacuation plan from scratch, brainstorming ways for the neighborhood to institute a rideshare program and laying plans to train residents as disaster first responders.

Looking back on the two spring-break trips to Broadmoor, Doug reflected, "Setting expectations was a key part of these two weeks." Under his leadership, the students sought to strike a difficult balance. "What came out of Harvard," he later wrote, "was the pushing of the residents to come up with big ideas, but ideas that were also not fantastical."

Now, weeks after the student teams departed, residents were encountering a harsh reality. Though their initial planning work showed promise, Doug told them, they had not put enough thought into how their plan would be implemented. It was not enough to simply list the goals the neighborhood hoped to achieve.

Some residents felt discouraged and suggested hiring professional help to flesh out the plan. As Father Jerry later explained, Doug wanted the plan "in urban-planning speak and we didn't know how to do that. And so we wanted to hire a technical writer and Doug said he would quit if we did." Father Jerry paraphrased Doug's response: "You will have to figure out how to put it in urban-planning speak. It's *your* problem. You have to figure it out for yourself because it's got to be bottom-up. No outside people; it's your plan."

Doug's feedback was harsh, but there was method to his madness. While many in New Orleans were operating under the assumption that billions of dollars in infrastructure recovery aid was bound for the city, Doug had traced congressional appropriations and grilled aides to the state's two U.S. senators. "There was no 'there' there," he later explained; the money was not on the horizon. If Broadmoor's plan was to come to fruition, it would have to be something that residents could directly implement.

Doug stuck to his guns, and eventually, residents began to come around. "It was a real power struggle and crisis," Father Jerry recalled, "and it was exactly what Doug needed to be doing. I mean, it was great coaching from Doug." As residents began to wonder what to do next, he explained his feedback in different terms. The plan's vision for Broadmoor's recovery was wonderful and compelling, he said, but that was not enough. "You have to work backward on this," remembered Father Jerry, paraphrasing Doug's advice. "This is where you want to go; how are you going to get there? You know, a plan is not [only] where you want to be, it's [also] how you're going to get there." The committees returned to work, in search of difficult answers to this relatively simple question.

⚜    ⚜    ⚜

As Broadmoor residents rallied against the green dot and began planning for their neighborhood's future, they were also engaged in a parallel struggle: convincing their neighbors to return home. Residents realized that they would have to reach out directly to their neighbors, convincing them to take the risk of moving back to a neighborhood whose fate was far from certain. Moreover, it became increasingly clear that they would have to build the neighborhood's capacity to help poor families rebuild their homes. This latter task would take time, but the former could begin immediately.

After the BNOB Commission branded Broadmoor with a green dot, Virginia Saussy received a phone call from a woman named Lisa, the daughter of one of Virginia's elderly neighbors. Lisa was considering whether to fulfill her mother's wish to return to her Broadmoor home; she had the financial means to renovate her mother's house, but only if she sold her own home and moved in with her mother. In light of the green dot, she told Virginia on the phone, such a move seemed like too big a risk. "I think I'm going to wait and see what happens to the neighborhood," she said. Virginia was distraught. "Beth, you can't do that," she replied. "If you wait and see, then we're going to fail the [Bring New Orleans Back Commission's] four-month test to bring the neighborhood back to life. It's a self-fulfilling prophecy. This 'wait and see' stuff, you're going to kill the neighborhood by doing that."

Ultimately, the neighborhood's fate hinged on whether residents decided to return to their homes. There would be thousands of such decisions, made one household at a time, and each decision would depend upon the outcomes of all the others. If a substantial number of residents took the early risk and decided to return, they could in turn influence their neighbors, and these decisions could snowball into a sustained recovery. Conversely, if the green dot convinced a number of residents to stay away, Broadmoor's recovery could sputter and ultimately fail.

The three-hundred-person rally, and the five-hundred-person Broadmoor Improvement Association meeting that followed it, sent strong signals to all those present that their neighborhood was coming back. However, there was much more to do. Many residents were displaced far from New Orleans; finding them and luring them back to the neighborhood would be a challenge. Moreover, it was one thing to see a large crowd at a meeting, but another to see block-by-block tallies of returning households that proved the neighborhood was on the mend. As Broadmoor residents organized in the wake of the green dot, these tasks fell to the newly formed repopulation committee.

Virginia cochaired the committee with Kelli Wright. Kelli, a mother of two teenage boys, had just taken her real estate exam but had not yet started working. The two brought different approaches to the committee's work. Virginia, with her corporate background, later explained that she "was thinking marketing, marketing, marketing." Repopulating the neighborhood, in Virginia's opinion, required "selling" skeptical Broadmoor residents on the idea that their neighborhood was on the mend.

Kelli also had a marketing background but took a different approach to the committee's work. She focused on collecting data about residents' plans to return to the neighborhood, knowing that that this information would become a substantial motivator for residents and send a powerful message to City Hall. When the Bring New Orleans Back Commission called for flooded neighborhoods to undertake four months of planning before deciding whether to rebuild, it had set out one specific criterion to gauge neighborhood viability. "We should know that most residents are committed to return," stated the recommendation—"at least half." Kelli took this requirement to heart. "We wanted to cross fifty percent," she said, "to show this city that had made us a green dot that we were viable."

When residents told repopulation committee members that they intended to return, Kelli recorded the data on her computer, but also tracked the neighborhood's progress by coloring in a three-foot-by-four-foot map of Broadmoor. She colored properties orange when residents reported that they were returning home, blue when they reported that they were not coming back, and red when properties were condemned.

Broadmoor residents proved far more interested in Kelli's data than the city did; the map became the center of attention at a number of neighborhood meetings. "I would take it to every meeting," Kelli said, "and people would go, 'Aw, but my next-door neighbor is coming back,' because they wanted their block to be orange. And I'd be like, 'Well, I don't have a report from them, could you have them call me?'"

At a time when most houses in Broadmoor remained vacant, the map showed residents that the neighborhood's recovery was nonetheless under way.

In order to gather information from across the neighborhood, the repopulation committee recruited block captains to contact their neighbors and report on their intentions to return. However, the system proved cumbersome. Far more efficient, Kelli found, were attempts to reach out to residents at large venues. For example, on the day of the city's mayoral election in April of 2006, Kelli and other committee members set up at Broadmoor's polling location. "Tons of people were coming in from out of town," she said. "We stopped everybody, every single person who went to the polls."

While Kelli and her data-collection team took stock of the residents planning to return to Broadmoor, Virginia was ramping up efforts to "market" the neighborhood. After unveiling her giant "Broadmoor Lives" banner at the green-dot rally, the phrase had become an oft-used slogan for the neighborhood's recovery. "Broadmoor Lives," Virginia thought, could be the basis for a major neighborhood marketing campaign. The only limitation was money.

Doug Ahlers helped her solve that problem. Drawing on his connections, Doug partnered Broadmoor with a Boston-based marketing firm called Digitas. Beginning in March of 2006, Virginia worked with graphic designers from Digitas to create an updated "Broadmoor Lives" template, with white and yellow lettering against a green background. Altering the template, she settled on designs for "Broadmoor Lives" yard signs, streetlight banners, and bumper stickers, and even a "Broadmoor Lives" billboard. With this work complete, Digitas donated $25,000 to turn the marketing campaign into a reality.

It was an instant success. "Broadmoor Lives" yard signs sprung up across the neighborhood as residents eagerly acquired them at neighborhood planning meetings. Streetlights along the neighborhood's boarders and main avenues sported "Broadmoor Lives" banners, in what Virginia later claimed was "the single largest light-post banner campaign in the city's history." When the neighborhood unveiled its

"Broadmoor Lives" magnetic bumper stickers, they proved so popular that residents reported having them stolen off their vehicles. LaToya began referring to her car as the "distribution center" after six of the magnets disappeared from her trunk. Eventually, the neighborhood also secured donated space on a nearby billboard for a large "Broadmoor Lives" advertisement.

Looking back on the marketing campaign, Doug Ahlers later reflected that its message might not have rung true at first. "People began saying 'Broadmoor Lives' when the neighborhood still looked pretty bombed out and dead," he said. Nonetheless, the campaign became part of a self-fulfilling prophecy. Residents identified strongly with the signs and took their message to heart.

"I love that green color, and I love yellow," said resident Lynda Ireland, gushing about the signs. "I love them. They make me feel so good. I've got one on my desk, one on my car, I mean, I do not know how to put it, but I was like, I was totally abandoned, and had no identity. I lost my job, I lost my house, I lost my city, lost stuff, my daughter had to go away, and then just everything Broadmoor gives me an identity."

⚜  ⚜  ⚜

"We, the residents of Broadmoor, have come together as neighbors to rebuild our lives and our neighborhood. . . . This is no ordinary plan." So opens the Broadmoor Redevelopment Plan, a 320-page document that the Broadmoor Improvement Association unveiled in July of 2006. Mayor Nagin, though late, joined hundreds of residents and more than a few members of the press at an event heralding the plan's completion. The mood was festive as residents voted overwhelmingly to approve the plan, but LaToya Cantrell and other neighborhood leaders who spoke at the event took pains to drive home an important point: Broadmoor had come a long way, but it still had a very long way to go. Completion of the plan did not mark the end of Broadmoor's recovery; it was merely the end of the beginning.

After months of meetings, the task of assembling Broadmoor's plan fell to a group of residents who called themselves the final report committee. Their task had been to assemble the work completed by each of Broadmoor's planning committees, and to combine this work into a single document. It was arduous. Though Harvard students created a template for the plan and the planning committees generated its content, the final report committee had to synthesize numerous strands and ideas, bringing them all together into a single, coherent, and compelling vision of how the neighborhood would recover.

Because the final report committee did not have the luxury of treating problems in isolation, committee member Lynda Ireland reported, "Sometimes we'd have to go back to square one and do brainstorming." Nonetheless, the plan came together, and the committee approached its work with a healthy mix of lightheartedness and determination. LaToya usually showed up with pizza, inside jokes proliferated, and committee members who had not known one another became good friends. As time wore on, Lynda explained, the committee grew increasingly anxious to release the report. "One week," she reported, "[we] said, 'We're meeting every night until we finish this.' But it was really fun; I loved doing it."

Committee members found it gratifying to watch the community vote to adopt the plan. Residents who had been involved in earlier stages of the planning process were stunned to see their work pulled together in such a seemingly professional document. The color green—appropriated first from the green dot and then from Virginia's "Broadmoor Lives" signs—became the plan's unifying graphic motif. The plan's spiral-bound pages were vibrant and colorful, full of photos, diagrams, and sketches. (Local architects had completed the drawings; their contract with Broadmoor referred to them as "graphic communicators," lest there be any confusion as to who was in charge of the planning.) When printed, the plan had an impressive heft. Thumbing through the document for the first time provided a tactile and visual rush, leaving residents with a visceral sense of pride: "Wow, we did *this*."

First impressions aside, the plan's content was wide-ranging, detailed, thoughtful, and ambitious. To help residents unable to return to their flooded homes, the plan proposed the creation of a Broadmoor community development corporation, the formation of a partnership with a national housing nonprofit like Habitat for Humanity, and the partial transformation of Father Jerry's Annunciation Church into a one-hundred-bed volunteer center. To reopen the neighborhood's Andrew H. Wilson Elementary School, which had been low-performing prior to Katrina, the plan proposed the creation of a Broadmoor school board to independently reopen Wilson as a charter school. To address the poverty and social problems that plagued Broadmoor prior to Katrina, the plan proposed the creation of a Broadmoor social services provider, which would help residents with everything from disabilities support to vocational training. To enhance the sense of a Broadmoor "center," the plan proposed the creation of an "educational corridor," anchored on one end by the school and on the other by the neighborhood's library, which the plan envisioned reopening as a multiuse facility with books, a community meeting space, and a coffee shop. The list went on.

More impressive, for each of the plan's many proposals, residents gave serious thought to how they could turn their visions into reality. This "planning for implementation" revolved around a simple, one-word strategy: partnerships. Recognizing that Broadmoor lacked the internal resources to spur its full recovery, residents took stock of potential sources of outside support. In what became known as the six-point redevelopment strategy, they envisioned Broadmoor's recovery as a collective endeavor undertaken by residents, faith communities, developers, universities, private-sector donors, and higher levels of government. Cultivating this network would take time, but if well nurtured, these partnerships could be the basis for the neighborhood's rebirth.

The best part about the plan was that it gave residents a firm sense of where to begin. As they left the festivities surrounding the plan's unveiling, residents knew that the road ahead of them would be long and daunting, but they were not paralyzed because they had already taken stock of the upcoming challenges and given significant thought to how those challenges would be overcome. Just as important, Broadmoor was already mobilized. The plan called for the neighborhood's planning committees to become implementation committees, and indeed, residents were already champing at the bit to see their initiatives put into action. Soon after the plan's release, for example, members of the neighborhood's education committee founded Broadmoor's school board and began work on the state's arduous nine-hundred-page charter school application. Hal Roark, after cochairing the revitalization committee, began laying the groundwork for a Broadmoor-based community development corporation. And after months of work with the final report committee, Lynda Ireland joined the neighborhood's new library committee, "because I *love* the Keller Library. I adore that library."

# CHAPTER 9

# The Lower Ninth Ward: "Always a Question, and Then a Dead Silence"

Entering October of 2005, most of New Orleans remained under curfew from 8 p.m. to 6 a.m. National Guard troops in tan and green Humvees patrolled the quiet streets. Buildings across the city bore fresh, spray-painted markings left by search-and-rescue crews. These marks, usually in the form of an X, quickly became iconic both for their omnipresence and for their blunt, utilitarian aesthetic. They displayed the date of search, the rescue unit's designation, and the numbers of corpses and animal carcasses found within the building in their four quadrants.

As zip code after flooded zip code reopened for "look and leave" visits, and families across the city returned to the postapocalyptic remnants of their neighborhoods, one area of New Orleans remained entirely sealed off. It would be another two months before the Lower Ninth Ward reopened; the severity and breadth of devastation there eclipsed that of any other neighborhood in the city. In an area measuring nearly three quarters of a mile by a mile—a swath of land that encompassed hundreds of city blocks—the force of water from the levee breach in the Industrial Canal had been so great that houses had been knocked off their foundations and piled atop one another. Some of the scenes of destruction were so incongruous that they seemed almost impossible; near the levee breach, for example, a two-hundred-foot-long barge was splayed diagonally across several blocks, resting atop a partially crushed school bus and the debris of a number of homes.[1]

Toward the river, the damage in the Lower Ninth Ward was less catastrophic, but severe nonetheless. In Holy Cross, where Pam Dashiell had rented a home for many years, most buildings had been flooded between three and five feet. Though they remained structurally intact, their interiors were ruined by the extended submersion. With the neighborhood still under curfew, the houses sat untouched, rotting from the inside as mold proliferated and stagnant puddles of mud and water festered in the heat.

After weeks living with her daughter in St. Louis, Pam had returned to temporary quarters in New Orleans. Though she could not move back to her flooded house, she had business to attend to in the city. As president of the Holy Cross Neighborhood Association, she was gravely concerned by the discussion of the Lower Ninth Ward's fate among government officials. She recalled, "It was really clear from what was coming out of City Hall, and the feds, and the state, that we were in real danger here in Lower Nine." The national media, and even some residents in other parts of the city, seemed to be turning against the neighborhood. The sentiment, she later explained, was, " 'Get rid of Lower Nine.' Or, you know, it's going to be a drainage ditch for the rest of the city."

On Tuesday, October 4, Pam Dashiell was one of four guests on NPR's *Talk of the Nation*. The question posed for the hour's discussion was simple: "What should become of the Lower Ninth Ward? Should it be bulldozed and its residents transplanted, or can it be recreated in a new form?" Given the circumstances, the ensuing discussion was not purely academic. After Mayor Nagin's September 30 unveiling of the of the Bring New Orleans Back Commission, residents across the city were nervous. It was widely expected that the commission's report, which was due within ninety days, would make firm recommendations regarding the fate of many of the city's flooded neighborhoods. Scott Cowen, president of Tulane University and a newly announced BNOB Commission member, was a guest on the program along with Pam.[2]

A caller from the Upper Ninth Ward phoned in, complaining that her neighbors in the Lower Ninth were being singled out. Why, she asked, was no one questioning the future existence of other vulnerable neighborhoods, like Lakeview? Cowen was quick to respond that the BNOB Commission would treat all neighborhoods fairly and equitably in its recommendations, keeping in mind that each neighborhood was beloved by its residents.

For Pam, this response did not go far enough; the very fact that neighborhoods' fates lay outside their residents' hands, she pointed out, was problematic. "I believe that the people of Lower Nine, and the people of Lakeview, and the people of every other neighborhood need to be absolutely involved and made aware of what's going on in this process. . . . It seems that some of the commissioners are the folks who were running things before—and who perhaps didn't run them as well as they could have."

Joseph C. Canizaro was likely among those commissioners to whom Pam was referring. A multimillionaire developer, Canizaro would wield considerable power over the city's post-Katrina blueprint as chair of the commission's urban planning committee. A *New York Times* article published a day before the commission's unveiling described him as "perhaps the single most influential business executive from New Orleans. One fellow business leader calls him the local Donald Trump."[3] Canizaro was certainly committed to the city; several years before, he had chaired the Committee for a Better New Orleans, which brought together community leaders and local businesspeople to create a plan for improving the city's failing schools, combating its high crime rate, and reversing blight. Still, neighborhood leaders like Pam worried that Canizaro would have business interests—not community interests—in mind as he led the charge to plan for the city's future. Residents of flooded neighborhoods grew nervous when he commented that the city had "a clean sheet to start again."[4]

In the weeks following her appearance on the radio show, Pam set to work with members of the Holy Cross Neighborhood Association and other interested stakeholders to lay the groundwork for the neighborhood's return. One outsider with interest in Holy Cross was Darryl Malek-Wiley, a longtime Sierra Club activist and organizer with a bushy, snow-white beard. Prior to the storm, many within the HCNA had worked closely with Darryl to combat the proposed expansion of the Industrial Canal lock. After the levee breaks, the Sierra Club asked Darryl to spend the bulk of his time working closely with the HCNA on recovery efforts.

Because the Lower Ninth Ward was still sealed off, Darryl arranged for a meeting space in an Uptown church. "We just started meeting every Thursday," Darryl recalled, "and the word just got out that the neighborhood association was meeting." At first, fifteen to twenty people came to the weekly meetings. Residents were encouraged to see Cynthia Willard-Lewis, their city council representative, in regular attendance. Discussion ranged from sharing the latest information from FEMA and the Red Cross to commiserating about the difficulties of returning to a flooded city. As Pam later noted, however, it never took long for residents' conversations to circle around to the core worry on everyone's minds: how Holy Cross could "figure out a way to survive."

⚜  ⚜  ⚜

The Uptown meetings were reassuring for Lower Ninth Ward residents who remained in the city, but most had scattered farther afield. For them, there was distressingly little information about the neighborhood. Tricia Jones, a black, twenty-eight year-old accountant who had lived most of her life in the Ninth Ward, was stranded in Atlanta with her husband and two young daughters. Her tall, athletic build perfectly matched her take-charge personality. Waiting helpless in Atlanta was agonizing for Tricia; all she could do was piece together information from news reports and hearsay from her family and neighbors. What little she heard was not encouraging.

"I think the main thing on my mind," Tricia recalled, was that "this is going to be a repeat of history." Tricia's grandfather had been "bought out by eminent domain. He owned a piece of property in the Upper Ninth where all the railroad tracks are. And they forced a buyout from everybody in that area. He never did go back into home ownership."

With her family's experience of a "skipped generation of wealth," the thought of losing her own home was particularly painful for Tricia. The oldest of fifteen children, she had spent most of her childhood in the Florida Avenue housing projects in the Upper Ninth Ward. Then, when she was seventeen, her father took her to see a nearby house he had purchased. "My dad was able to buy a house that was dilapidated by anybody's regular eyes," Tricia remembered. "I was like, 'Dad, you can see freakin' grass through the house.' He just said, 'I can fix that. Don't worry about all that. This is doable.'" As time passed, she said, "He built that house from collecting wood as people built houses in the neighborhood."

Several years later, at Tricia's wedding, her father pulled her aside. "I'm like greeting everybody, kissing, and crying," Tricia recalled.

"As soon as you can," he told his daughter, "buy a house." Tricia continued hugging well-wishers, overwhelmed by the joyful onslaught of family and friends. Her father was not satisfied. "Are you *listening* to me, Aliska?" he asked, employing the nickname he often used with his eldest daughter.

"What is it, Daddy?"

"I'm *serious*," he said, reminding her of her grandfather's lost house and of his own lifetime of struggles. He did not want Tricia and his new son-in-law to suffer the same way. His earnest resolve struck a chord. Beginning on the day after the wedding, Tricia recalled, she and her husband embarked on a quest to buy a house. It took them three years. In 2000, they signed papers for a modest clapboard home in the Lower Ninth.

They quickly fell in love with their surroundings. "There was sixty percent home ownership back here in Lower Nine," Tricia later explained. "We didn't have expensive houses—they were basic family homes. But families lived around the corner from each other, and that was the social unit we used to support each other, with baby-sitting, groceries, parties. It's a walkable neighborhood at two square miles. You don't have that [elsewhere] around the city."

Now displaced in Atlanta, Tricia desperately missed the neighborhood, wondering whether it would ever again be the place she remembered. Each passing month grew more difficult to bear. Finally, in November, though the Lower Ninth Ward remained completely sealed off, Tricia and her husband could wait no longer. "I gotta see," Tricia said. She and her husband rented a truck, left their daughters with friends, and hit the road. "We were so full of adrenaline, we drove through the night, and got [there] at daybreak," Tricia recalled. Using his electrician's badge, Tricia's husband talked his way past the checkpoints and into the Lower Ninth.

"When I saw the neighborhood," Tricia recalled, "I was so in shock, I was like, 'This can't be.' It was so quiet. I never felt the aloneness of a neighborhood. Not in Lower Nine. Because everybody walks, and everybody speaks and talks. [But] there was no one here, [and] the sky, the trees were brown. There were no birds flying. There were power lines everywhere. There was mud over everything."

Not long after that first fateful visit, Tricia's husband moved back to New Orleans, where electricians were suddenly in very high demand. Tricia had planned to stay with the girls in Atlanta, but the separation soon took its toll. Her husband had "always been an active father," Tricia said. "Every day, it was, 'When's Dad coming?'" Reluctantly, she reunited the family in New Orleans.

The move was difficult. Though her husband worked consistent sixteen-hour days, the family was barely making ends meet. Between the mortgage on their flooded house, the rent on their temporary New Orleans apartment, and the rent they had been paying in Atlanta, their income disappeared. Worse yet, there were few signs of progress in the Lower Ninth. "I questioned a lot that I had made the right decision to come back," Tricia recalled.

Many days seemed hopeless. Tricia's daughters, she recalled, were scared for their friends. "I'm trying to counsel them. I'm all messed up mentally. [My husband is] messed up. We haven't even found all of our family yet. And we're broke. And we've lost all that we had. It was rough to find yourself."

By the new year, the neighborhood had reopened for visitation, but a strict curfew remained in effect. Tricia worked to clear her house during the day, but felt a sense of urgency each evening as the sun began to set. There was no power in the neighborhood, so "when it got black, it got *black*," Tricia recalled with a shudder. "It was a very scary feeling." She had to wrap up her work and cross the Industrial Canal before nightfall.

In February of 2006, she found a small reason to hope. A neighbor told her about informal meetings taking place at the Sanchez Community Center, just a few blocks from her flooded house. Every Saturday at 11 a.m., the windowless building on Caffin Avenue became a quiet hub of activity amid a swath of deserted streets. Some residents drove in just for the meeting; others, like Tricia, used it as a late-morning break from gutting their houses.

Soon, the meetings at the Sanchez Center became an anchor for each tumultuous week. "It was like an AA meeting," she explained. "I would say, 'I'm Tricia Jones and I live at 1012 Lizardi.' And then it was dead quiet. And then somebody else would say, 'Mary Smith and I live at 1310 Egania.' It kept going in circles.'" In hindsight, Tricia has trouble conveying what it was about the meetings that seemed so powerfully important. "I can't tell you what was drawing me back," she said. Inside, the building, "the smell reeked unbelievably. . . . It was mold on steel and dry water. There were no lights in there. And [we] were sitting around on some rusty chairs." But every week "I kept coming." The meetings seemed to fill a hole. She explained, "My social network of how we deal with issues and crises—all of that was gone. And so you're trying to manage protecting your kids." The only way she could stay strong, and let out pent-up frustration, was "by talking to an adult who's sharing in the same way."

Residents began to bring water, fried chicken, and snacks to the meetings. Sometimes, representatives from an outside organization called the People's Hurricane Relief Fund showed up and tried to push an agenda, but residents like Tricia were tired and skeptical. "They were telling us they were organizers," she said. "First time I'd heard this word, 'organizer.' Organizer, you know, what is that? And they said, 'Well, we just wanna make sure people have the right to return.' You know, they were ready to fight. I was just ready to get

some wood in my house. I wasn't on this whole social justice mode. . . .
I just needed to get home."

Though the organizers' agenda did not gain traction, residents
did find themselves increasingly worried about what to do for the
neighborhood. "As the weeks continued to pass," Tricia remembered,
"we were like, 'Well, what we gonna do?'" Meeting after meeting, the
question went unanswered. It was always, "'I don't know!' 'What you
think?'" she explained. Then, inevitably, the conversation would turn
back to missing neighbors. "'Oh my God—did you hear about Amy?'
'Lord, did Charles make it?' Always a question," Tricia explained,
"and then a dead silence. Every round. But people kept coming."

⚜  ⚜  ⚜

"Why would people ever come back to the Lower Nine?" This was
a question, Pam Dashiell recalled, that she and her neighbors heard
incessantly in the months following Katrina. It was haunting, hanging
over every conversation, every phone call, every meeting about the
neighborhood's future. To opinionated outsiders—and the city was
full of them in Katrina's wake—it certainly seemed the obvious question to ask.

It was late April in 2006, eight months after the storm, and little
had changed in the Lower Ninth Ward. The neighborhood's northern reaches—branded by the BNOB Commission with a green dot—
remained in ruins. Higher ground in Holy Cross was less damaged,
but still largely devoid of inhabitants; an overnight curfew remained
in effect, and utilities had not been restored to many blocks within
the neighborhood.

As Pam and other residents gathered for an intensive three-day
planning process during the last week in April, their neighborhood's
singular predicament was difficult to stomach. The curfew in the
Lower Ninth Ward was the last in effect in Orleans Parish; the rest
of the city had reopened. Moreover, in what was both a blessing and
a curse, the neighborhood had become a national symbol of the pain
and destruction left by Katrina. The publicity garnered the neighborhood no shortage of charitable help, but also no shortage of scrutiny.
All eyes were on the Lower Ninth Ward as residents considered their
options, and many observers believed that the neighborhood should
not be rebuilt. Residents knew that they faced an added burden of
proof as they plotted their neighborhood's future.

Charles Allen, Pam's neighbor and Holy Cross Neighborhood Association colleague, was the ringleader of the planning process. Five months before, from his job at a New Orleans environmental think tank, Charles had caught wind of a Department of Energy grant that would help one neighborhood "recover along energy-efficient lines." After the BNOB Commission's recommendation that neighborhoods undertake their own planning processes, Charles applied for the grant on behalf of Holy Cross. A meeting with state officials sealed the deal; Holy Cross would undertake a planning process to determine how to bring the neighborhood back as a model of sustainability.

This focus, Charles and many other residents soon realized, was strategic. In light of the chorus of spectators claiming the Lower Ninth Ward was too vulnerable to rebuild, they would have to create an alternate vision that was more compelling. "If we were going to reconstruct and recover our neighborhood," Charles explained, "we had to do it in some better manner. It had to take on some unique, smart approach. . . . We would have to prove to ourselves and the world that what we're doing here is promoting a better Lower Ninth Ward."

Sustainability, it seemed, could be the neighborhood's magic bullet. The concept was already a buzzword among architects and planners across the country, who were interested in building communities that were more walkable, more energy efficient, and less resource intensive. Moreover, the term captured the concept of resilience. In the Lower Ninth Ward, rebuilding sustainably would mean rebuilding in anticipation of future floods. As Charles later explained, "It's all about, how do we capture that water? Or how do we build higher—in the event that we have a flood, the home perhaps won't be flooded."

Over the three days of planning in April, the assembled residents crafted a vision of a sustainable recovery in Holy Cross and the Lower Ninth Ward. A trio of sustainability consultants from around the country facilitated the meetings. Their job was to help residents apply sustainable concepts like energy efficiency, use of renewable building materials, flood-resilient construction, and planning for walkability as they envisioned their neighborhood's future. Over the three days, discussion remained grounded in the neighborhood's immediate needs. At a previous meeting in February, residents had undertaken a "situation analysis," in which they had catalogued the many hurdles facing the Lower Ninth Ward's recovery. Now, residents and facilitators worked to find solutions to these problems, applying principles of sustainability whenever they could.

Although the planning maintained an emphasis on Holy Cross, much of the discussion focused on the fate of the Lower Ninth Ward as a whole. Residents from both sides of St. Claude Avenue attended the meetings, and began hashing over a sensitive topic: whether the lowest-lying and worst-hit areas of the Lower Ninth Ward should be rebuilt. The BNOB Commission had unleashed a firestorm of criticism and controversy by placing a green dot on the neighborhood's upper reaches. In the intervening months, the Holy Cross Neighborhood Association had stirred further resentment by not coming out forcefully against the BNOB suggestions. Turning the worst-flooded part of the neighborhood into parkland, residents who lived north of St. Claude objected, would mean more money and rebuilding resources for Holy Cross. The decades-old tension between Holy Cross and the rest of the Lower Ninth Ward seemed to have opened a new chapter.

Interestingly, though, all of the residents assembled for the April planning process seemed to agree that concentrating future development in Holy Cross was a good idea. The consensus took Pam Dashiell slightly by surprise. "What was interesting," she said, "was that the people from the north side who participated really came to see why that was so. And fairness was an issue, but the logic of it was—I mean, it was stark." If homeowners in the northern portion of the neighborhood could be fully and fairly compensated for their properties, attendees agreed, moving those individuals into Holy Cross could be a good idea.

Those at the planning meetings were satisfied with this aspect of the document, but upon its release, many Lower Ninth Ward residents who had not come to the meetings were furious, feeling that the plan had sold them out. As Pam later explained, the plan "exacerbated the tensions, and there were many, many meetings and discussions about—saying that it was not fair. And we're still dealing with the repercussions of that." Moving forward with a coordinated rebuilding strategy in the Lower Ninth Ward would require a great deal more consensus than this plan had generated.

On less-contentious issues, though, the plan outlined approaches on which nearly all residents could agree. It called for new architecture in the Lower Ninth Ward to remain true to the neighborhood's vernacular, while also incorporating cutting-edge, energy-efficient design. It highlighted the need for improved infrastructure throughout the neighborhood, such as repaved streets and overhauled storm drainage. It proposed a variety of ways to lessen residents' dependence upon cars, from clustering businesses near homes to improving bus service to widening sidewalks.

The plan was vague about how to implement many of its recommendations, but its goals were not grandiose. With organization and hard work, many seemed achievable. Moreover, the Lower Ninth Ward—and Holy Cross, in particular—now had what Charles Allen termed a "marketable niche." Residents were determined to make their neighborhood a model for sustainable recovery, harnessing the nation's newfound enthusiasm for green building and putting it to work for its residents.

⚜ ⚜ ⚜

"When you came over the bridge [into the Lower Ninth Ward]," Tricia Jones recalled, "you felt very alone." It was late spring in 2006, and though cleanup operations were well under way, most streets in the Lower Ninth remained eerily deserted. Close to the levee break, blocks were still littered with the splintered, upended remains of houses. It would take at least another year for all the debris to be hauled away and for utilities to be restored. When this finally happened, families in these areas would be starting from scratch. Recovery in less-damaged areas of the city seemed difficult but attainable, Tricia thought; in much of the Lower Ninth Ward, by contrast, recovery often seemed impossible. Tricia turned these thoughts over in her mind as she engaged in what was now a familiar routine. "I would just drive around the neighborhood. From the river to Florida Avenue," she said, "just thinking, using a lot of gas."

After weeks of attending meetings at the Sanchez Community Center—where residents had commiserated about their problems and worried about the future without getting organized—Tricia had taken matters into her own hands. Outside organizers from the People's Hurricane Relief Fund (PHRF) had been trying to convince the residents to join a national campaign on behalf of disaster survivors, but Tricia thought that the neighborhood's limited energy could be better spent. "I know that we were all mentally exhausted, and we could have been diverted in so many different ways. It's the mercy of God that we came back to the real issues," she recalled.

Tricia was the one who got the group on task. "No matter what happens with PHRF," she told the assembled residents, "there needs to be a group of us just dealing with the issues of Lower Nine. And if we don't bring this focus in, the neighborhood is dead." The residents at the meeting liked the idea of creating a formal Lower Ninth Ward recovery organization. Tricia promised to come back to the group the following week with better-fleshed-out ideas.

That week, she wracked her brain, thinking about how this new organization would take shape. Days later, after pensive drives around the neighborhood's devastated blocks and nights lying awake in bed, Tricia settled upon the contours of the group's mission. It was embodied within its name—the Neighborhood Empowerment Network Association, or NENA for short. NENA, as Tricia conceived of it, would reach out to displaced residents and offer them assistance with the bureaucratic hurdles and red tape that were preventing many of them from rebuilding. Although Tricia was slowly helping her own family clear the hurdles that would one day allow them to return home, she knew that many of her neighbors were getting stuck—encountering trouble with finances, permitting, insurance, and utilities.

"I'm a young and resourceful person," Tricia observed, "[but] where does that put someone who's borderline illiterate?" It pained Tricia to think of the resources available to help homeowners recover that many of her neighbors were unable to access. The Louisiana Recovery Authority—an arm of the state government set up after Katrina—had recently announced the creation of a homeowner grant program called The Road Home. Using billions of dollars in funding from the federal Department of Housing and Urban Development, The Road Home would provide money to flooded-out homeowners who didn't have adequate flood insurance. The application process, however, was grueling. It required persistence, resources, and wherewithal that Tricia feared many residents, especially elderly ones, lacked.

The next Saturday at the Sanchez Community Center, Tricia presented her idea for NENA, and received an enthusiastic response. On the spot, she asked residents in attendance to form a board of directors. "We don't have a pot to piss in and a window to throw it out," Tricia quipped, "[but] I will commit to you that we will do everything honestly, honorably, and respectfully." Five residents immediately signed on. Tricia realized that this high resident interest represented a strong start for NENA, but she worried about next steps. NENA did not have a staff; it did not have funding; it did not even have a building.

❧   ❧   ❧

"This was supposed to be a quiet neighborhood ceremony," Tricia mused. It was Memorial Day, 2006, and in addition to the hundreds of residents now gathering around the patched Industrial Canal levee in the Lower Ninth Ward, Tricia saw a line of TV news trucks, their satellite dishes extended to beam coverage of the day's proceedings into living rooms across the country.

The day's ceremony had grown out of Sanchez Center meetings. While Tricia moved ahead with her plans for NENA, she and other residents believed that the neighborhood faced unfinished spiritual business. "In order for this community to come back," Tricia explained, "we can't disrespect those who were lost. We had to acknowledge them."

As the crowd reached a critical mass, preachers from across the neighborhood delivered eulogies for the lost lives and decimated communities Katrina had left in her wake. Volunteers solemnly read names from a list of 1,500 people killed in the storm and subsequent levee failures. When the service drew to a close, a New Orleans brass band struck up traditional "second line" jazz funeral music, leading mourners past wrecked houses on a ceremonial march through the neighborhood's empty streets. Tricia wished she could join them, but found herself cornered. News crew after news crew angled to snag an interview with her.

In the weeks since proposing NENA at the Sanchez Center, Tricia had begun to lay groundwork for the organization. With each passing day, she seemed to find new residents in need of assistance, whether with Road Home applications, insurance claims, or emotional difficulties. Tricia helped them all, latching onto the empowering opportunity to connect with her neighbors. Those who knew her were increasingly coming to see Tricia as a community leader. Outsiders were beginning to take note as well—and not just the news crews.

In recent weeks, representatives of the Oregon nonprofit Mercy Corps had been attending the Sanchez Center meetings. Determined to help New Orleanians rebuild, Mercy Corps aimed to foster relationships with emerging neighborhood leaders and help them develop the organizational capacity they needed to rebuild their communities.[5] After one of the meetings, Tricia explained her work to a Mercy Corps representative. "We're helping our neighbors fill out forms, [and] passing out information so they can know how to get home," she said, reminding the representative that Lower Ninth

Ward residents remained displaced all over the country. She stressed that she and her neighbors were committed to bringing about a practical, achievable recovery. "We're not trying to think about pie-in-the-sky redevelopment," she said. "We're trying to get water [service restored to our houses]."

"Write that down," said the Mercy Corps representative, clearly impressed. Soon thereafter, Tricia received a call from another Mercy Corps official, who promised to buy food for the neighborhood's memorial service and bankroll NENA's early expenses. With a $6,000 Mercy Corps check, Tricia bought folding tables and chairs for community meetings, hoping that more funding was on the way. Indeed, the Mercy Corps representatives who attended the memorial service were impressed with the self-assured leader they saw in front of the news cameras that day, and privately resolved to keep close tabs on her work. Meanwhile, in subsequent days, Tricia returned to the basic organizational challenges facing NENA. "I still didn't have a building," she recalled.

One day, she explained, "I drove down Caffin [Avenue] coming back from one of my thinking sessions." Overcome by the sights out the window and the tremendous challenges NENA faced, Tricia subtly bowed her head. "God," she prayed, "we need a hub. We need a space to work out of. . . . And it's gotta be in the Ninth Ward. And it's gotta be somewhere where people can meet." God, it seems, was listening. "I turned down Marais Street," Tricia recalled, "and there was Father Joe."

Father Joe was the priest at St. David's Catholic Church, located several blocks away. He oversaw another parish on top of his responsibilities at St. David's, so he had been difficult to track down in the months after the storm. Tricia pulled over and started a conversation. Father Joe was excited to hear about her work with NENA. On the St. David's campus, behind the church building, sat a one-story cinderblock building that could house NENA's offices. Father Joe told Tricia that he would be glad to host the new organization on the church's campus. There was only one catch. "Have you actually seen it on the inside?" he asked.

Soon thereafter, Tricia and Father Joe stood in the building's open doorway. Tricia gulped at what she saw. The building had not been fully gutted, mold crawled up the walls, and the roof was partially collapsed. She put on a brave face. "We'll make it work," she said.

CHAPTER 10

# Neighborhoods and Citywide Planning: "Promises Are Made, and They Are Not Kept"

On July 5, 2006, Mayor Ray Nagin's office and the city council announced an agreement to launch a third citywide planning effort for New Orleans. The eight-month-old Louisiana Recovery Authority (LRA), a state body responsible for distributing federal recovery funds throughout the state, spearheaded this new initiative. Known as the Unified New Orleans Plan (UNOP), the process would follow in the wakes of two other planning efforts. The Bring New Orleans Back Plan—the first planning initiative undertaken in the city—had succumbed in February to lack of funding and to outrage over its calls for a building moratorium in flooded neighborhoods.[1]

The second planning effort, begun in April and spearheaded by the firm Lambert Advisory LLC, had its own flaws. Aside from scattered complaints of heavy-handedness and steamrolling by planning facilitators, the Lambert process suffered from a lack of credibility and too narrow of a scope. The city council had circumvented the mayor's office by awarding Lambert Advisory a no-bid contract and had allocated funds only for planning to take place in flooded areas of the city. Without the backing of the city's executive branch—which would be the driving force behind the implementation of any citywide recovery effort—the Lambert process seemed unlikely to deliver an actionable plan. Moreover, the state-run Louisiana Recovery Authority would not release money to parishes until each one submitted a comprehensive redevelopment plan. Because the Lambert process did not produce a plan that encompassed all of Orleans Parish, it was unacceptable for submission to the LRA.

The Unified New Orleans Plan, as its name suggested, sought to bridge the gaps in the previous planning efforts to create a single recovery plan for Orleans Parish on which all parties could agree. The Rockefeller Foundation put up $3.5 million in funding for the project, and the LRA pledged that the UNOP plan would take the results of all previous planning efforts into account. Even so, it took three weeks of negotiations and some political arm-twisting for LRA representatives to convince both the mayor and the city council to sign off on the new initiative.[2]

⚜   ⚜   ⚜

Like the Lambert plan before it, the UNOP process relied on teams of planners to solicit resident input and create plans for the city's neighborhoods. Reaction to the new planning process was mixed among residents and neighborhood leaders. Some were furious at having to start their plans over again, seemingly from scratch. In Lakeview, where the District 5 recovery council had worked closely with the Lambert facilitators, the arrival of a new team of UNOP planners came as a slap in the face. "It pissed people off," Martin Landrieu said, "when the UNOP people came in and said, you know, 'I'm Mr. Smith from Wisconsin and we're in charge of the planning. What would you like to see happen in your neighborhood?' And your head wants to explode, because you've done it for the last eight months and somebody wants to start over, and you say, 'I don't want to do this over.'"

Other neighborhoods saw UNOP as an opportunity. The Vietnamese community in New Orleans East had settled on its recovery priorities through its design charrette, but wanted to ensure that its plan was endorsed by the city and the LRA. Pushing the community's priorities during the UNOP process, neighborhood leaders realized, would legitimize the neighborhood's planning process. As one of the community's organizers later explained, "We already had our [community] plan; then we were involved in the Lambert plan. And then the UNOP plan came up, [and we said], 'Okay, we have to make sure that we're on the map.'" Added another resident, "We followed the community plan and the charrette through all the UNOP meetings. We stayed focused with what we wanted."

In addition to providing a means of legitimating the community's planning process, UNOP gave Village de l'Est residents the chance to find their voices in a citywide dialogue about recovery. For decades, geographic separation and the language barrier had kept Village de l'Est isolated from the rest of the city, but UNOP gave residents from across New Orleans several chances to come face to face and talk. During three "Community Congresses," in late 2006 and early 2007, residents who had returned to New Orleans gathered at the city's convention center, while those who were still displaced joined over the Internet and via video conference from remote sites in Baton Rouge, Dallas, Houston, and Atlanta. With the help of electronic voting pads and facilitators, residents who took part in these Community Congresses could express their preferences and vote on the plan's content.

During the first community congress, Village de l'Est residents who required interpretation services were herded into a separate room, effectively cutting them off from the dialogue taking place on the convention floor. This sparked a concerted campaign, led by community leaders in Village de l'Est, for UNOP to provide direct interpretation for residents at future gatherings. With the help of headset-based interpretation services, the UNOP facilitators complied. "By Community Congress two and three," a resident explained, "the community was fully involved in what was going on." This marked a first for the normally isolated neighborhood and raised awareness throughout the city of the needs of non-English speakers. At future meetings, community leaders proudly reported, city agencies made concerted efforts to provide Vietnamese and Spanish interpretation services.

Meanwhile, Broadmoor residents kept a close eye on the UNOP proceedings, but did not engage directly in the new planning effort. Before the Lambert planning process began, neighborhood leaders had negotiated an agreement to have Broadmoor's resident-driven plan incorporated as-is into the Lambert plan's final draft. "Hal and LaToya went to work lobbying the city council in this regard," Doug Ahlers explained, "and I immediately began work on lobbying the LRA." By the time the Lambert plan fell by the wayside, Doug continued, "Broadmoor had already established itself as political player to be courted [and] contended with. So, the UNOP needed Broadmoor's buy-in. . . . Broadmoor's endorsement of the UNOP process came with the condition that the Broadmoor plan be adopted as is into the final UNOP plan." This concession allowed Broadmoor residents to focus purely on implementing their plan, rather than attending a series of redundant planning meetings held on their behalf.

Elsewhere, the UNOP plan inflamed tensions and widened rifts that had already begun to form within recovering neighborhoods. In the Lower Ninth Ward, for example, the Association of Community Organizations for Reform Now sparked a controversy when it applied to be hired as the official planner for the Lower Ninth Ward. ACORN had been organizing in the neighborhood for years prior to

Katrina, and its national housing wing had experience with community planning and affordable-housing development, but many prominent residents believed that the organization was too partisan and confrontational in its approach to facilitate good planning.

ACORN's ideological bent and confrontational tactics, Holy Cross Neighborhood Association president Pam Dashiell later explained, "didn't reflect everybody. It certainly didn't reflect the way I, Pam, wanted to proceed." Pam was also concerned about a potential conflict of interest—ACORN was seeking to redevelop hundreds of properties in the Lower Ninth Ward, and its dual role as a planner and a developer seemed likely to muddle the planning process. Other Holy Cross residents agreed, and HCNA, which had just released its sustainable-recovery plan, came out against ACORN's planning bid.

The move was not well received. As Pam explained with a bemused laugh, ACORN "released a plan of their own in which I was called a 'gentrifying Caucasian.' I'll never forget that—that's in print—that's a high point or a low point depending on how you want to look at it." The description was comically vitriolic, as Pam was a black woman who had spent much of her working life fighting to improve the quality of life in poor communities. Suffice it to say, the conflict "got really, really nasty," Pam said.

Hollygrove had seen its own share of planning drama, after the Lambert plan facilitators offhandedly dismissed residents' home-grown planning efforts and insisted on starting from scratch. UNOP, by contrast, did not arouse residents' passions. Many in the neighborhood were simply tired of planning. They correctly inferred that the UNOP proceedings represented an exercise in wishful thinking. "We want to help crime," one man recalled with a roll of his eyes. "We want a police substation. . . . It was sort of a grab bag. You picked and chose what you wanted."

Although the UNOP process was praised for its widespread and representative citizen involvement, the plan it produced was a disappointment. It amounted to little more than a long wish list with a $14 billion price tag. A New Orleans watchdog nonprofit, the Bureau for Governmental Research, said that the plan's system for prioritizing recovery projects was "vague and bewildering," citing, for example, that repairs to historical forts ranked at the same level as basic infrastructure improvements and school repairs.[3] The Bureau for Governmental Research lamented that, "in the end, the [UNOP] document fails to deliver a cohesive, workable roadmap for recovery. Instead, it proposes a sweeping list of ninety-one projects, without placing them in a realistic financial context. As for recovery strategy it offers a continuation of the indecisive and confusing approach that has characterized New Orleans' recovery for a year and a half."[4] The UNOP plan's completion unlocked federal funds that had been withheld by the Louisiana Recovery Authority, but it did not produce a workable path forward for the city's recovery.

⚜  ⚜  ⚜

So, in the spring of 2007, the city's planning mantle came full circle, landing back in the mayor's office. At the beginning of the year, Mayor Nagin had hired Edward Blakely, a well-respected scholar of development and disaster recovery and a former city official in Oakland, California, who had helped the city rebuild after the 1989 earthquake. Blakely was confident that he could kick-start recovery in New Orleans, promising that there would soon be "cranes in the sky" over the city. "He went and he looked at all of the plans" Councilwoman Cynthia Hedge-Morrell said, and identified "plans that are doable . . . [and] plans that are dreams."[5]

From the plans, Blakely identified seventeen projects throughout the city that he and his Office of Recovery Management (later renamed the Office of Recovery and Development Administration) would help to fast-track. Using a combination of direct funding and tax credits, Blakely's office would quickly push these projects to fruition, in hopes that they would, in turn, spur recovery in the surrounding blocks. Among other priorities, Blakely promised substantial support for rebuilding in the Lower Ninth Ward; tax credits to help business recovery at sites in Hollygrove, Lakeview, and Village de l'Est; and prioritization and funds to turn Broadmoor's "educational corridor" into a reality.

At the outset of Blakely's plan, observers praised it as a realistic and sensible way to begin coordinated citywide recovery efforts. The president of the nonprofit Bureau of Governmental Research, which had criticized the UNOP plan as unfeasible, said, "It's promising to see somebody who is giving us a program that's based on a realistic assessment of potential resources." Unfortunately, however, Blakely's efforts quickly became bogged down. Private investment dollars proved more difficult to attract than anticipated, Blakely publicly complained about racial infighting among his two hundred staffers, and state ethics rules prevented money from being quickly spent.[6] More than a year after the seventeen target zones were announced, *The New York Times* summed up the initiative's progress: "A modest paved walking path behind a derelict old market building is held up as a marquee accomplishment of the yet-to-be-realized plan."[7]

The article quoted a New Orleans resident who was frustrated after nearly three years of false starts: "They come up with these plans that look great and sound great. They give people hope. Then, they fall into the background. Promises are made, and they are not kept."[8]

⚜  ⚜  ⚜

Citywide recovery planning efforts in New Orleans offer a host of lessons for cities facing similar predicaments. After the levee failures, most planners engaged in their work with the best of hopes and intentions for the city; they simply found their efforts derailed by a challenging confluence of circumstances to which their skill sets and repertoires proved difficult to adapt. In the years since, most New Orleanians have been happy to forget the roller coaster of high hopes and dashed dreams that characterized planning efforts in Katrina's wake. Others are less forgiving. Broadmoor's Hal Roark did not mince words when asked about the subject. "I hate urban planners" he said, only half kiddingly.

Broadmoor residents' aversion to professional planning, born of distrust sewn by the green dot and intensified by the neighborhood's homegrown planning success, is an extreme reaction. Most residents, even many in Broadmoor, will concede that cities need professional planners after a disaster; they simply wish that planners had gone about their jobs differently after the flood. The contrast between stymied citywide planning attempts on the one hand, and comparatively fruitful neighborhood-based planning efforts on the other, sheds light on how urban planners might modify their repertoires to better respond to future disasters. Because disaster recovery involves myriad stakeholders and demands complex social and physical restoration, postdisaster planners could stand to take cues from the discipline of community organizing.

Community organizing is the process of bringing people together to achieve a goal that is in their common interest. Whether it involves campaigning for civil rights or coordinating a flooded neighborhood's reconstruction, the core principles of organizing remain the same. Organizing begins when people come together to identify common values and interests. It progresses as these individuals and groups build upon their common ground, growing collective capacity to affect change. Outsiders can organize communities of which they are not a part, but they must do so mindfully. Values and priorities must flow from the community, not from the organizers. Moreover, organizing is never about doing something for a community; it is about helping that community do something for itself.

In the United States, postdisaster planners must recognize that power is diffuse. New Orleans neighborhoods' fates lie in thousands of hands, including those of city administrators, commercial developers, school officials, and, most important, residents themselves. At the end of the day, residents would vote with their feet, deciding their city's fate one household at a time. Neighborhood-based recovery planning efforts were closely attuned to this reality, and better off for it. Planners should heed their example.

Moreover, planners should recognize that recovery is not merely about restoring buildings, spaces, and infrastructure; it is about resurrecting every aspect of life in a place. Residents know better than anyone else what their lives were like prior to a disaster and how, if at all, they want them to change afterward. Hal Roark frequently said that he and his many neighbors were "the world's leading experts on Broadmoor," and he was absolutely right. Disaster recovery planning must tap this expertise.

The city's most successful planning efforts were, at their core, community-organizing efforts. Especially in Broadmoor, Lakeview, and Village de l'Est, planning took place within a broader context of neighborhood mobilization. As residents came together to envision their neighborhoods' futures, they simultaneously worked to build the community capacity required to enact their plans. It was a virtuous cycle, resulting not only in better-prepared neighborhoods but in better plans; residents approached the task of planning more constructively and seriously when they realized that they themselves would be carrying the plans out.

New Orleans neighborhoods' post-Katrina planning experiences suggest a simple set of guiding principles for neighborhood-based planning, especially postdisaster planning. Planning processes must begin with widespread buy-in and consistent participation from residents. In Broadmoor, Lakeview, and Village de l'Est, neighborhood leaders pulled residents into planning processes early, using large meetings and church services as recruitment venues. Extensive, on-going resident participation in these neighborhoods' planning efforts ensured that the plans reflected the values and interests of the entire cross section of each neighborhood's inhabitants.

When residents partner with outside planners and experts, these partnerships must build community capacity to plan and execute recovery. The role that University of New Orleans advisers played in Lakeview's planning effort perfectly embodies this principle: the advisers partnered with resident-staffed committees to consult on decisions and provide guidance, but residents remained in control. Similarly, Doug Ahlers and the Harvard Kennedy School found cre-ative ways to support Broadmoor's planning efforts, but did so in a way that pushed residents toward self-reliance.

Moreover, visions of recovery and plan content must come from residents themselves, not from outsiders. Not only will resident-generated content better reflect community needs, but it will also en-sure that residents become invested in seeing the plan through. Such investment is important, because much of the impetus for recovery lies on their shoulders.

Indeed, successful community-based planning must maintain a laserlike focus on implementation. While government assistance for neighborhood recovery efforts in New Orleans was starkly lacking, even well-supported community development initiatives will fail if residents simply create wish lists. The "implementation-oriented" outlook that Trang Tu found "built into the psyche" of the Vietnam-ese community in New Orleans East, for example, proved vital for that community's recovery success. "A plan," as they say in Broad-moor, "is not where you want to be, it's how you're going to get there."

In order to foster a focus on planning for implementation, and in order to build a community's capacity to implement its plan, resi-dents must have a say not only in the plan's content, but also in the planning process. When the locus of control for planning lies with residents, they take ownership of and responsibility for the plan that they produce. In Broadmoor, resident control of the planning process ensured that it did not descend into an abstract, facilitated exercise in wish making. It also gave residents a sense of ownership over their fi-nal product that was lacking after other planning processes. As Doug Ahlers wrote, "The Lambert Plan (in some cases) and UNOP (pretty much across the board) were planning processes that involved heavy input and participation of residents, but they were not citizen-led efforts. At the end of the day, these plans belonged to someone else—the residents participated, but they did not *own* the plans."

Communities should, in fact, own the plans they produce, viewing them as living documents, to be referenced, revised, and updated as time passes. When Martin Landrieu introduced the District 5 recovery committee's plan to a packed meeting in June of 2006, he referred to it as a "first draft" that would be "a work in progress for years to come." Similarly, Broadmoor residents often refer to their plan as "the Broadmoor plan Version 1.0." Plans that are intended for implementation—not for gathering dust—require updates over time as their goals are met and new ones emerge.

By adhering to these community-based planning principles, cities facing landscape-scale disasters could avoid many of the pitfalls that derailed recovery planning in New Orleans. These principles alone, however, are not enough. Effective recovery planning requires more than the simple devolution of planning power and initiative to the level of neighborhood groups. An aggregation of very good neighborhood recovery plans does not, in and of itself, make for a good citywide recovery plan. Indeed, New Orleans continues to face an array of challenges that neighborhood-based planning could not solely address. Neighborhood groups, for example, could not craft the plans for the comprehensive wetlands restoration and levee system improvements needed to prevent the city from flooding again. Nor could they, on their own, address the challenge of overhauling the city's failing public school system. Though work is now moving forward on these fronts and many others, New Orleans residents have played at best a limited role in crafting the plans behind these efforts. Some in New Orleans argue that the city's overriding focus on neighborhood-based planning has left residents with a myopic recovery outlook. One man, worried about the safety of rebuilt levees and concerned by the possibility that many of his neighbors would rebuild without sufficiently elevating their homes, argued that neighborhood planning efforts "take our eyes off the ball."

This critique of the neighborhood-centric recovery planning undertaken in New Orleans, while valid, does not undermine the basic notion that communities should be empowered to plan for their futures in a disaster's wake. Neighborhood planning and citywide planning can and must coexist. Such coexistence would not have been impossible in New Orleans, under the right circumstances. If Mayor Nagin and the city council had immediately embraced and fostered emergent community-based planning efforts, following the broad principles outlined above, New Orleanians would also have been able to focus on issues facing the city as a whole. Citywide recovery planning in New Orleans was derailed by power struggles and unrealistic dreaming, not by the hard work that residents undertook to plan for their neighborhoods' futures.

Whether at the neighborhood level or the city level, any plan is only as good as its outcomes. Disaster recovery plans must not only create visions of recovery that communities can embrace; they must also position communities to bring their visions to life. For this reason, postdisaster planning sets the stage for the rest of the recovery. The best-recovering New Orleans neighborhoods started with the best recovery plans.

PART III

# A Ringing Bell

CHAPTER 11

# Broadmoor: "Bring Life Back"

EARLY MARCH OF 2007, a year and a half after Hurricane Katrina, was an in-between time for New Orleans. Though the days grew longer, the coming warmth had yet to blow away the last vestiges of winter. People were coming down off their Mardi Gras highs and enduring the forty days of Lent that precede Easter, Jazz Fest, and all that was glorious about their city in the spring.

For Nancy Isaacson, the passing days felt like a state of limbo for another reason. After months of frenetic work as a member of the Broadmoor charter school board, the fate of the neighborhood's school now lay entirely out of her hands. Waiting was not something that Nancy, a transplant from Boston who had cut her teeth teaching in alternative schools for expelled youth, in any way savored. The rapid-fire cadence of her speech, devoid of $r$'s despite years away from her Massachusetts home, reflected her irrepressible energy.

Nancy was a relative newcomer to New Orleans. After living elsewhere in Louisiana and Mississippi, a second marriage brought her to a stately white home in Broadmoor, where she enjoyed playing with her young grandchildren on a wide front porch overlooking Napoleon Avenue. She quickly fell in love with the neighborhood and believed strongly that reopening the Andrew H. Wilson Elementary School would boost her community's recovery. "I think that when you see a successful neighborhood, you see a successful school, and visa versa," she said.

Nancy had joined the school board in October of 2006, as its members raced to meet the December charter application deadline. "Everything, day and night, was [spent] getting that application done," she said. Broadmoor residents, like their peers in Village de l'Est, had realized quickly that the impetus to open a functional new school in their community would have to come from them. As Nancy later explained, "The Broadmoor school board came about because the city at the time had no way to support education. It had no way to support anything. We knew that it would maybe be years, and when the school opened again it would be same old-same old. . . . Broadmoor didn't want the same old-same old, and so the idea, through the education committee, was to have a charter school here in Broadmoor."

Broadmoor's eleven-member school board was a strong contender to win a state charter. Its chairwoman, Connie Yeaton, had decades of experience as a teacher and principal in Orleans Parish schools. Sheila Thomas, another board member, was also a veteran New Orleans principal and educator. Even this strong board, however, had decided that it needed help as it put a new school together. Months before, board members opted to partner with a private, for-profit school-management company, Edison Schools, Inc.

Edison, they knew, was not without controversy. Several years earlier, the company seemed poised to make vast inroads in public school management, before an accounting scandal and a tumbling stock price lowered expectations for the company. Edison and other for-profit school operators also faced a chorus of objections from parents and observers who condemned the incursion of capitalism into public education. As Nancy Isaacson explained, "Edison makes money on a per-pupil basis. The state gives Wilson Charter School X amount of money per student. That money goes into the operating budget. [Then] Edison charges us a fee for the students, and we pay that up to a certain percentage a year." Company leaders responded to criticisms of this arrangement by arguing that Edison managed to do more with less, running extended days and longer school years, applying the latest curriculum and teaching advancements, and pulling up test scores in the schools it managed.

Edison representatives had convinced Broadmoor school board members that the company could help to make Wilson a better school. Board members also knew that their partnership with Edison would have a flip side. Edison made money only after all of the school's other expenses—from teacher salaries to books to busing fees—had been covered. Moreover, Edison could cover the budget deficits that often challenged charter schools in their early years, acting as a financial safety net to ensure that the Wilson School would remain open despite scarce funds.

Board members also liked Edison's openness to community engagement. The Edison-run schools that board members visited seemed superbly integrated into the communities where they were located. As Nancy later explained, their buildings were used for "after-school and evening programs, adult ed, elderly ed, lots and lots of activities. . . . They encourage that and invite it." The model of the school building as a community hub fell closely in line with Broadmoor's plans to use the Wilson School as an anchor for its "educational corridor." Edison would help them turn this vision into a reality.

Edison's curriculum was also a draw, saving board members from having to create a curriculum from scratch. "It's set in place, and it's standard, and it's non-negotiable," Nancy said. "This is what Edison does, they do it well, and that's what you have to take." Edison fit because Broadmoor's school board did not aim to reinvent the wheel; it simply wanted a good school for the neighborhood. "Of paramount importance to Broadmoor was that it be a Broadmoor school board," Nancy explained, "and that the school be in Broadmoor."

Though board members enjoyed a bit of a respite after completing the charter application, they could not afford to wait around for the state's approval. With nine months before the beginning of school in September, they would have to select a principal, write bylaws and school policy, begin their search for a building, and craft a plan for recruiting 450 students—all before learning whether the Louisiana Department of Education would give them a green light.

Thankfully, at the end of March, the green light came. When the dust settled, the board's application was one of only nine from across the state that won approval. After a search, the board decided to hire their school leader from within, selecting retired principal Sheila Thomas to lead the fledgling school. Sheila resigned from the school board and came out of retirement to tackle the task, beginning the long process of hiring staff members and interviewing prospective teachers.

Meanwhile, other board members began a long search for a suitable school building. Ultimately, residents hoped that the school would return to its original location in Broadmoor, a beautiful three-story school building with large windows and a red-tile roof. The building, however, had remained untouched since the storm; for the time being, the Andrew H. Wilson Charter School would have to find a temporary home. As Nancy recalled, the board looked at "archdiocese buildings, at public buildings, at shopping centers, churches, office buildings, [and] houses. . . . At one point I said, 'Let's put circus tents out,' because it was getting down to the wire and we needed to have a building."

As the months passed, much remained up in the air, but the board members were relentlessly determined. "Wilson School was going to be open for [that] year," Nancy recalled. "No matter what."

❧  ❧  ❧

It was a hot summer's morning in June of 2007, and Father Jerry Kramer had just given notice that he planned to resign as the Episcopal priest at Broadmoor's Church of the Annunciation. He sat slumped in a folding chair in LaToya Cantrell's office, squinting as sunlight streamed in through the window. With a light knock on the door, LaToya entered bearing a troubled look. She had just heard the news. Fixing her gaze on Father Jerry, she dropped her heavy handbag by her side and took a deep breath.

"People are just sick, thinking . . .," she trailed off, but her meaning was clear. Father Jerry was a beloved and integral part of Broadmoor's recovery effort. He left decisions about the neighborhood up to LaToya, Hal, and other residents, taking it upon himself to ensure that the neighborhood had the space and resources it needed to succeed. During Broadmoor's planning process, easels and neighborhood maps shared space with hymnals and a communion chalice at the church's temporary home in a double-wide trailer. Now, the Broadmoor Improvement Association enjoyed its own offices in which everything—the building, the furniture, the computers, the pencils and paper—came from the church. LaToya worried for Father Jerry and fretted about the setback his departure would deal to the neighborhood. Father Jerry met her anxious expression with a sly grin.

"Well, make some noise," he said.

"We love you," she replied.

"Make some noise. Make a hell of a lot of noise."

"Okay! Okay, that's good." LaToya caught on. Father Jerry had something up his sleeve. With enough help, he would not be going anywhere.

"Basically, we're at a power-struggle moment right now," Father Jerry explained, referring to the state of his congregation. Some in the church thought that its charitable work had gone too far. "I need the congregation to decide to commit to the direction we're going in," he said. "Because I can't do what we need to do and have this tug constantly pulling us in the other direction."

In the nearly two years since Katrina, Father Jerry had been hard at work. The church's relief operation had proved all-consuming. As Father Jerry explained, "There is no longer-running, busier relief operation in the Gulf South. We have served seventy thousand people

from our parking lot since the storm." Expanding the church's relief activities had been difficult, Father Jerry said, because "this is a
working-class parish." Church members, he said, "are either elderly,
disabled, or working. So I don't have discretionary time or cash from
our natural constituency."

To keep resources flowing into Annunciation's recovery efforts,
Father Jerry had begun to visit churches around the country. He was
a phenomenal preacher and storyteller, weaving his congregation's
post-Katrina experiences into sermons that were at once reflective,
riotously funny, and inspiring. At the churches where he preached—
picturesque stone buildings nestled in the mountains of Tennessee,
evangelical mega churches in Dallas, well-heeled and reserved congregations in Washington, DC, and New York City—he asked for
prayers, money, and volunteers. All were sorely needed, and they
flowed in.

As the months wore on, Father Jerry and others at the church
began to consider next steps for Annunciation's work. Its relief operation would not be needed forever; eventually, demand for food, clothing, water, and bleach would dry up. Other needs, too, would emerge,
as residents struggled to rebuild their homes. As Broadmoor carried
out its planning process, residents began to envision a new role for
the church.

"We have a big problem," Father Jerry remembered, paraphrasing
the neighborhood's request. "We need a mechanism for being able to
deal with the blighted homes in Broadmoor. And you guys have been
really good. You know, you've run the relief center, you've given us
the office space, the resources, the meetings. You've been great. Now
we're asking you to give us the whole campus for ten years. We're
asking you to rebuild it, fix it up, and we're asking you to bring in
one hundred volunteers at a time for ten years, and feed them, and
organize their work details, and you have to pay for all the renovations and things."

Father Jerry embraced the seemingly impossible challenge, which
he called "an incredibly stupid idea for Jesus." As he saw it, Annunciation "didn't have a choice." More than half of the city's churches had
shuttered since Katrina, succumbing to flooded buildings, displaced
congregants, and financial turmoil. For Annunciation to survive and
thrive, Father Jerry believed, it would have to remain outwardly ori-
ented. "Any church right now that's going back to the way it was is
going to die," he explained. Supporting a volunteer center would re-

quire the church to make tremendous sacrifices and take a profound financial risk, but as Father Jerry saw it, bearing this cross would lead to Annunciation's rebirth.

"So basically I had to walk into the trailer one Sunday," he remembered, "and tell folks, 'OK, we've just taken out a $1.2 million loan to buy up the block, minus three properties that aren't for sale. We can't really afford the note, but we're not really going to worry about that today. Oh, and the other thing is that we're not going to really go back to being a stained-glass chaplaincy here. We're all going to be about serving Broadmoor and the greater community. And that's the way it's going to be.'"

This was another shock for a church that had already changed substantially since Katrina. "Some of the old guard don't like it, and still struggle with it," Father Jerry said. "Some of them have already left." It also meant that the reliable stream of income from the church's downtown property was now being diverted to pay a bank note. Annunciation would have to raise even more money to cover its daily expenses and its ongoing relief efforts. Father Jerry knew that it was a leap of faith.

A year after selling the downtown property, as Father Jerry sat in LaToya's sundrenched office, his faith seemed well placed. Renovations to the church building were complete. Former Sunday school classrooms and church offices had been converted to bunkrooms, and its function hall-cum-warehouse was now a large dining hall; the church could house and feed up to 125 volunteers at a time. This new volunteer center, called Annunciation Mission, also boasted a large, diverse, and dedicated staff. Many, with nowhere to turn after the storm, had begun working at the church's relief operation, receiving room, board, and a weekly $100 stipend. As the church's mission evolved, they became the backbone of the volunteer center, mixing paint, cooking meals, and shuttling volunteer groups to and from the airport. Better still, Annunciation's attendance was growing, attracting members who had been displaced from other churches. By Father Jerry's estimate, the congregation had as many Baptists and Catholics as it did Episcopalians. He loved it. "I'm not here to make Episcopals; I'm here to make disciples," he said. "I don't give a crap if you ever become Episcopalian, couldn't care less."

Unfortunately, miracle working was exhausting. Father Jerry had just returned from yet another whirlwind fund-raising tour, and the past two years of work were taking their toll. "I am *fried*," he said when asked how he was doing, rubbing his eyes with an open palm. "I could barely get dressed today. I am so tired." It was hard enough to keep going with the total support of the congregation and the neighborhood, but some parishioners at Annunciation continued to question the church's new role. For Father Jerry, it threatened to become the straw that broke the camel's back. If it continued, he would have to leave—a signal he sent clearly with his letter of resignation. The letter, he knew, would rally a great deal of support to his side.

"This dispute is like a power struggle in a marriage," he said. By bringing the conflict out into the open, he hoped to resolve it once and for all. It was exactly his style, and it had certainly worked before.

⚜ ⚜ ⚜

The Broadmoor Improvement Association's offices were nondescript, located in the second story of a gray stucco duplex on the Annunciation Church campus. It was a bright midsummer's day in 2007, and the neighborhood felt more alive than at any point since the storm. Children were beginning to zip down the streets on their scooters. Once-overgrown yards were now well-kept, bursting with color from rows of flowers. It seemed that every other house was under construction, with stacks of plywood out front, music blaring from paint-spattered portable radios, and puffs of sawdust wafting out of open windows.

Behind the bright-red door, at the top of the stairs, a large open room was abuzz with activity. Seven people, all in their twenties, sat around a long, cluttered conference table, transfixed by their laptop computers. In the corner, a fax machine spat out reams of paper, and two women conferred about the design of a flyer. Across from them, two high school boys wearing mud-stained T-shirts and work boots downed cans of Pepsi and wiped sweat from their foreheads.

Hal Roark emerged from a back hallway, happily surveying the busy scene. These days, nearly a year after the Broadmoor recovery plan had been released, Hal spent a lot of time with a big grin on his face. The neighborhood's K–5 charter school was set to open in late August in an off-site location with 450 students, and Hal was entering his seventh month at the helm of the newly created Broadmoor Development Corporation. The plan was coming to life.

The people hard at work around the conference were BDC interns—college and graduate students from around the country who had come to New Orleans for the summer. They had a variety of jobs, many of which aimed to build the BDC's capacity to accomplish its work in the coming years.

The BDC's work would not be easy. Helping the neighborhood's poorest families find the resources to renovate their homes would be a daunting challenge. Moreover, for many families, recovery would require much more than fixing damaged property; it would mean tackling problems like hunger, chronic medical conditions, and unemployment, which had often existed well before Katrina. The "neighbors helping neighbors" approach that Lakeview's Beacons of Hope used so effectively would not cut it in Broadmoor; the neighborhood needed professional social workers and a comprehensive case-management system.

Broadmoor residents lacked the resources to mount a housing recovery initiative or run a social services department on their own. As a result, Hal knew, forging and cultivating relationships between the neighborhood and outside partners would be central to BDC's work. This had been part of the neighborhood's plan from the early days, when residents devised the "six-point recovery strategy" that envisioned partnerships among residents, faith communities, developers, universities, private sector donors, and higher levels of government. The number of students assembled around the table was proof that university partnerships were bearing fruit, and the neighborhood was finding success on other fonts, as well.

Residents had recently received word, for example, that a number of partners in the Clinton Global Foundation had committed to a goal of raising $5 million for the neighborhood in cash and in-kind donations. Walter Isaacson—who had grown up in Broadmoor before going on to lead *Time* magazine, CNN, and the Aspen Institute think tank—had used his connections to help seal the deal. Broadmoor also benefitted from a new partnership with the Shell Oil Corporation. Shell, one of the few Fortune 500 companies that maintained a substantial presence in New Orleans, had given the Kennedy School a half-million-dollar grant to expand its partnership with Broadmoor. Some of the money went to pay rent and stipends for Harvard interns, a number of whom now sat around the conference table.

The interns were helping Sheila Thomas, the Andrew H. Wilson Charter School's new principal, prepare for the school year. Others were creating an online database for resident case management, setting up a free legal clinic, and laying the groundwork for the neighborhood's educational corridor. By the end of the summer, Hal thought, Broadmoor would finally be ready to get down to business. In the year since the plan's release, much of the neighborhood's work had centered on building capacity, and this summer was a capstone to those efforts. Soon, Broadmoor residents would finally begin to enjoy the fruits of their labor. These initiatives would help the neighborhood's population continue to climb steadily upward.

❧ ❧ ❧

The din of excited young voices rose above the low rumble of diesel engines as a line of yellow buses rolled slowly up to the large brick school building. Inside the buses, children fidgeted in nervous anticipation, zipping up new backpacks, twisting in their seats, and peering out with wide eyes at the crowd of parents, teachers, school board members, and fellow students that awaited them. Outside, a sign read, "Wilson Charter School—Opening Sept. 4." Its forest-green hue matched the color of the new collared uniform shirts that all the students had donned that morning.

The swell of voices grew louder in each of the buses as their double doors swung open and the children began to disembark. Teachers and administrators greeted the students, shouting out names from attendance forms and shepherding their charges into the appropriate lines. Some of the children proceeded hesitantly, tears of anxiety welling in their eyes as they beheld the sea of unfamiliar faces. The adults, however, were glowing. Nancy Isaacson, LaToya Cantrell, Hal Roark, and the other school board members stood amid the crowd, smiling at one another as teachers began to lead their students inside.

"It was a very happy day," Hal recalled. "It was the culmination of a dream." Hal had been at the planning meetings, a year and a half before, when Broadmoor's ad hoc education committee hatched the idea to reopen the Andrew H. Wilson Elementary School as a charter school. Back then, sitting around a table in a donated trailer, surrounded by scenes of tremendous destruction, the notion of creating a fully functional, 450-student school from scratch had seemed farfetched. Yet now, as the pandemonium subsided and teachers coaxed their classes into the school, there was no denying that the committee's work had been a wild success.

As the school day began, principal Sheila Thomas was everywhere at once, shaking hands with parents, kneeling down to reassure timid kindergarteners, and conferring with members of her staff. Entering the school building, heels clacking in the narrow hallways, Sheila felt optimistic about the coming year. After all of the stress and difficulty of finding a suitable location, Wilson had landed in a marvelous temporary home—a three-story, 130-year-old school building in a quiet neighborhood less than two miles from Broadmoor. The city had only recently opened the building, so the past weeks had been a blur of assembling new desks, hanging posters, and standing atop ladders to paint the high ceilings. Sheila's newly hired forty-person staff attacked the challenge with vigor, assisted by a small army of Broadmoor neighborhood volunteers. The school was ready in time for its scheduled opening.

Making her rounds, Sheila was pleased to see many full classrooms—the result of an intensive, summer-long student recruitment effort carried out by school board members and Wilson staffers in Broadmoor and across the city. This year, in order to fill all 450 slots, Wilson was drawing its students from all over New Orleans. In the years ahead, board member Nancy Isaacson explained, "We're hoping that the school will transition to a more community-based, less city-based school." She hoped that after more school-aged children had returned to Broadmoor, and after the school had reopened in its original building, this transition would be easy. "That may not happen," she conceded.

What seemed sure about Wilson's student body was that it would remain almost entirely black, and predominantly poor, for years to come. Attracting higher-income students, both black and white, would require proving that the quality of its education was at least equal to that of the city's parochial and private schools. Such a change would be key if Wilson was to one day become a true community school serving all of Broadmoor.

⚜ ⚜ ⚜

In late 2008, Annunciation Mission had operated steadily for a year and a half, recruiting, housing, feeding, and dispatching volunteers for Broadmoor's recovery. Father Jerry, having prevailed in his power struggle, remained at the church's helm. On busy weeks, the dining hall buzzed with the din of more than a hundred people. At lunch, church youth-group members from around the country sported paint-splattered coveralls and rubbed shoulders with longtime Annunciation parishioners, Broadmoor AmeriCorps workers, residents, and Mission staff.

Hal Roark usually wandered into the dining hall from his office around noon, happily accepting a full plate of food from the Mission's friendly cook. Hal remained busy as ever. The Broadmoor Development Corporation now employed a staff of case managers, social workers, and housing specialists, who together served hundreds of neighborhood clients. In partnership with Annunciation and the national housing nonprofit Rebuilding Together, BDC had helped to renovate dozens of homes, and had painted hundreds more. An agreement with the Salvation Army would build up to fifty new energy-efficient houses in Broadmoor for teachers and first responders. Eighteen months before, the Carnegie Corporation had pledged $2 million to renovate Broadmoor's historical library, and Hal now advocated for the project as the city dragged its feet.

A prodigious multitasker, Hal split his time during lunch between heckling his overworked underlings, firing off e-mails from his prized new iPhone, and holding good-natured theological debates with Father Jerry. With the end of lunch, volunteers would pour out of the Mission's side door, padding down its concrete steps in stocking feet, searching for recently discarded boots. Hal would wander back to the neighborhood offices, where the twenty open windows on his laptop would vie for his attention, and where the CDC staff was already back at work.

⚜  ⚜  ⚜

AUS. The three letters left a pit in LaToya's stomach. After they were announced, the cavernous hallways of Broadmoor's newly renovated school building grew eerily quiet. The letters were a call to action, and if that action proved insufficient, they would become a death sentence. AUS. Academically Unacceptable School.

In late September of 2010, the Andrew H. Wilson Charter School was just over a month into its fourth year of operation. LaToya could sense what she called a "lack of momentum" in the building. The energy and enthusiasm of the school's founding year were gone, and trouble was written across the faces of administrators and teachers. Students were quickly catching on, with bullying and other destructive behaviors crowding out learning. LaToya was determined to turn things around.

The Louisiana Department of Education had branded Wilson with the Academically Unacceptable School label that summer, drawing on a combination of test scores and attendance numbers from the

previous school year. The solid gains Wilson students achieved during the school's first two years of operation, when test scores climbed
well above the school's pre-Katrina averages, no longer mattered.
Without rapid improvement, Wilson's charter would be revoked. The
hard work that hundreds of residents, teachers, parents and administrators had put into the school would have been for naught.

As LaToya saw it, the trouble had begun midway through the previous school year, after a harried and stressful move from the school's
temporary building into its newly renovated permanent home. "The
move had a tremendous impact," she asserted. Aside from the lost
learning days and the distraction of packing and unpacking, the massive new space also hampered student progress. It seemed to swallow
the sense of community that the older, tighter quarters had fostered.
"The culture had shifted," LaToya explained. "It was a completely
new environment. We went from thirty-nine thousand square feet to
ninety-five thousand square feet. We were in building before where a
teacher could look out the door and talk to her colleague and go watch
a class. Moving into the new building, it didn't provide you that."

The renovated space was gorgeous, with polished bamboo floors,
wide hallways, spotless white walls, and tall picture windows. With so
little time to move in, however, teachers had been unable to make the
thousands of homey touches that make classrooms warm and inviting learning environments. Too many parts of the building felt vast
and blank. A teacher described her students bumbling through school
days in a state of "awestruck distraction."

"When our testing in that building [happened]," LaToya said,
"that's when [our results] did not come back well at all." It was no help
that Sheila Thomas, who had come out of retirement to serve as Wilson's founding principal, had fallen fell ill and resigned just as testing
occurred. It was a perfect storm.

The board installed its chairwoman, Connie Yeaton, as acting
principal. Then, LaToya said, "we had to think about when is the best
time to hire a new school leader. . . . Normally, principals are looking
for jobs around April. That was around the time that our principal
took ill." They had just missed the hiring window. "It was not a good
time to be searching for a principal," LaToya said, adding that she
and the board decided, "It was time to be prepared for the new year."

The coming academic year would be tough. Connie was a veteran New Orleans educator and principal, but she was blind and had
limited mobility. That she could even consider taking the helm at

WE SHALL NOT BE MOVED                                    149

Wilson with such disabilities testified to her tremendous experience and indomitable will, but LaToya knew that Connie would need help. She anticipated the objections that teachers and parents might raise.

LaToya wanted to nip any such objections in the bud. She would be at the school every day. "I was pretty much there to offer support for Connie, and show a united front. The board is not only supportive of the new direction that we're going in, but the board is driving it."

⚜   ⚜   ⚜

For LaToya, the year that followed passed as a blur. Attempting to recall the work, she remarked, "The times get all twisted up." Calm reflection was not a luxury she typically afforded herself. When she did slow down to think, a surprising torrent of memories issued forth.

One day, she opened an e-mail from a staff member at Annunciation Church. "He was being very critical of some things going on," she explained. "Like, 'LaToya's not at the office anymore, and I can't get what I want out of the website, and there's an issue with crime.' All of these things, right? . . . I'm like, 'Look, for the past ten months, I have led an executive search for the BDC, had to go through that process of hiring, I had to deal with the issue of the Broadmoor Improvement District starting, running an election, doing that whole campaign piece, a new *board* for the BIA, the whole process of an interim principal at the school. Then that led to a strategic-planning process with the school. Then that led to a principal search.' It's like, dude, I've been doing all of this in ten months. Riding three horses with one behind. Give me a break!"

Looking back on the enormity of her undertakings, LaToya stopped and drew in a breath. Then came two whispered words that captured her sense of emotional vertigo. "Holy shit."

LaToya was alone now. For years, she, Hal, and Father Jerry had been Broadmoor's trifecta. They were the Holy Trinity or the Three Stooges, depending on the storyteller and the day. No longer.

Father Jerry hit the wall first. Years of marathon fund-raising, declining health, and clashes between his conservative religious outlook and his vestry's socially liberal inclinations took their toll. By the summer of 2009, dollars were drying up and volunteer teams were not coming as frequently; supporting the mission became an unbearable burden. Most of its staff was let go, and more often than not, the dining hall sat silent. In a sermon he gave shortly after the storm,

Father Jerry had promised to "go to the cross for Broadmoor." Several years later, the words seemed prophetic. Physically and emotionally spent, Father Jerry had resigned, moving his family back to Africa midway through 2009.

Hal lasted a bit longer, but found himself equally drained. "I'm tired. Exhausted. Depleted," he wrote in May of 2010 to the neighborhood e-mail list. Like Father Jerry, Hal found himself bound for a venue from earlier in life—a place that would allow him "time and distance and freedom to recuperate. I need time to heal and rejuvenate with my family." Yale Divinity School had accepted him on a full scholarship. "I hope to eventually be ordained a priest in the Episcopal Church and work with people who have gone through traumatic life experiences, to help them use the tools of their faith to move from death to new life," he wrote.

LaToya had no plans to go anywhere. "I say I'm in this web," she explained. She chaired the board of the Broadmoor Development Corporation and the Broadmoor charter school board. She was the Broadmoor Improvement Association president. Some days, it felt as if a whole house of cards would come tumbling down without her. She found the prospect troubling. "I'm trying to get myself out of the web," she said, while "making sure though that there's leadership in place."

Building self-sustaining leadership for the neighborhood had become the defining theme of LaToya's work. It began with a nationwide search for Hal's successor. After rounds of applications and interviews, the BDC board settled on a Philadelphia transplant, Santiago Burgos. His work in community development and city government made him an ideal candidate to implement the multimillion-dollar homebuilding projects in the BDC's pipeline. Santiago took over the BDC in August, just in time for LaToya to turn her attention to reinventing the Broadmoor Improvement Association.

The BIA was due for a change. Even through the busiest days of the recovery, the BIA had been a dues-paying organization. Every year, a few hundred residents paid the $25 membership fee, and only they could vote for the organization's governing board. Moving forward, if the BIA was to truly represent the entire neighborhood and sustain its ambitious operations, the organization would have to adopt an updated model.

With the Louisiana legislature's blessing, LaToya and others put their new plan on the November 2, 2010, election ballot. With residents' approval, each property in Broadmoor would be subject to a $100 annual parcel fee. Resulting funds would sustain the BIA, whose board would consist of nine members—three from each geographic subgroup—elected in an annual poll open to all residents. In the campaign leading up to the ballot initiative, the "t-word" was firmly off limits. "Never call it a tax!" one resident told prospective phone bankers. "It's a parcel fee."

Residents came out of the woodwork to support the new plan. In addition to phone banking, they knocked on doors, distributed fliers, and produced a promotional YouTube video. As a nonprofit, the BIA could not participate in this electioneering; residents ran the campaign from their homes. After the polls closed, campaign leaders celebrated when the initiative passed by a margin of more than 2 to 1.

Righting the ship at the Wilson Charter School, LaToya knew, would require a more protracted effort. As the new school year kicked off in the fall of 2010, she could sense that staff members were deeply unhappy. "I began to have the board host events for teachers to build morale," she said. Kicking back over margaritas and burritos, the teachers, administrators, and board members enjoyed the chance to relieve stress, reflect, and get to know one another better. The events were a small step in the school's renewal, but a start nonetheless.

Teachers were not the only ones running out of steam. "We started having a board that was just nonresponsive," LaToya recalled. "It's burnout. People are tired." She realized that the board needed some fresh perspective and renewed energy. "I brought on four new members," she said. She knew that the school would not survive with a board where she "was the only one [working]."

New blood and reinvigorated workers would not be enough to save the school, LaToya knew. Wilson needed a plan. Tapping a parent and a respected teacher to cochair a new strategic-planning committee, LaToya kicked off a six-week process that would lay the groundwork for the school's future. With numerous subcommittees holding frequent open meetings in the spring of 2011, the process in many ways mirrored that of the Broadmoor recovery plan, which Broadmoor residents had authored five years before.

Over the course of sixty meetings, parents, teachers and board members tackled changes to school curriculum, professional development, building maintenance, special education, classroom management, and more. Some of the resulting changes were sweeping; others were simple. Acting on faculty recommendations, the curriculum subcommittee overhauled Wilson's math program. A student from the Harvard Kennedy School, assigned to the transportation subcommittee, consolidated school bus routes, saving the school thousands of dollars a month.

The planning's impact proved greater than the sum of its parts. "It ignited the faculty. It gave them a way to plug in, letting them know that they mattered, and letting them know that they could be a part of what we create," said LaToya. Parents and administrators felt the same way. For the first time in well over a year, the Wilson community seemed genuinely optimistic. It remained to be seen whether the positive new vibes would translate into better instruction and higher test scores. The school's fate depended on it.

# CHAPTER 12

## Village de l'Est: "Everybody's Connected"

In late August of 2006, Mary Tran was savoring her first victory as executive director of the Mary Queen of Vietnam Community Development Corporation. Her young staff had taken the lead in the community's protest against the landfill. Now that the dump was closed, her organization could turn its attention to the neighborhood's future.

Mary had lived in Village de l'Est for her entire life. She was in her mid-twenties, but looked younger, with a slight build, an unassuming demeanor, and a pretty face that flashed easily into a wide smile. Her appearance belied a rock-solid toughness. The oldest of four children, Mary had supported her siblings since age twelve, when her mother passed away. "I was kind of like the backbone of the entire family," she said. Growing up, while her father worked his job at a company called New Orleans Cold Storage, Mary found time to cook and clean for the family, attend school, and get her homework done.

When Mary finished high school, she recalled, "the thought of going to college elsewhere wasn't even an option." She enrolled at the University of New Orleans and studied management. "I found a degree that didn't involve a lot of studying," she explained, "because I had other duties at home." During her senior year, Mary took a position as an assistant manager at a Walgreens. It paid well and offered good benefits, but it still felt like a dead end. Mary watched as her friends from Village de l'Est and her classmates from UNO left New Orleans, diplomas in hand, chasing better job prospects in Texas and California.

The levee breaks dealt her family a harsh blow. New Orleans Cold Storage did not reopen after the flood, and Mary's father lost his job. While her family members regrouped in Texas, Mary called contractors and began putting her family's house back together. One day, Mary's phone rang, and Father Vien The Nguyen greeted her from the other end of the line. "At this point," Mary explained, "I didn't know Father Vien; I just knew him as a pastor." Mary had attended church her entire life, and taught Sunday school classes in Vietnamese, so Father Vien knew her by reputation. He asked her to consider coming to work for the church, helping to coordinate the neighborhood's recovery. The pay would be low, but Father Vien told Mary that the community needed her help. As Mary explained, Father Vien "has the power to persuade you to do anything." She accepted his offer.

Mary's new post traced its origins to a meeting Father Vien had held several months before. Shortly after the community's successful planning charrette, Father Vien met with a representative from Enterprise Community Partners, a foundation that supported housing initiatives across the nation. As they discussed ways for Village de l'Est to implement its plan, the representative suggested that the community consider forming a community development corporation. Father Vien had never heard of such an organization. As he later explained, he associated the acronym "CDC" with the Centers for Disease Control. Indeed, community development corporations—though a fixture of the urban landscape in many cities across the United States—rarely gain high profiles outside of the neighborhoods in which they operate. Like the Broadmoor Development Corporation, CDCs most commonly work to redevelop the poor urban neighborhoods in which they are based. Developing high-quality, affordable housing is often their primary mission, but they undertake projects ranging from small business assistance to social programming.

At Father Vien's urging, Mary began to look into the possibility of founding a CDC in Village de l'Est. She read books, consulted with lawyers, and visited existing organizations to gain insight into how a CDC in her community could be structured. It seemed that such an organization would be viable in Village de l'Est, and a plan began to take shape.

The community's new CDC would be closely tied to, but distinct from, the Mary Queen of Vietnam Church. As Mary and other residents began to write the organization's charter, they decided that the head priest at Mary Queen of Vietnam Church would serve as president of the CDC's board. Raising money from charitable donations and grants, the CDC would hire a small staff and carry out its work. It would be the entity on which Village de l'Est pinned its hopes; the organization would be responsible for bringing rebuilding resources into the community, providing needy residents with social services, and carrying out the development initiatives outlined in the neighborhood's plans.

Working with a lawyer who specialized in founding nonprofits, Mary navigated the mountains of paperwork required to create such an organization. Before they could complete the paperwork, they would have to identify an executive director for the organization. Father Vien hemmed and hawed, Mary explained, promising to do a "mass callout" in search of suitable candidates for the position but puzzlingly not following through. Weeks passed, and eventually, Mary recalled, "I came back to Father Vien and I asked, 'Have you found an executive director yet?' He was like, 'No, you're going to be the executive director.'"

Managing a Walgreens was one thing, but running a fledgling nonprofit would be something else entirely. "I *did not* want to be the executive director," Mary recalled, "because I had no experience. [I] did not know how to run a nonprofit." As usual, though, Father Vien the persuader prevailed. "This is for the community," he told Mary. "You'll step up. You'll learn on your way." With goading and prodding, Mary accepted the challenge.

Mary Queen of Vietnam CDC was incorporated in May of 2006, less than eight months after Katrina. Mary worked with three other staffers, including Cam Tran, the woman who had moved to Village de l'Est from Denver to help her husband's family rebuild. "At the very beginning," Cam later explained, "we were volunteers." She and another woman worked one-on-one with residents, interpreting for them and helping them navigate the difficult path toward restarting their lives.

Meanwhile, Mary attacked the challenge of developing the new nonprofit. She cultivated a relationship with the National Alliance of Vietnamese American Service Agencies (NAVASA), hoping to learn from individuals who had already formed organizations like her own. NAVASA's regional director, a man who had previously worked for a groundbreaking Vietnamese CDC in Boston known as VietAID, worked closely with Mary. "He was kind of my coach," she said. "He helped me through forming staff policies, finding an office space, running programs, and all these other things."

Mary also began to take stock of the work that Mary Queen of Vietnam CDC would undertake in the years ahead. Its social services for individual residents would doubtless continue, but would become a less urgent component of the organization's mission as time passed. As the organization grew and developed capacity, it would shift more of its focus to opening new neighborhood institutions and improving the community's built environment.

Getting any of this work done would require a great deal of organizational capacity, which Mary and the rest of the staff would have to slowly build. They got off to a good start when Catholic Charities agreed to pay the staff's salaries. "We don't make a lot," Cam later explained, "but it's better than just volunteering and not making anything." Mary also began cultivating relationships with national nonprofits like NeighborWorks America and the Kellogg Foundation, which could provide the CDC with guidance and funding in the years ahead. Using her connection to NAVASA, she also lobbied to receive a number of the alliance's paid fellowship slots. Mary Queen of Vietnam CDC received five fellows—recent college graduates who would work in Village de l'Est and receive stipends from NAVASA. When the fellows arrived in June of 2006, the CDC's staff more than doubled in size, just in time for the campaign against the nearby landfill.

Now, with the landfill beaten, Mary and her staff could turn to implementing the plans laid forth laid out during the neighborhood's November 2005 planning process. Residents hoped to found a charter school, revitalize the neighborhood's commercial corridors, bring affordable medical care to the community, create a retirement center for the elderly, and perhaps even start an urban farm.

⚜  ⚜  ⚜

Cam Tran knew that the stakes were high. Soon after moving to Village de l'Est from Colorado to help her husband's family rebuild, she began work to found a neighborhood school. Now, on this February day in 2007, she and other members of the Mary Queen of Vietnam CDC education committee were finally sitting down for a formal interview with Louisiana Department of Education officials. The interview would help determine the fate of the Intercultural Charter School, which board members hoped to open that fall.

Back in October of 2005, Cam had been busy distributing food, interpreting for residents who could not read their insurance forms, and helping her parents-in-law gut their house. It was a complete change of pace from her former life as a grade school teacher in a Denver suburb, but Cam was doing her best to quickly adapt and meet the community's needs in any way she could. In late 2005, Cam had asked Father Vien, "Okay, now I'm doing the social work. I'm doing all of this [relief work]. What else do you need?"

"You need to open a school for me," he replied.

At first, the request caught her off guard. "Okay, well I'm a teacher," she thought, "but I've never opened a school. I don't know anything about it." The need, however, was pressing. None of the public schools in eastern New Orleans had reopened, making it difficult for the parents of school-aged children to return. On top of her other responsibilities, Cam vowed to investigate what it would take to open a school in the neighborhood.

Within a few months, she secured a meeting with Robin Jarvis, the superintendent of the state-run Recovery School District, which controlled most of the city's public schools even before the storm. "We desperately need a school to be opened in our area," Cam told her. "That's what's holding our parents from coming back, because there's no school." Years later, she would still vividly recall the exchange that followed. One of Jarvis's aides replied:

"We went around the community. We went to see how many people were back—and your community isn't back."

"How can that be?" Cam asked. "When did you do the survey? Because we were back in October."

"Well, we did it in November."

"Can you show us the survey?"

"Oh, no, it wasn't an official survey."

Cam was disappointed, but not truly surprised. "[We] knew right away that they—just like everybody else in the city—did not think about us. Did not even realize that we were here." It seemed unlikely that the Recovery School District would open a school in Village de l'Est. This year, students from the neighborhood were being bused to schools in other parts of the city. If parents in Village de l'Est hoped to once again have a school that their children could walk to every morning, they would have to open a school of their own.

As the months went on, Cam and other residents began to hear talk in the city about charter schools—schools funded with public tax dollars but run by boards of parents and community members. At first, Cam explained, "I had no idea what a charter school was," but she began to research the option. She trawled the web, attended an education conference in California, and spent hours in meetings with Louisiana education officials.

Applying for a state charter, she discovered, was an arduous task. "You have to have a mission statement," she later explained. "What is your vision of what your school's going to be? Then they ask you for your curriculum." The questions continued for hundreds of pages. The state needed to know about staffing and hiring policies, budgets and financing, school hierarchy and governance, special educational—everything required to run a school. For Village de l'Est to pull this off, Cam would need some help.

In late March of 2006, Cam and Father Vien began to recruit members for a school committee to work through the application. Eventually, the committee grew to five people. "We were teachers," Cam explained, "but we've never run a school. We had no idea how to run a school." Working off advice from former colleagues and school district officials, the committee members split up tasks and began to tackle the application.

As they worked, their vision for the new school began to come together. Cam had originally wanted to start small, with a pre-kindergarten-through-second-grade school that could grow by a grade level with each passing year. "But realistically," she conceded, "funding would not be there" for such a model. The committee decided that a standard kindergarten-through-fifth-grade school would best serve the community's needs, and stood the best chance of winning approval.

One of a charter school's strengths, the committee members knew, was relative flexibility to determine a curriculum. The committee members did not aim to develop groundbreaking pedagogy, but they did want their school to serve the particular needs of Village de l'Est. They decided that in addition to a standard grade school curriculum, students would take Vietnamese language classes.

As the months passed, committee members also hashed out a plan for school governance. They decided that the Mary Queen of Vietnam CDC board would also be the school board, to ensure that the community's voice remained front and center in important school decisions. They would serve as the board's education subcommittee, carrying out duties like hiring a principal and overseeing the school's operation.

The charter application was due in mid-December, and the committee worked down to the wire to complete it. After nine months of work, they handed it in on time. "We thought the application wasn't the best, but it was good," Cam recalled. "We thought for what we had put together, it was good."

In mid-March, a month after their nerve-wracking Department of Education interview and nearly a year after the committee had first convened, Cam and the rest of the board got the news. "We didn't get it," she said. The disappointment was sharp and hard-hitting, but it did not come as a complete surprise. The state maintained high standards, and it had rejected a number of other applications on this round. As committee members reviewed the state's comments, they discovered potential to improve upon the application. Their reviewers were uncomfortable with the notion of one board overseeing both a community development corporation and a school. "They didn't want that," Cam later explained. "They wanted one board just to focus on education, on the charter school alone." Already, committee members were gearing up for the next fight. "We said, 'Okay, we'll have to form the charter school board,'" Cam recalled.

There was also another, more intractable problem with the application from Village de l'Est. The state was hesitant to give the fledgling school committee a charter, Cam explained, because "we didn't have any experience in terms of running a school. Which is very true. We [did] not have any experience." After a year of work, during which community members did everything in their power to lay the groundwork for a school, they had run up against a wall. To successfully move forward, they would need help.

⚜   ⚜   ⚜

By the summer of 2007, the Mary Queen of Vietnam CDC seemed to be staffed by seasoned pros. Despite their brief time on the job, Mary, Cam, and the other CDC staff were already veterans of numerous planning processes, the charter school effort, the landfill campaign, and thousands of hours of direct social service provision. It was easy to forget, in the cheerful but no-nonsense culture of the office, the tremendous personal struggles each staff member had to overcome to show up at work every morning. They were not ones to dwell on hardship.

Mary, forgoing the salary that would have accompanied private-sector work, remained her family's backbone as she shouldered the community's recovery. After gutting her family's house, Mary "was the person that actually called contractors" while her father and step-mother cared for a newborn daughter. Rebuilding the house with no construction experience, Mary contended with the same issues as the neighbors she served at the CDC. "One of my mistakes was that I shouldn't have put the sheetrock on so early," Mary recalled. "It was like, well, how was I supposed to know?"

The neighborhood's long-term volunteers faced their own host of daily struggles. Mai Dang, the recent college grad whose trial by fire came during the landfill campaign, undertook her own rebuilding effort. Upon arriving in Village de l'Est in the summer of 2006, she and her fellow volunteers learned that their apartment had not yet been gutted. As they walked through its rooms, taking shallow breaths of the moldy air, Mai and the others were struck by the juxtaposition of destruction and mundane signs of daily life. "I remember coming in and there was still a Bible sitting on one of the beds," Mai recalled. They were informed that they would have to renovate the space themselves. "We spent the first couple weeks gutting it," she said. They installed their own insulation and hired neighbors for help with tasks that were over their heads. "It gave me a good sense of what community members had to go through."

Settling into such a tight-knit community presented another set of challenges. Even Cam, moving from a Vietnamese American community in Colorado, was taken aback by the neighborhood's strong bonds. "When I first came down," she explained, "I was really surprised at how everybody seemed to know everybody's businesses. It was very uncomfortable for me at first." If her car wasn't back in the driveway by early evening, she could count on neighbors asking, "Why are you coming home so late?" It took time for her reservations to diminish. "As you live in a community like this, you realize, people actually care about you," she said. "They're watching out for you. So it no longer bothers me."

⚜  ⚜  ⚜

*Lo! the apostolic train, Join the sacred Name to hallow;*
*Prophets swell the loud refrain, And the white robed*
  *martyrs follow;*
*And from morn to set of sun, Through the Church*
  *the song goes on.*

"I think they sound good!" Father Vien exclaimed with a knowing smile. The cavernous sanctuary at Mary Queen of Vietnam reverberated the choir's full, confident sound. At this 11 a.m. Sunday Mass in the spring of 2008, Father Vien surveyed the congregation and beheld the typical sea of white, black, and Vietnamese American parishioners. However, the choir behind him, which continued belting out verse after confident verse, was entirely Vietnamese American. Father Vien was not one to gloat, but he knew he had won the fight.

The issue of language at the eleven o'clock service had been a contentious one since the storm. With other parishes in eastern New Orleans closing their doors, Mary Queen of Vietnam found itself absorbing a diverse array of new parishioners. "We are the only parish in the U.S. where it's mixed, yet the mother church is Vietnamese," Father Vien later explained. "Elsewhere, the mother group is always English, and then the Vietnamese group would be attached to it."

The parish had recently added a Spanish-language service, a move the church's Vietnamese American majority easily embraced. "Remember what we were like more than thirty years ago," Father Vien counseled his congregation. "Remember how Americans embraced us. Remember the struggles that we went through. The Latinos are going through the same thing. So, as the Americans opened up their arms to embrace us, it would be proper for us to embrace these people, and see in them ourselves more than thirty years ago."

Adding an English service proved more difficult. Parishioners objected on the grounds of linguistic and cultural preservation. Father Vien chalked their reticence up to latent insecurity. "It is a colonialist mindset," he explained. "We viewed the Latinos as being less than us in terms of being integrated into the community. So it's easy to deal with them, easy to be magnanimous. But we've always had this colonialist view. We've always viewed non–Vietnamese Americans as superior."

The parish's powerful choirs put up a particularly vigorous fight. Along with the ward presidents from across the neighborhood, the choirs held their own seats on the parish's pastoral council. The members were tight-knit enough to have coordinated their own evacuation caravan before Katrina. At first, the idea of singing in English was a non-starter. After some digging, Father Vien discovered that they were afraid of mispronouncing words in front of native speakers. "That colonialist view," Father Vien reflected, shaking his head. "We have no problem with the Latinos, but when it comes to English, our fear is that the English-speaking people will judge us."

The English service was only one of four services that would take place every Sunday, and Father Vien stayed firm. "Eleven a.m. *will* be English. So you can sing, or you cannot sing. If you want to [just sing at] six a.m., fine." He offered to let them ease into their new role, starting with one English song per week, then working up to two, and so on. "So finally, the eleven o'clock choir gave in," Father Vien said. Months later, he was convinced they sounded better in English than in Vietnamese; the former language's long, open vowels lending themselves easily to choral music.

This gradual acceptance of non-Vietnamese language and culture into the parish was part of a broader trend of increasing cross-cultural and cross-generational understanding kick-started by Katrina. Relations between older adults and youth began to improve during the initial recovery, and were then completely transformed by the anti-landfill campaign.

"There's a mutual appreciation and respect now," Father Vien reflected. The neighborhood's aging adults had come to see their children and grandchildren as leaders. "To see people in their twenties come up to give direction to the old people," proved powerful and transformative," he said, whether it was a protest at the landfill or a march at city hall. The youth, in turn, had come quite a way from the years when "they were so embarrassed walking around with [the elders]." Their prior attitude, Father Vien explained, was "'these people are just like country bumpkins.'"

"Now," said Father Vien, "they are proud to walk with their parents."

⚜   ⚜   ⚜

Katrina put an end to many eras, but few were as close to the hearts of New Orleanians as one institution's reign, begun by a French shipbuilder on his deathbed, which continued uninterrupted for nearly three centuries. On November 16, 1735, Jean Louis wrote a fateful will bequeathing funds from his estate "to the founding of a hospital for the sick of the City of New Orleans."[1] With the stroke of his pen, Charity Hospital was born. Over the years, it served the city's poor through fires, deadly bouts of yellow fever, floods, and wars. Generations of Crescent City children, including many first-generation Vietnamese Americans from Village de l'Est, were born in the hospital's maternity ward. The institution was in its sixth building, a vast, Depression-era art deco edifice with more than two thousand beds, when floodwaters from the levee breaks crept up Tulane Avenue and snuffed out its venerable flame.

Sentimentality aside, public health experts agreed that Charity epitomized many of the problems with New Orleans' dysfunctional health-care system. Large hospitals like Charity operated on a centralized model, dealing with a flood of inpatients whose unchecked medical conditions demanded hospitalization.[2] New Orleans was beset by the chronic illnesses that plague America's urban poor—obesity, diabetes, asthma—and it lacked accessible local clinics to provide the preventive care its residents so desperately needed. This system left New Orleanians particularly vulnerable when many of the city's hospitals failed to reopen after Katrina. "There are no hospitals in New Orleans East right now," Mary Tran worried, expressing the concern and frustration shared by many Village de l'Est residents as years passed in the storm's wake. Doctors had been "really hard to find" for community members, and emergency care was dangerously far away. Mary Queen of Vietnam CDC caseworkers reported that inaccessible medical care was one of the residents' most intractable problems.

On August 14, 2008, Village de l'Est took a step in a new direction on health care. Mary Queen of Vietnam CDC had partnered with Tulane's School of Medicine and New Orleans Children's Hospital to found a community health clinic. With cameras flashing, residents, local politicians, Tulane representatives, Father Vien, and the CDC staff assembled to officially open the facility. It was located amid the Vietnamese shops and taco trucks of Alcée Fortier Boulevard, in an office chosen by community members because it had formerly housed a doctor's office.

Mary Tran knew what a difference the clinic would make for her clients. "A lot of our community members are low income," she explained, adding that if "you don't have insurance, you only have to pay $10 to be seen by a doctor, which is really great." The CDC would provide Vietnamese and Spanish interpretation services, working along the clinic's doctors to ensure that medical services would be accessible to all residents.

An operating health clinic was not the CDC's only pending triumph. Four days hence, doors would open at the community's Intercultural Charter School, whose application the state approved after a second round of submissions. Cam Tran had led the effort to correct the flaws that doomed the community's first attempt.

Hoping to learn from Broadmoor's successful application, Cam met with several members of the Wilson charter school board. They praised Edison, explaining the ways the company had assisted with the charter application and lent an experienced perspective to the neighborhood's effort. Cam and other board members had considered partnering with an educational management company, but initially decided that "it wasn't a good match." However, after speaking with Edison representatives, Cam realized that "they pretty much shared our philosophy of education."

"We went and we reapplied a second time," Cam explained, "this time with Edison and with a new board. So we were accepted." Intercultural Charter School would operate out of the Sunday school building at Mary Queen of Vietnam Church, the same edifice that had sheltered residents from Katrina three years before.

With the school about to open and the health clinic in place, Mary and the rest of the CDC's staff began turning their gaze to the future. Plans to build an assisted-living center for the neighborhood's seniors proved difficult to fund, but the efforts would continue. They hoped to open an urban farm, where the community's vibrant Vietnamese agricultural tradition could flourish. The progress Village de l'Est had made in thirty-six months was dizzying, but in her typically humble fashion, Mary declined to claim any credit. She maintained that the community's strong bonds were the prime reason for its success. "Everybody's connected," she explained. "For the Vietnamese community, that's how we rebuilt so fast."

# CHAPTER 13

## Hollygrove: "Slowly but Surely"

I MADE EIGHTY YEARS OLD in July, and I've seen *a lot*," said Phil Harris, drawing out the sentence for emphasis as he reclined in his chair. It was the summer of 2007, and Phil sat happily in his recently renovated dining room, clearly at ease after a lifetime of hard work. Of his life's many challenges—from Navy service to raising children to working his way up from laborer to supervisor at Shell Oil—none was harder, he said, than moving back to Hollygrove after Katrina. And Phil was among the lucky ones.

Unlike a number of his neighbors, Phil had flood insurance on his home. Across the Gulf South, residents with hurricane insurance policies were surprised to learn that their insurance providers were refusing to cover flood claims; insurance companies insisted that flooding from the levee breaks did not technically constitute hurricane damage. While many of Phil's neighbors struggled to find money to rebuild their homes, he forged ahead with his work.

As Phil hired men to rebuild his house, he also managed to avoid another pitfall that ensnared many desperate residents across the city. In the storm's wake, New Orleans was crawling with dubious contractors. Some were scam artists, presenting residents with forged credentials, collecting large down payments for renovation jobs, and then disappearing without a trace. Others did such slipshod work that it did not pass inspection and had to be redone. Phil, however, was friendly with a number of honest and competent contractors. "I was lucky," he said, "because all of the guys that was working, they'd worked for me. I knew them all. We all came from the same area; we was all raised up together."

As the months passed, Phil's house came together. Contractors, plumbers, and electricians did much of the work, but Phil also received help from volunteers. Trinity Christian Community, Phil remembered, sent "some people over to paint the side of my house. They did a lot of work around this house for me." Phil was grateful for the help, but even more grateful for the organization's role in Hollygrove's rebirth. "That's a good organization. Kevin and they [are] very sincere [about] what they do."

Indeed, the help that Phil received on his house paled in comparison with the work that TCC volunteers and AmeriCorps workers performed for hundreds of residents across Hollygrove. TCC did not apply strict criteria when deciding which homeowners to assist, but as Kevin Brown later explained, "Our rationale is poor, elderly, uninsured, underinsured. This is a mercy ministry."

Nearly every week, volunteer teams from churches, schools, and universities would arrive in the bare-bones bunkrooms of TCC's hastily renovated office. In a pinch, the building could house forty people, and it often did. Kevin worked right along with the volunteer teams. "We'd be working morning to night," he later remembered. "We'd have breakfast together, we'd work all day, have dinner together, have evening wrap-up, then go to bed, and the next day do it all over again."

In 2006, TCC's volunteer teams spent much of their time gutting houses in Hollygrove. Under the guidance of the organization's AmeriCorps workers, volunteers donned Tyvec suits and respirators as protection against harmful mold spores, and set upon houses with shovels and crowbars. Their work provided a helpful head start for residents who were unable to gut their houses on their own and could not afford the thousands of dollars required to hire private help for the job.

As time went on, though, TCC began to move beyond gutting, tackling more substantial construction projects for needy residents. Volunteer teams erected interior walls, installed flooring, and hung drywall. An eighty-year-old resident named Ms. Ricks had her entire roof replaced. As construction wound to a close on one house after another, volunteer teams did more and more painting.

All of this work did not come cheaply. TCC's budget ballooned by millions of dollars, buoyed by a flood of giving from churches, national nonprofits, federal grants, and foundations. The organization hired a full-time staffer to keep track of its finances. "It was a very steep learning curve," Kevin later explained, "because we went from a quarter of a million in federal funding to almost $2 million. And with that, we had different requirements; namely, we had to have it audited every year. So that's been one of the biggest challenges—trying to get the organization ready for audit every year."

The extra red tape and bureaucratic headaches, however, proved well worth it. TCC's work on houses throughout Hollygrove began to have a cumulative effect greater than the sum of its parts. As Kevin later explained, "Wherever we redid a house . . . if we do one or two houses on the block, that block would come back. And so we'd move to another block and do one or two houses, and that block would come back. And you can tell. Right now, I mean, if you were to drive with me through Hollygrove, you could tell where we did a house because the neighbors are all back. And you can tell where we didn't do a house because those blocks have maybe one, two people on them."

⚜ ⚜ ⚜

Shortly after the levee breaks, Trinity Christian Community's executive director Kevin Brown recruited one hundred AmeriCorps volunteers to the city. Now, in the summer of 2007, the organization had secured its second AmeriCorps wave, keeping some of the workers in Hollygrove and dolling the rest out to neighborhood groups and schools around the city. Those who remained in Hollygrove coordinated large groups of short-term volunteers.

Every evening, an onslaught of steamy air and excited banter diffused the air-conditioned quiet at TCC's headquarters. High school and college volunteers, soaked with sweat and covered head to toe with dust and paint, would race one another up the stairs toward the shower stalls. Others would sit cross-legged, exhausted, slowly untying the muddy work boots that just days before had been immaculately clean—newly purchased for the mission trip down to New Orleans. Soon, savory whiffs of chili or spaghetti sauce or red beans would come wafting out of the cramped kitchen. Wet-haired volunteers in clean T-shirts and flip-flops would meander back down the stairs, curling up with books or starting card games. Chords, strummed tentatively on an acoustic guitar, might emanate from one of the bunkrooms.

TCC ran like a well-oiled machine. Its volunteer housing was booked solid for the entire summer, and reservations for the fall remained strong. The organization was getting a lot of work done. Under the tutelage of its AmeriCorps workers, TCC's volunteer teams were gutting, framing, mowing, drywalling, and painting their way through block after block of Hollygrove's flooded houses. The amount of work remained overwhelming, but TCC had found a workable model that would, over time, get much of it done. There was just one problem.

"I don't want to be doing housing," Kevin explained. "I don't want to be gutting houses and building houses for twenty years. It's not in this organization's DNA." Kevin's heart still lay in TCC's previous community-based youth work. "Our way of changing the neighborhood prior to the storm was to envision what it would take for a contingent of young people to be transformed so that they could transform the neighborhood," he explained. Before the storm, the model had been working. Graduates of TCC's youth programming had gone on to college and started successful careers. Some, Kevin said, had "outgrown Hollygrove," but others had returned and committed themselves to bettering their neighborhood. Two even worked on TCC's staff.

Though residential development was not in TCC's genes, Kevin said, "it *is* in this organization's DNA to start things and launch them. We've got a track record of building capacity in organizations and then launching them." Indeed, several months before, TCC had helped to launch a new organization known as the Carrollton-Hollygrove Community Development Corporation, named both for the neighborhood in which it was based and for a major commercial corridor—Carrollton Avenue—that bordered the neighborhood to its east. The CDC's executive director, Paul Baricos, was not a Hollygrove resident, but had years of experience at the New Orleans Neighborhood Development Collaborative, a nonprofit that provided training and funding to small CDCs across the city. "There were no strong CDCs [in New Orleans] prior to the storm," he explained, but he was excited to see the blossoming of community-based development across the city as the floodwaters receded. Paul had consulted closely with Hollygrove during its planning process, and eventually approached Kevin with the idea of creating a CDC for Hollygrove, under TCC's umbrella. As Paul had envisioned it, he would work for Kevin.

"Why would you come and work for me?" Kevin had replied. "And why would I have a community development corporation as part of my operations? Why don't you start your own 501c3 [nonprofit organization]?" Kevin was serious. "[Paul] though I was brushing him off," he later explained, "but really what I had envisioned was a spinoff organization."

Not long after their conversation, Paul set up shop at a downstairs office at TCC's headquarters and begun the work of building a CDC from the ground up. Some of his work had already been taken care of. As Kevin explained, "He moved into the building, he trucked off of our phones, he used our Internet, we paid his utilities, and all he does is work. He doesn't have to think about the worries of developing—except for getting his own 501c3 and raising his own funds."

In the months since, Paul had been plotting the Carrollton-Hollygrove CDC's agenda. It would not grow into a large organization overnight, and Paul knew to start small. Working in concert with Carol Dotson and others at the Hollygrove Neighbors residents association, the CDC began an effort to recruit a resident from each block of the neighborhood to act as a block captain. These individuals, he knew, "would have a vested interest in seeing everybody else in that block return." They would also become conduits of information among residents, the CDC, and the neighborhood association. Block captains, Paul said, could share information with their neighbors about "what resources are out there, available, to get back into their homes." Likewise, they could keep Hollygrove Neighbors and the CDC informed about the evolving needs and concerns of residents on their blocks.

As Paul's fledgling CDC began to take root, Kevin received another good piece of news. Rebuilding Together, a home renovation nonprofit that served poor, elderly, and disabled people living in substandard housing, had decided to partner with TCC and expand its operations into Hollygrove. Rebuilding Together was a national organization with more than two hundred chapters across the country. In New Orleans, it traced its roots back to a home-renovation initiative spearheaded in 1988 by the city's Preservation Resource Center (PRC). The organization's New Orleans chapter was now among the largest in the country. It remained under the leadership of the PRC, a powerhouse nonprofit with a $6 million annual budget that had been working for three decades to preserve and restore the city's historical neighborhoods.

In light of the overwhelming housing challenge facing post-Katrina New Orleans, Rebuilding Together was rapidly expanding its operations in the city, and promised to be a strong ally in Hollygrove's recovery. Clients who qualified for Rebuilding Together's services used their insurance proceeds, plus any payout they had received from The Road Home program, to have their houses renovated. If these funds proved insufficient, Rebuilding Together raised money to make up the difference. In a city crawling with incompetent and untrustworthy contractors, it offered needy homeowners peace of mind. It also kept its costs down by using volunteer labor and re-cycling building materials from deconstructed properties elsewhere in the city.

As 2007 wound to a close and the new year began, Kevin watched as Rebuilding Together established its operations in the neighbor-hood. The organization, he later explained, "got really active back here. They got very excited about Hollygrove. And frankly, some-times I feel as though I've been left out of the process. It's like Re-building has taken over so much that they talk about Hollygrove as if it's their idea in the first place." Then again, he quickly reminded himself, "It's not about who takes credit, it's about, 'Does the work get done?'"

Hollygrove's future lay with its young people, and Kevin was de-termined to prepare them to become a positive force in their com-munity. As TCC began winding down its housing initiatives, it threw itself back into its youth programming work. It re-started its after-school program, began planning a youth leadership initiative, and secured slots at sleepaway summer camps for neighborhood youth. Soon, dozens of grade school and middle school children were lining up outside of TCC every day after school.

Once again, TCC was working toward its ultimate goal. "There will come a day," Kevin said, "after we develop enough leaders and enough programs, that I will sit in my office one day and think, 'What am I doing here? Why am I even here?'"

⚜  ⚜  ⚜

A marketing expert might say that Hollygrove had a branding prob-lem. Name recognition was not an issue; everyone knew about the neighborhood, but the associations were not always positive. Holly-grove's most famous resident, the talented multiplatinum rapper Lil Wayne, had grown up in the neighborhood in the 1980s and '90s, attending nearby McMain High School. His verses included frequent heartfelt tributes to his childhood home, painting a far different pic-ture of life on its streets than Phil Harris remembered from his youth. In one song, Wayne wistfully recalled riding down Hollygrove's streets on a bicycle as a child, with a pistol tucked in his pants and packets of crack cocaine in his mouth.

Paul Baricos, director of the young Carrollton-Hollygrove CDC, was acutely aware that most New Orleanians associated Hollygrove with this type of imagery. By contrast, the name conjured few preconceptions in the minds of the one hundred volunteers who now stood before him. These were Starbucks employees, bused into the neighborhood for a scheduled stint of community service—just one item on their agenda at a massive downtown convention. On this sunny afternoon in late October of 2008, the assembled baristas, flown in from places like Sacramento and Tallahassee, knew little of either Phil's or Wayne's Hollygrove. They only knew what they saw before them, which, in Paul's words, "was a wreck. . . . There was debris everywhere."

The vision, already well on its way to reality, was to transform this derelict site on Olive Street into the Hollygrove Market and Farm. The volunteers would clear a two-foot layer of chipped oyster shells (a frequent fill-in for dirt in an alluvial city where real soil is always at a premium) off a half acre of ground, to make way for truckloads of topsoil.

The idea for a produce market, Paul reflected as he watched the volunteers fan out onto the site, had grown rapidly from inception to implementation. During Hollygrove's many planning processes, lack of available fresh food had been a tangential but recurring topic of discussion. Like many poor neighborhoods in New Orleans, Hollygrove was what urban planning parlance had taken to calling a "food desert"—an area where healthy, inexpensive food was hard to obtain. The neighborhood had plenty of corner stores, but these sold mainly sold junk food. Residents had no choice but to drive miles to buy their groceries, or pay a hefty premium for food from a recently opened specialty market in a richer abutting neighborhood. The inconvenience caused many families to compensate with fast food and junk food, contributing to astronomical levels of obesity and diabetes.

Food had been on Paul's mind as the CDC came into being, but it seemed likely to be a side project. Perhaps, he brainstormed, the CDC could organize a farmers' market for the neighborhood. The idea had not gained traction; farmers' markets often fail if they do not gain a wide following, and their clienteles are usually well to do. A program that sold fresh produce from neighborhood corner stores sounded more promising, until Paul visited the stores and discovered wilted fruits and vegetables on small, ill-tended shelves. Then, he and a partner happened upon an idea that stuck. "Why don't we open our own corner store and focus on fruits and vegetables?"

They discovered the largely derelict future home of the Hollygrove Market and Farm on a drive around the neighborhood, and contacted the owner, who maintained an office on the untouched second floor of the property's formerly flooded building. Surprised that anyone would want to rent the remainder of his property, the owner did not drive a hard bargain, and Paul signed a lease in September of 2008. "We started paying rent," he said, "so we had to have some income." The market began by offering boxes of fruits and vegetables, grown in city gardens and on farms in southern Louisiana and Mississippi. The boxes, with enough produce to last two adults for a week, sold for $25 apiece.

The market's clientele in these opening weeks had been largely white and well-off. For Paul, though, demographics were not an immediate concern, because the new service was generating a lot of buzz, and its customer base was quickly expanding. The brisk business had provided a huge boost for the market's physical transformation. Teams began refinishing the downstairs portion of the site's building; after the drywalling and painting, it would host displays of produce, a community kitchen and meeting space, and the Carrollton-Hollygrove CDC's new offices.

More dramatic than the building's renovation was the transformation of the landscape now underway before Paul's eyes, as the Starbucks volunteers carted their wheelbarrows under the bright sun. The New Orleans Food and Farm Network (NOFFN), one of Paul's partners in this endeavor, had big plans for the little site. Through a combination of fresh topsoil and raised growing beds, NOFFN would convert the small wasteland into a lush microfarm, complete with classes on gardening and sustainable agriculture for the community. As Paul saw it, the stream of outside money flowing into the market would help to create a green oasis that would sustain and enrich the neighborhood for years to come.

As the volunteers wrapped up their work, Paul reflected on another reason for optimism. Some of the market's founding members, knowing Hollygrove's reputation, had been initially skeptical about the market's chosen title. "Do we want to scare people away by using the name Hollygrove?" one asked bluntly. Paul was adamant, insisting, "That's why we're here—to promote this neighborhood." Indeed, after receiving substantial press coverage upon opening, the

Hollygrove Market and Farm was now the talk of the town. No one seemed scared away; in fact, the name seemed to conjure up imagery that flew in the face of Hollygrove's longstanding reputation. Perhaps, Paul thought, the market would help everyone see the neighborhood in a new light.

⚜   ⚜   ⚜

Though the humid late-summer air had not cooled noticeably with the setting sun, the game's pace was quick. Shekiel LeBlanc, the boy who had lived with his aunt in Atlanta while waiting for his mom to be released from jail, was now seventeen. He leapt as the ball ricocheted off the unforgiving rim. Three bodies collided in air, forming a momentary tangle of arms and dreadlocks and rubber. Halogen court lights illuminated the aerial struggle in an otherworldly white glow. Though not the strongest of the contestants, Shekiel was the fiercest, and he hit the concrete with the ball clasped firmly to his chest. Dorian Johnson, Shekiel's younger neighbor, was already running down court. He was sixteen now, with shoulder-length dreads and a keen eye for developing plays. He joined the fray under the net.

Behind the scrum, a hand-painted sign lay perched against a shed: "Welcome to Trinity Christian Community. Please honor our code of conduct by not cussing . . . and *please* keep your pants up." Like most rules in New Orleans, these held limited sway. Exposed boxers and muttered curses came with the territory in the rough-and-tumble world of street ball, although the self-officiated game remained remarkably clean and fair.

It was August of 2011. In three years, Pressing On Basketball Ministries had become Trinity Christian Community's largest program, with dozens of neighborhood men in their teens and twenties showing up each week to play. The basketball was top caliber. Most on the court had played seriously for years; one trained daily with New Orleans Hornets point guard Chris Paul. Between games, the men gathered for a brief basketball-inspired sermon and prayer.

The ministry was Ben Aronin's brainchild. A short, energetic white player on a court of tall black men, Ben held his own with hustle and a thorough command of the game's fundamentals. After moving to New Orleans from Wisconsin in 2007 for a yearlong volunteer stint, Ben had joined the growing ranks of Katrina volunteers who opted to stay in the city. He lived with his wife and their one-year-old son in a house on Palm Street, a few blocks from the court.

Dorian and Shekiel respected the passion Ben brought to the game. "I consider him my mentor," Shekiel remarked, contemplating the years they had played together. Ben's example had helped both young men keep their heads up through the preceding years' trials and tribulations.

Dorian was still contending with the previous school year's bitter end. Leaving middle school, Dorian had passed the rigorous entrance exam at Benjamin Franklin, one of the top public high schools in the United States. The trouble started soon thereafter. "There was no library" near Hollygrove, he explained. "I had no computer or Internet. So I just had to do everything on my own. I would get home really late coming from the library, and my mom didn't like that. We didn't have a car, so I had to catch the bus."

Midway through the year, one of Dorian's friends was shot. "He was walking to my house, and a car crept up on him," Dorian explained. "He started running, and they started shooting." Hit in the hip, Dorian's friend survived, but the incident did little to bolster Dorian's psyche or change his mother's mind about his late arrivals from the library. Although Dorian maintained an A average in his difficult freshman math class, he failed out of Franklin when the school year ended in June.

Sophomore classes at McMain High School seemed easy by comparison; the opening weeks of the school year helped Dorian restore some self-confidence. He knew he was capable of whatever he set his mind to. "I love math," Dorian reflected. "I was thinking about doing engineering." Harboring Ivy League aspirations, Dorian was determined to make the most of his second chance. It remained to be seen, however, whether McMain's light homework and comparatively lax classes would prepare him for a top-tier university.

One thing was sure—both Dorian and Shekiel were mastering the art of gliding between worlds. They could switch effortlessly from the dropped consonants and constant ribbing of on-court banter to the clear enunciation, respectful tone, and eye contact of professional conversation. From the first firm handshake, either one could nail a job interview. This agility, this knack for transcending fixed roles, sometimes felt lost on the neighborhood's elders. "I make a point of saying hello to old folks on their porches," Dorian explained. "Sometimes, they seem afraid and go inside."

Shekiel's life in post-Katrina Hollygrove had not proved much easier than Dorian's. With his mother's release from prison, Shekiel found himself suddenly shy. After three and a half years, it was as if he did not know her anymore. As his mom became reacquainted with her children, Shekiel's older sister began a battle against a brain tumor. It seemed a minor miracle that Shekiel still greeted each day with a smile.

Hollygrove's gradual rebirth gave Shekiel reason for optimism. For years, he watched as residents and volunteers put the broken pieces back together. "You just see a bunch of people coming from different places," he recalled. "Kevin [Brown] had teams coming up. Every week, he had teams coming up building houses. People started coming back. Slowly but surely, you saw a lot of houses and a lot fewer trailers." Shekiel naturally projected his optimism into the future.

"I'd like to be a sports physician," he said. Though he was thrilled with Hollygrove's progress since the storm, Shekiel planned to settle elsewhere in the city. "I want somewhere where it's quieter," he reflected, "somewhere you can raise a family." This impulse, shared by many young people in Hollygrove, marked an important challenge for the neighborhood. Until its best young minds felt sufficiently safe and invested in the community to settle there, Hollygrove's rebirth would remain incomplete.

# CHAPTER 14

# Lakeview: "A Whole Different Ballgame"

Even at its low point after Katrina, with its schools shuttered and its businesses derelict, Harrison Avenue retained every bit of its vibrancy in the memories and imaginations of Lakeview's adults. "Memory Lane and Harrison Avenue most definitely intersect for anyone who has grown up here, raised a family here, or both," wrote one Lakeview father.[1] In the years following the storm, the commercial boulevard that many referred to as "downtown Lakeview" played host to a rapid, but uneven, recovery.

Scenes on the street, especially to nostalgic eyes, were sometimes jarringly incongruent. Parents watched as their children emerged happily from a temporary modular library with stacks of books, their smiles framed by the ruins of the old library behind them. As families lined up outside Nick's Snowballs and Gelato in the August heat on the storm's second anniversary, they caught whiffs of moldy, decomposing carpets from the neighborhood's still-unsecured, formerly award-winning Edward Hynes Elementary School.

Through the large windows behind her desk at the newly renovated Gulf Coast Bank, Nancy Lytle had a front-row seat on Harrison Avenue's gradual rebirth. Nancy, a middle-aged woman with graying blond hair and an eager smile, was far from a spectator in the process. Her employer had long ago realized that Nancy's civic engagement bolstered the bank's reputation and drew in business; the bank did not begrudge the long phone calls, unannounced visitors, and impromptu meetings that seemed to define her work. Nor did they mind her word-of-mouth advertising with customers. "Come to Lakeview Fest!" she told them. "Sunday, September 16, St. Dominic's School Yard." Most needed little reminding. The last year's festival, in the fall of 2006, drew five thousand people.

Nancy, a single mother who had spent a decade at home with her disabled son, had been organizing Lakeview Fest for seven years. Her ever-alert posture and lively eyes reflected her indefatigable energy. "I'm not a person who can just sit around doing nothing," she explained. Every year, as the festival approached, preparations began to feel like a second full-time job. The year 2005 had been Lakeview's centennial, and Nancy had been pulling out all the stops for Lakeview Fest when ten feet of stagnant floodwater led many to question whether the neighborhood's hundredth year would be its last.

Lakeview Fest 2006, then, was an extraordinary vindication. Though the neighborhood remained largely empty, more people attended the celebration than ever before. "It actually pulled people in," Nancy later explained. "No matter where they were, they came in for that day. . . . It was packed." Nancy had arranged for contractors, cabinet vendors, flooring specialists, and other construction businesses to set up displays in the St. Dominic's school gym, so that Lakeview families could shop for home renovation options as they considered how—and whether—to rebuild. On the latter question, the festival's high turnout seemed to have swayed residents' decisions. "With everybody coming together," Nancy remembered, "it just grounded everyone. [People said,] 'I'm coming home; you're coming home. Now I know I'm not alone.'"

Nancy, for one, had known early on that she was committed to returning to Lakeview. In January of 2006, Nancy had started her job at Gulf Coast Bank. "There was no phone service, no heat, no air, no computers, and no traffic. It was very quiet," she recalled. That winter, tellers kept ledgers on sheets of paper, recording transactions as a slow trickle of homeowners arrived to sort out the finances of rebuilding.

A milestone came in May of 2006, when St. Dominic's parish school reopened several blocks away. Parents played an integral role in the school's quick return, quickly reenrolling their children after the storm, washing classrooms at the school's temporary site, and caravanning books and furniture back to the Lakeview campus when renovations were complete. On the first day of school in the reopened building, Nancy and other bank staffers smiled as they saw the street and the schoolyard once again full of uniformed students.

After a sweltering summer, during which Lakeview's recovery began to gather steam, St. Paul's Episcopal School reopened just across the street from St. Dominic's. There too, enthusiastic parents drove the school's quick return, laboring alongside hired contractors and reassuring Father Hood that they would enroll their students in the fall. They knew that time was of the essence; without tuition money to run St. Paul's, staff would quickly dissipate, and families would begin enrolling their children in other schools. Terry Miranda, who helped dozens of neighbors gut their homes, lived nearby St. Dominic's and St. Paul's. He was not surprised by their quick return. "They're a small business, and their commodity is education," he explained. "You don't open, you don't have anything to sell, you get closed."

As St. Dominic's and St. Paul's reopened, Hynes Elementary continued to lie fallow. In the auditorium, an upright piano lay across several rows of warped auditorium seats. In a hallway, a large tree branch, a wheelchair, and a rusty stack of tables sat splayed beneath a bulletin board reading "PTO Welcomes Back the Magic." In the library, bookcase after overturned bookcase littered the room with the moldy, bloated pulp of torn books. Prior to Katrina, Hynes had been one of the city's best public schools. Though the will existed to do it, the Orleans Parish school board did not allow parents or administrators to gut the school, citing liability concerns and the need for an accurate damage assessment from FEMA and insurers. Members of the Hynes community had gone on to open a charter school at a location miles from Lakeview, but even two years after Katrina, as St. Paul's and St. Dominic's wrapped up their first full school year in newly renovated classrooms, the Hynes building on Harrison Avenue remained untouched.[2]

Like most Lakeview residents, Nancy Lytle was unhappy with the progress at Hynes, but felt that its recovery was largely out of her hands. She was more hopeful, however, about another derelict building along Harrison Avenue. Nearly two years after Katrina, Lakeview's fire station remained unrepaired, like dozens of others across the city. New Orleans firefighters were being housed near their stations in temporary trailers, as the cash-strapped fire department struggled to come up with the funds to renovate the buildings.

True to form, Nancy had taken it upon herself to reopen the station, and to do as much as possible to renovate stations in other parts of New Orleans. The beginning of hurricane season lent her work a sense of urgency, because the firefighters' temporary trailers were particularly vulnerable to high winds. A few months before, in February of 2007, a tornado had torn through neighboring Gentilly and "flipped a trailer with three firemen in it," Nancy said. "Needless to say it's been a priority for me to get them out of the tin boxes."

The city had condemned some of its fire stations, leaving eleven in need of renovation—a staggering challenge to undertake without municipal backing. Nancy was undeterred, asking large local businesses for substantial donations. "I'm not gonna just ask you for a hammer," she told them. "I need you to adopt a firehouse." So far, her overtures had met some success. The Lowe's home improvement chain donated thousands of dollars worth of plumbing, electrical fixtures, and kitchen cabinets to the cause. Robert Lupo, a local commercial developer, adopted Lakeview's station, donating $5,000 and two weeks of free labor from a local construction firm. Nancy used the money and labor to repair the station's concrete slab, which had cracked after Katrina.

Nancy also hoped to make headway with individual donations. She hung a sign from Lakeview's station, advertising a "celebrity bartender night" fund-raiser, and urging residents to "Donate Now! Volunteer Now!" At her prompting, the Lakeview Civic Improvement Association was selling firehouse T-shirts, at $20 apiece, to raise funds for the station. For her part, Nancy attacked all of the work with a cheerful gusto. Only occasionally did she stop to reflect on the peculiar nature of her firehouse work—raising private funds to reopen a vital but neglected public building.

"You know, a lot of people get upset, and it would be nice to see money flowing and more happening," she explained. The best anyone could do, she thought, was to learn from Katrina's example. "I think everyone may have come to the conclusion that this disaster was just unprecedented," she said. "Shame on the United States if we don't learn from it and put systems in place in other cities after seeing what's happened here."

⚜ ⚜ ⚜

With the passing months, a steady trickle of returning businesses restored much of Harrison Avenue's former vibrancy. Not all of Lakeview's homes followed the same trajectory. In October of 2008, a striking letter went out to the more than one thousand owners of these properties. "We've given you three years," summarized Al Petrie, then in his seventh month as president of the Lakeview Civic Improvement Association. "Now you're on our target list."

This was a marked change in tone for the LCIA, which had bent over backward until that point to help the owners of derelict properties. Al wanted there to be no doubt that his organization would now play hardball. His message was clear. "Make up your mind to fix or sell this property, or we are going to have it expropriated and sold."

The letters marked a culmination in the LCIA's work to guide the neighborhood's recovery. Prior to taking the organization's helm, Al fretted over its relationship with the Beacons of Hope—a relationship that was fast deteriorating. The Beacons, flush with cash, had rapidly expanded their mission's scope onto turf that some old-guard members of the LCIA viewed as theirs alone. The organizations were duplicating each other's efforts on repopulation surveys, blight remediation, business incubation, and events planning; residents were becoming confused about their respective roles.

"We were sort of stepping on toes," Denise Thornton later conceded. It didn't blow up, she asserted, because she and then–LCIA president Bari Landry both were women, and "women don't have the egos that men have." There may not have been a blowup, but resentment simmered.

"It reached just this peak of anxiety between Beacon and LCIA," Al reflected. Breaking the icy status quo, he called Denise in January of 2008 and asked for a meeting. He was frank when they sat down: "If we can't work this out, I'm gonna resign. Because I'm not going to go home every night stressed because we're not communicating, and because you think somehow we're trying to undermine you, and [an LCIA board member] thinks, somehow, you're trying to undermine him."

"We have to work as one entity," he continued. "Whether it's Beacon of Hope or LCIA, that's not the point. We can't have two competing organizations in a neighborhood that's recovering." He pointed to the future, noting that the LCIA would be the organization serving the neighborhood over the long haul. Then, he laid out a plan for a vast expansion of the LCIA's mission. Historically, the organization's fifteen-person board had tackled the lion's share of its work, but Al wanted to expand the LCIA with a set of large new committees that would bring in fresh blood and assume much of the recovery work that the Beacons had pioneered.

"A recovery, once it's got its legs, should be able to stand on its own," he explained. The neighborhood was at the point where it could sustain progress under its own power. The Beacons could take their resources and expertise farther afield, leaving the LCIA to pick up the slack. Denise agreed: "Al, if you can do that, we're outta here. Because you will have accomplished what no one else has done, which is to figure out how to merge together all of these committees and active people who used to be [divided]."

With Denise's blessing, Al turned his attention to convincing the LCIA board to endorse his plan. He realized that, once again, he was on delicate turf. "I didn't want the committee chairs to be board members," he later explained, "because that was how I was going to get new people into the organization. [The LCIA board] didn't quite get it, but I knew what I was trying to accomplish."

He laid out his vision for LCIA committees, which would have eight to ten members, and tackle issues like blighted properties, infrastructure, and green space. "The board should be strategic," he said, "and the committees should be execution." His plan received a polite, but skeptical, reception. "They said, 'Well, Al, that's a great idea, but do you know how hard it is to get people?'"

Then, he played his full hand. "What they didn't know was that I already had all of my committee chairs together," he said. "I already had at least eight to ten people on every committee volunteering. Once I told them that, they were stunned." The board gave its blessing. When Al assumed the presidency in March of 2008, the LCIA took up much of the Beacons' previous work.

Fortuitously, the transition came just as Beacon administrators noticed declining demand for recovery services in Lakeview. As the spring of 2008 wore into summer, St. Paul's Homecoming Center director, Connie Uddo, the former tennis pro who ran the Episcopal church's Lakeview recovery operations, found herself surprised at the slower pace of recovery work. "We really, truly are doing less work here," she said, "because there's really less work to be done." She also was relieved to have some of the Beacon's more peripheral duties taken off her hands. "I told Al, 'I can't maintain neutral grounds anymore. I'm just too tired. We need a committee to do this."

The slackening demand at the Beacons showed that the nature of recovery work in Lakeview had changed, requiring less carrot and more stick. Homeowners had been given three years to begin rebuilding or sell their properties if they did not plan to return. "It's a whole different ballgame," Al explained. "You hate to be that way, but you do get to the point . . . [where] the neighborhood says, 'Okay, we've reached out to you for three years and you've refused that help. Now you're *hurting* us.'"

The city's code enforcement office, which could fine the owners of derelict homes and repossess their properties, was just beginning to find its poststorm footing. The LCIA made a point to expedite its work in every way. Its newly formed blight committee kept a detailed list of noncompliant properties in Lakeview, delivering updated versions to the city every few weeks. It also dispatched Rita Legrand, an energetic retiree whose work as a Beacon administrator won her the admiration and fierce loyalty of her neighbors, to sit in on every Lakeview blight hearing brought before the city.

Legrand, who was eventually dubbed the "Blight-blaster" by the New Orleans *Times-Picayune*, sat through hundreds of adjudication hearings at City Hall.[3] Often, when a property owner claimed that she or he was taking steps to board broken windows or cut tall grass, Rita would counter with recent photographs or testimony from neighbors that proved otherwise. This relentlessness slowly but inexorably began to eliminate blighted properties from the neighborhood.

⚜ ⚜ ⚜

Something about the phone call caught Connie Uddo's attention. The voice on the other end of the line "sounded a little distraught." The woman asked for help painting her house, and Connie promised to connect her to the Beacons' resources. Connie paused for a moment after she hung up. She rarely found time to follow up in person with individual homeowners, but on a lark, she decided to make an exception.

This homeowner, like an increasing number of the clients at St. Paul's Homecoming Center, lived in Gentilly. Connie drove the mile-long greenway through City Park that connected Lakeview to its less-affluent neighbor. What she found, when she arrived at the address, broke her heart.

An elderly black woman emerged from a FEMA trailer to greet her. Then, she showed Connie into her house, which did not need just painting. "She hadn't started her rebuild," Connie recalled. Her husband, a veteran and Purple Heart recipient, had recently suffered a massive stroke. To make matters worse, "They literally had been turned down by Road Home the day of the stroke."

Soon after her visit, Connie packed up the office at the St. Paul's Homecoming Center and moved the entire recovery operation to Gentilly. The move had long been in the works, but this couple's story seemed emblematic to Connie of the rationale behind her decision. Three years after Katrina, there simply were not many people with similar plights left in Lakeview.

It was now May of 2009, six months after the St. Paul's center in

Lakeview had closed its doors, and the pace of recovery work in Gentilly remained brisk. From the Homecoming Center's new location in a small yellow bungalow on Gentilly's Filmore Avenue, Connie's volunteer teams had been painting houses at a rate of almost one per day. Like the couple in the FEMA trailer, many of Connie's clients were people who, in one way or another, had "fallen through the cracks."

"There are some people who just ran out of money. Didn't have enough money to finish. We saw a lot of contractor fraud," Connie explained. Happily, not all of her clients were still stuck in FEMA trailers. Many of her requests were for painting or yard work, and came from residents who "are in their houses and are 90 percent there. . . . And that's very important stuff, because they want to drive up and feel good about where they live. This is a quality-of-life issue, and it's also how things used to be. They want to drive up [to their home] and feel complete."

While Connie, her caseworkers and volunteers continued their work in Gentilly, their former headquarters in a two-story clapboard house behind St. Paul's Church in Lakeview underwent an emblematic transformation. Freed from its gritty, paint-splattered former life as a refuge for rebuilding homeowners and exhausted volunteers, the building assumed a new, upscale identity in keeping with the commercial developments around it. It now played host to the Sweet Life Bakery and Yogurt Factory on one side, and the NOLA Pilates Studio on the other. In Lakeview, this was the real face of recovery.

⚜   ⚜   ⚜

A metal spike protruded from a telephone pole in front of Terry Miranda's rebuilt house in Lakeview, six feet above the street. "That's sea level," Terry explained with a grin one day to incredulous out-of-town visitors. Happily back home, Terry had mixed feelings when he contemplated the "new normal" of post-Katrina life.

There was certainly tremendous progress to celebrate on the storm's fifth anniversary in August of 2010. With Terry's help, many of his neighbors had returned. The Edward Hynes Elementary School building was finally demolished, making way for the new campus that would replace it. Nancy Lytle's firehouse fund-raising had paid off; the station was back in use. In what Terry and others believed was one of the most crucial developments in the neighborhood's recovery, the new Lakeview Grocery had recently opened its doors on Har-

rison Avenue. Still, the progress could not help Terry shake a sense
of emptiness. "Lakeview was purged; the city of New Orleans was
purged," Terry said.

Some of the changes were obvious. "The big loser in Lakeview,"
Terry reflected, "is we lost our elderly. My mother lived over here;
she was eighty-six years old. She'll never live over here again." The
neighborhood's physical character had also shifted—whether for better or worse lay in the eye of the beholder. Yards expanded as residents bought the empty lots adjacent to their properties, filling the
spaces with pools, gardens, and garages. Families took the opportunity to replace the postwar bungalows that had been the backbone of
Lakeview's architectural vernacular with much larger houses. Some
towered on pedestals up to fifteen feet high, designed to withstand
future flooding.

Terry, on the other hand, rebuilt his house at grade. Much to his
chagrin, the LCIA had endorsed a zoning change that designated
his Harrison Avenue property as a commercial tract. "I went to a
series of meetings and protested," Terry said. "It did no good." He
could reside on the property as its current owner, but would have
to sell it to a business owner. "My house will have no residential re-
sale value, because the lots will be commercial," he explained. "I just
need someplace to live for the twenty years that I have left on earth."
Without an elevated house, he said, "I'll be paying through the
nose in flood insurance, but the numbers just didn't make sense any
other way."

Partially as a result of his decision, the "new normal" of Terry's
life involved a constant, vague uneasiness. "I'll never have confidence," he reflected, "because I'm going back in the same situation I
was in. There'll be that little fear in my head all the time."

Day to day, though, Terry got back to the important work of enjoying the freewheeling spirit of the city he loved. He was a fixture at
the city's many festivals, biking the half dozen miles from his house
to the French Quarter for New Orleans classics like the Red Dress
Run, Dirty Linen Night, and Krewe de Vieux. He reveled in the joy-
fully irreverent ethos that fueled much of the city's culture, taking it
upon himself to spread it wherever possible.

After joining a retirees' society in Lakeview, he was horrified to
hear about the group's mundane social events schedule. "Bingo?" he
incredulously asked one organizer. "I would rather take a stick in my
eye." Soon thereafter, he founded the group's Casino Night, complete

with distinctly New Orleanian twists. "If anyone wins a hand with three sixes," he announced before a poker game, "I will give you five dollars on the spot. Here's the catch: you have to use it for something evil. Maybe buy a devil's food cake, or make a donation to the Louisiana politician of your choice."

Displaying one of the qualities that made him such a force in the recovery, Terry refused to get bogged down rehashing the difficulties and losses wrought by Katrina. "Nothing could have prepared us for this in a thousand years," he replied, when asked what lessons the storm held. "Nobody knew what they were doing. I made some good choices, and some bad choices. I was lucky that the good ones outweighed the bad."

Though he did not wish to dwell on it, Terry saw the suffering as a part of life in the city—it had always been there in one way or another, and it always would. "New Orleans, when it was founded, had floods in the spring, yellow fever in the summer, hurricanes in the fall, and fires in the winter," he explained. "When you got to Mardi Gras, you were celebrating because you'd survived another year."

CHAPTER 15

# The Lower Ninth Ward:
# "I Feel So Good When I'm Home"

Tricia Jones glanced out of NENA's new headquarters and was surprised to see that the line of residents had grown considerably. It was late summer, 2006. On days like this, Tricia thought, it felt like she and her organization were living a miracle. In the months since residents held their nationally televised memorial service by the Industrial Canal levee break, NENA had secured substantial funding, hired staff, and moved into its newly renovated headquarters on the St. David's campus. This breathtaking success, taking place over a few short months, buoyed Tricia's spirits. Though the surrounding blocks remained largely abandoned, NENA's headquarters felt like an oasis of hope and possibility. Now, more than anything else, Tricia wanted clients for her new organization, and this particular day was proving to be a windfall.

Most of the residents who now gathered at NENA's headquarters had come to sign up as claimants in a class-action lawsuit against the U.S. Army Corps of Engineers. NENA had offered to help residents complete the process, and as Tricia explained with a smile, "word got around." The suit had residents talking, and it was getting them in the door at the center. Tricia knew that if she and her newly formed staff helped the residents in a professional and courteous way, many would come to see NENA as an organization they could trust.

The day's work was possible because NENA had recently received a $100,000 grant. Representatives from the Oregon nonprofit Mercy-Corps, impressed with Tricia's work in the Lower Ninth Ward, had kept in touch with her after the neighborhood's memorial ceremony. When Tricia told them she had found a potential headquarters, Mercy Corps committed the funding, allowing NENA to renovate the building and hire local staff. "That [grant] was the beginning of our capacity," Tricia explained. Building that capacity, however, required a great deal more than money. The past few months had been a blur of hard work. Tricia and her board members had partnered with outside volunteer teams to gut and renovate the organization's office on the St. David Parish campus. It was still bare-bones, with a concrete floor and cinderblock walls, but the single large room could accommodate both office work and larger meetings. Securing the grant money had also required a legal and bureaucratic dance; Tricia had scrambled to register NENA as a federally recognized 501c3 nonprofit. She had also worked hard to hire and train her staff members, many of whom were not as familiar with office work as Tricia was.

Now, as Tricia walked around the room, she was happy with what she saw. Staff members and residents sat together at folding tables and chairs. The staffers helped residents one at a time, working with them to fill out the forms. As they did, they also asked each resident for basic information about his or her family and recovery status. In this way, Tricia later explained, "you have a history of a client being built in a nonassuming, nonthreatening way." Staffers made copies of all the paperwork, and created folders for each family.

Before residents left the center, staffers encouraged them to come back in for help with other recovery needs. "Look, The Road Home [program] is coming up," Tricia later paraphrased, explaining the approach that her staffers took. "Come in with these documents and we'll help you apply. And make sure your grandma comes with you. We're going to help both of y'all do y'all's applications."

One of NENA's greatest assets, it seemed, would be the flexibility to directly meet the evolving needs of Lower Ninth Ward residents. For one thing, Tricia later pointed out, "we had a competitive advantage with other nonprofits, because ones that are already established, they had to do some internal struggling to decide [whether to change] their mission." For another, the resident staffers were going through the same rebuilding process as their clients. "You look ahead from a personal perspective on what's coming along the horizon," she explained. Tricia, for one, knew that she was having trouble restoring water service to her house. "So if water's the issue at my house," she said, "it's the issue at everybody's house. So, an organizing piece was around water. Another organizing piece was around getting power." In this way, NENA could "get prepared" for upcoming challenges "very easily, because you know what's hitting." As new challenges arose in the coming years, Tricia was confident that NENA would be able to meet them.

⚜   ⚜   ⚜

TOURIST
Shame On YOU
Driving By Without Stopping
Paying TO SEE MY PAIN
1600 + DIED HERE

The message, painted on a large piece of plywood, was displayed prominently in front of a small cape-style house on the 1700 block of Deslonde Street. This was ground zero, less than a hundred yards from the massive levee breach along the Industrial Canal in the Lower Ninth Ward. The house, owned by an organization called Common Ground Relief, was one of only a few in the vicinity still standing; most of the others had succumbed to the cascade of floodwater that swept over the neighborhood on a fateful August morning nearly two years before.

Over the course of several months, dump trucks had hauled away the debris from the flattened blocks, leaving empty lots that quickly filled with grass. Residents had always likened the Lower Ninth Ward to the country, but now it really *looked* like the country. The only hints of the dense city neighborhood that had formerly occupied these blocks were ghostly concrete front stoops, which rose from the ground at regular intervals, leading to houses that no longer existed.

Common Ground's buildings on Deslonde Street were among the few in the area left standing. Down the street from its single-story cape, the organization owned a two-story building with office space, tool storage, a kitchen, and bunkrooms for volunteers. The block, which a week before had been overrun with fifteen passenger vans and college kids wearing paint-spattered jeans, once again felt devoid of life. April was drawing to a close, and with it came the end of spring-break season. For Thom Pepper, Common Ground's new director, it was a time to rest and reflect after an exhausting crash course at the helm.

Common Ground was an unlikely collaboration, an improvised series of partnerships forged across class and racial lines. Its origins lay in radical politics. Two of its founders, Scott Crow and Brandon Darby, were far-left-wing organizers from Austin, Texas; a third, Malik Rahim, was a former Black Panther who lived in the New Orleans neighborhood of Algiers, on the "Westbank" of the Mississippi. The three knew one another through their friendship with Robert King, a recently freed prisoner who had spent three decades in solitary confinement at the Louisiana state penitentiary known as Angola. They, along with Malik's partner, Sharon Johnson, founded Common Ground five days after the storm.

The organization began its work just after Katrina in the city's unflooded Algiers neighborhood, distributing food and water to residents who remained. From its earliest days, it depended on donations and volunteer labor that flooded into the city, expanding its outreach as new needs emerged and new resources arrived. Under the slogan "Solidarity, not Charity," it opened a free health-care clinic in the Algiers neighborhood eleven days after the storm, staffed by volunteers with medical training who arrived from around the country.

In December of 2005, Brandon Darby rented the small cape house on Deslonde Street in the Lower Ninth Ward. The surrounding blocks were a debris field, and there was neither water service nor power in the neighborhood. Before long, the Common Ground organization followed him. Brandon's house became a food-and-water distribution center in the neighborhood, serving residents who began trickling back in to work on their properties. Over time, it also built up a "tool-lending library," at which residents could check out weed whackers, saws, sledgehammers, and other implements of destruction required for the gritty work of gutting their houses.

Common Ground's volunteer coordination in the neighborhood developed slowly. At first, it housed and fed individuals, who trickled into the neighborhood from points around the country, looking to volunteer. Slowly, larger groups began to arrive: college service trips, hippies traveling the country in vegetable-oil-powered buses, church youth programs, packs of gutter punks, employees of Fortune 500 companies in town for large conventions. The volunteers mowed overgrown lawns, dug ditches, administered surveys, distributed supplies, planted gardens, and—most important—gutted thousands of houses. As the months passed, they kept arriving in droves, becoming the lifeblood of Common Ground's operations in the Lower Ninth Ward.

The hand-painted message to tourists at Common Ground's Lower Ninth Ward headquarters, then, was only a facet of the organization's conflicted stance toward the outside world. To be sure, Common Ground's leaders resented the tourists who snapped pictures of the destruction from the air-conditioned confines of their buses. They were furious at the federal government, which had abandoned poor New Orleans neighborhoods while spending billions of dollars on overseas wars. They rejected the national mores that seemed to value profit and material comfort over solidarity and equality. For all of these reasons and more, it was tempting to renounce the world outside the Lower Ninth Ward. Such a move, however, was impossible. Common Ground depended on a steady stream of money, material donations, and volunteers in order to carry out its mission. Keeping these resources flowing required working with people and organizations of all persuasions. Radicals alone could not revive the neighborhood.

Although Common Ground's leaders initially embraced a decentralized approach to running the organization, idealism slowly gave way to realism as they realized that their approach led to poor communication and lack of accountability. When Thom Pepper first arrived at Common Ground as a volunteer in October of 2006, the organization was in serious debt. No one could account for how money had been spent, nor did anyone know how much each creditor was owed. Thom had bookkeeping experience, and began chasing paper trails and crunching numbers. "We discovered that we owed $300,000 to vendors and we didn't know how that number got to be so large," Thom later explained. "We had forty-two cell phones and a $6,000-per-month cell phone bill, and our payments were in arrears of like $17,000. It was just doing some housekeeping and figuring out how we were going to do all of that."

Thom knew how difficult disaster recovery could be. He had struggled to rebuild his own house after Hurricane Andrew, and experienced the frustrations of dealing with insurance companies and clearing bureaucratic hurdles. His management expertise, coupled with his experience with postdisaster recovery, seemed to uniquely qualify him to lead Common Ground out of its quandary. After finishing his volunteer stint and returning home, he received a phone call asking him to take over as Common Ground's organizational director. He accepted the offer.

By courting new donors and imposing more rigid spending rules, Thom paid off the organization's debt. Neighborhood leaders, who came to depend on Common Ground for volunteers, were impressed. "The expertise that Thom Pepper has is just amazing," said the Holy Cross Neighborhood Association's Pam Dashiell. "He's a born administrator. [He] brought order and accomplishment to chaos."

Meanwhile, Common Ground's volunteer operation continued to grow. "At the end of spring break of 2007, we had about five hundred volunteers a week coming through gutting houses," Thom said. "We were cooking eleven thousand meals a week on propane gas stoves behind a blown-out, abandoned school house over in the Upper Ninth Ward." The flood of volunteers accomplished tremendous quantities of work. As spring segued into summer, Thom said, the organization hit a crossroads. "The house-gutting program ended," he recalled. "There was really not that much more to do."

With its gutting mission complete, Thom and the rest of the crew at Common Ground began contemplating the organization's future. Across the Lower Ninth Ward, the focus was beginning to shift toward renovating and rebuilding houses. At NENA, Tricia Jones was gearing up her organization to help residents with the design and construction process. NENA could help residents with the finances, paperwork, and bureaucracy involved with building a house. Common Ground, it seemed to Thom, was better suited to help tackle the work of construction itself.

Common Ground's ability to recruit and deploy armies of volunteers had been ideal for tackling the mountains of unskilled gutting work in the Lower Ninth Ward, but it would prove less useful as residents slowly began to rebuild. In order to support the neighborhood's new wave of construction, Thom hoped to shift Common Ground's volunteer recruitment to focus on "quality over quantity." As the months passed, this new approach began to take hold. Common Ground required that its long-term volunteers know a construction skill, or at least be willing to learn one. Thom encouraged college groups to learn how to hang drywall before coming to New Orleans, so that they could begin working immediately upon arrival.

As skilled volunteers flowed into the Lower Ninth Ward, Common Ground began to refine its approach to construction assistance. It took a cautious, professional approach. The last thing the organization wanted to do, Thom later explained, was to "put the property owners in jeopardy again." Common Ground insisted that "people had their houses assessed properly, to make sure that they could even rebuild," Thom said. "Because there had been horror stories of people getting their insurance proceeds, starting to rebuild, and as soon as they brought inspectors in the inspectors were condemning their houses, because their houses weren't on their foundations properly."

Common Ground also partnered with a professional firm, Epco Construction, to carry out highly skilled work. "We wanted to make sure that the electrical and plumbing work was done by licensed general contractors that had insurance," Thom explained. Residents paid for Epco's services, but received other labor, like framing, hanging drywall, and painting, free of charge from Common Ground's volunteer teams.

Under Thom's leadership, and building on the creativity and initiative of its volunteers, Common Ground also began a number of environmental initiatives in the Lower Ninth Ward. The organization planted fields of sunflowers on empty lots, using the plants to soak up toxins and heavy metals that the floodwater had left in the neighborhood's soil. It built a trail along Bayou Bienvenue, the stretch of wetlands along the neighborhood's northern border. It also planted a number of community gardens, both on plots in the Lower Ninth Ward and elsewhere in the city.

Perhaps most important, Common Ground strove to support resident-driven recovery efforts whenever they needed assistance. Its volunteers helped to gut and renovate NENA's headquarters. As a reliable source of volunteers, it freed neighborhood leaders to concentrate on other matters. Pam Dashiell, for example, could attend to her work with the Holy Cross Neighborhood Association and with various sustainability initiatives, knowing that she could secure volunteers whenever she needed them. "Common Ground is the biggest resource and supplier for volunteers," she explained. "They're very high profile, and attract people from all over. They've also been a wonderful resource for the sustainability projects." She was even more impressed with "all the construction work that they do, and the actual rebuilding of people's houses. It's amazing."

Although Common Ground had sprung to life outside of the Lower Ninth Ward, and largely had been run by outsiders and transplants, it had nonetheless become integral to the neighborhood's recovery, providing extensive labor for hundreds of projects.

❧   ❧   ❧

Mornings in Holy Cross always brimmed with potential. As the sun crept over the horizon on this particular April day in 2008, a slight breeze blew in off the river, the roosters crowed on cue, and long shadows slowly receded to reveal peacefully empty roads. Pam Dashiell, an early riser, puffed a cigarette as she strolled down Lizardi Street. The Holy Cross Neighborhood Association, headquartered in a small office in back of the Greater Little Zion Baptist Church, was only a few blocks from Pam's apartment.

At times like this, in the gentle embrace of the city's streets, it was hard not to feel an almost organic rootedness in the place. Pam paused at the church's back stoop, taking one last puff and enjoying the sunlight, steeling herself for what would likely be a fifteen-hour workday. Numerous responsibilities vied daily for her attention. Though she had since passed on the presidency of the Holy Cross Neighborhood Association, she remained the director of the Lower Ninth Ward Center for Sustainable Engagement and Development (CSED), sat on several boards that worked on city- and statewide environmental issues, and kept constantly engaged with an array of recovery projects in the neighborhood. As one of her neighbors later wrote, "There isn't one, single, grassroots community-building project in the Lower Ninth Ward—and there are dozens of projects at one stage or another, almost all green—that Pam Dashiell was not involved with or supported."[1]

The seeds for CSED were planted shortly after residents completed the Lower Ninth Ward green rebuilding plan. At the same time Mercy Corps was in talks with Tricia Jones to support NENA, its representatives began showing up at Holy Cross meetings. "They would observe and ask questions," Pam said. What would residents do with funding? The neighborhood's answer was unequivocal. "We want to make this plan happen."

In "August 2006, we started working on a grant getting it all set up. And then the money came in December." It did not hurt that actor Brad Pitt, who called New Orleans his adopted home, had started showing up at neighborhood meetings and throwing his weight behind the community's recovery. "Brad came in during the summer of 2006," Pam explained, and "I think that probably revved up Mercy Corps."

Pitt aimed to undertake his own work in the neighborhood. He was particularly drawn to the devastated blocks near the levee breach, where empty concrete slabs provided the only hint of what had once been a dense community.

"It was obliterationville," Pitt said, in an interview with the historian and author Douglas Brinkley. "It was a blank, blank, blank canvas. . . . The place just looked like a giant eraser had come in and just erased away those homes."[2] Families whose roots and memories in the neighborhood stretched back for generations would likely bristle at Pitt's invocation of a blank canvas. But many realized that the actor, unlike the parade of politicians who made speeches and posed in the neighborhood for photo ops, was actually committed to articulating a vision for the neighborhood's most devastated reaches and seeing it through.

In December of 2007, Pitt had announced the creation of Make It Right, a foundation that aimed to build 150 architecturally innovative homes near the Industrial Canal breach. Thirteen architecture firms from around the world agreed to submit designs pro bono, and the organization began recruiting potential buyers among Lower Ninth Ward residents. NENA referred the first six Make It Right clients.

The incursion of brightly colored, avant-garde houses onto previously empty blocks was visually striking, receiving mixed reviews from residents who lived nearby. The high-profile houses, along with their high-profile spokesman, quickly became the best-known recovery effort in the city. Neighborhood leaders found themselves grumbling about the glut of donations Make It Right received. No one, however, could argue with the attention. "It's forced the city to address the infrastructure," said Thom Pepper. "So, now they're putting in sewer lines. And they're doing water lines. They're putting in gas lines. And it brings attention here; I mean the tour buses come by."

Not one to be starstruck, Pam had pushed hard in their meetings for Pitt to adopt the neighborhood's vision of a green recovery. Pitt would later call her "a guiding force in the recovery efforts;" Make It Right's overriding focus on innovatively resilient and energy-efficient design doubtless grew out of their meetings.

While Pitt's recovery effort remained nascent, the CSED found its legs and began charting an ambitious course. Almost immediately, Pam and her collaborators secured a donation of solar panels to install on houses throughout the neighborhood. Soon thereafter, they partnered with the Sierra Club to install radiant heat barriers in the attics of hundreds of Lower Ninth Ward homes. Pam was quick to point out that these "green" projects directly benefited residents, lowering energy bills for families who were often on low, fixed incomes.

The context of the neighborhood's destruction also lent a visceral, moral urgency to the task of a sustainable recovery. "I don't think anybody understands the effects of climate change and global warming better than the people of the Lower Ninth Ward and other parts of New Orleans," Pam was quoted in the local weekly newspaper *Gambit*. "We've lived the effects."[3]

Safeguarding the neighborhood from future storm surges, Pam understood, meant more than fighting climate change. For decades, the wetlands surrounding New Orleans to its south and east had eroded at an alarming rate. The construction of high levees down much of the Mississippi a century before had choked flooding that annually restored the wetlands with massive sediment deposits. A spiderweb of canals dug across the delta for fishing and oil exploration expedited the decay, allowing for saltwater incursion that killed plants and dissolved the root systems that held the precious soil in place. Without wetlands, hurricane storm surges could sweep right up to the city's levees at full strength.

Bayou Bienvenue, a former cypress swamp abutting the Lower Ninth Ward's northern frontier, was one of Pam's particular concerns. Except for old-timers who used to fish on the Bayou, most of the neighborhood's residents had not even known it existed before the storm. It lay behind train tracks and a high metal wall—nearly impossible for anyone to reach. "The first time when we were climbing over the sheet piling, and making piles of rocks and everything to get over there, it was amazing to see," she remembered. A beautiful expanse of open water, tall grass, and cypress stumps stretched out toward the northern horizon. It stood in stark contrast to the devastated urban blocks behind them.

Soon after Pam's visit, the CSED and other neighborhood groups defined the restoration of Bayou Bienvenue as a core tenet of the community's recovery efforts. A group of University of Wisconsin students built an observation platform overlooking the bayou, and for the first time in decades, residents gained a clear sense of the connection between their neighborhood and the surrounding wetlands. Pam threw herself into efforts to secure funding for the bayou, although to date, no funding had arrived.

Firm belief in the cause helped Pam sustain her daily grind, as did thoughts of the steady trickle of neighbors who returned to the community each week. Every Thursday, at meetings of the Holy Cross Neighborhood Association, newly returned residents rung the church bell in a joyous ceremony that had quickly become a poststorm tradition. Everyone knew that the ringing bell signified another neighbor coming home.

⚜  ⚜  ⚜

There was poetry in the cadence of Ms. Georgia Johnson's speech. Her sentences commenced with vigor, but then meandered lazily,

painting pictures in couplets that trailed soothingly off into a medita-
tive emptiness. "It's something you couldn't even *imagine*," she began. "When you're used to seeing a place that's so vibrant, and full
of life. Cars movin' and horns blowin'—and birds singin' and trains
goin'. And nooothing." She paused, her audience hanging on her every word. "*Ab*solute silence." Her audience *felt* the silence as the words
trailed off.

Georgia, perched happily on a couch in her renovated living room,
was a master storyteller. Today, she had a reason to smile. More than
three years after the Industrial Canal had spilled its muddy contents
through the front door of her cottage, Jourdan Avenue was no longer
silent. Georgia, along with many of her neighbors, had restored life
in the void that Katrina's floodwaters left behind. The October sun,
relenting somewhat after months at its blazing apex, cast a warm glow
across her broad front porch, illuminating a fresh coat of white paint
and handsome turquoise shutters. In a way, the property reflected
the artistry of Georgia's speech, at once vividly alive and serenely
timeless.

"I had custody of all eight of my grandchildren. Plus two more—
eight, nine, ten. And we all lived here," Georgia explained. She
grinned, anticipating the description that came next. Before Katrina,
"What they called it was the Raggedy Mansion. . . . We had every bit
of between fifteen and twenty holes in the ceiling." When it rained,
"everybody knew to get their bucket. You know, you gotta put your
bucket here, put your bucket there."

Many of Georgia's friends recognized a unique aesthetic in her
family's lifestyle. Shortly before this particular October afternoon,
Georgia received a CD recorded by her still-exiled neighbors, musicians Katie Euliss and Mike West, who together made up the band
Truckstop Honeymoon.[4] The CD's seventh track, dedicated to Georgia and her life partner, Blue, captured the joyful ethos.

> *Do your dogs still bark, do your roosters crow?*
> *Do your little gray car with the flat still go?*
> *Do your fishing poles hang out the back window?*
> *Do your hens still nest in the passenger's seat?*
> *Do they still lay eggs that your kids won't eat?*
> *Do you still love Georgia, and do she love you?*
> *What am I sayin'? Of course you do . . .* [5]

To Georgia, the song was a reminder of how whole she felt while at home. "I know all of my neighbors," she explained. The Blackwells, a family down the street, "have been here as long as I have. Our children grew up together." Being back among the friendly faces on her block was a welcome relief. "I've been home a couple months now," Georgia reflected, "and I feel really good. I was bein' really sick. I have severe asthma and bronchitis. I have emphysema. While I was in Mississippi, I was sick. I had to go to the doctor, if not every day, then every other day. But since I've been home, I've been to the doctor maybe twice."

The return had not been easy. When she and Blue first worked up the courage to drive back into the neighborhood, they were overwhelmed. "Ain't no way you could ever make this home again," she thought. Later, she found herself "sitting down, thinking, reminiscing about . . . the good times."

Much like Tricia Jones, Georgia remembered a lesson her father did his best to impart. "I thought about how hard the trouble was for my daddy when he first bought this house. And he told me, you know, it's the hardest thing in the world for a black man first off to buy a house, then to maintain the household. . . . He said, 'I want you to promise me that if anything ever happened to me, you'll keep this house.' " It was a promise she intended to keep.

With the help of a NENA caseworker, Georgia applied to The Road Home. "It took a long time," she explained, lapsing into one of her trademark pointed pauses. "It took a looong time . . . y'understand?" Georgia, like many residents whose houses had been in their families for generations, did not have her property's deed. Without a deed, all she heard was, "No. You've got to put your name down on the list. And you've just got to wait until it gets to you. And you've got 999 people ahead of you." Eventually, the paper surfaced, and "things kind of smoothed out a little bit."

One day, Georgia was pleased to discover a newly bolstered checking account, flush with the money for which she had applied. "It was enough to get started," she recalled, but more struggle lay ahead. Two different times, contractors promised to fix her roof and then ran with her money. One "showed me all this paperwork and this and that. Anyway, I got beat."

"I finally got with this guy. He's a New Orleans police officer. . . . He said, 'Ms. Georgia, I'm gonna help you all I can, because I

know you're on a tight budget, and I know you need to have a certain amount done.'" Like so many New Orleans builders, he sub-
contracted much of his work to a newly emerging class in the city.
"I didn't get a *contractor* contractor," Georgia explained. "I got a
Mexican guy."

She was thrilled with his work. Her roof was patched, her high
ceilings restored, and her floors refinished. NENA sent a team of
volunteers to paint her house. A $500 Lowe's gift card, a giveaway
procured at a Holy Cross Neighborhood Association meeting, helped
her to put on some finishing touches.

Eager to help others make the transition home, Georgia signed
up to be a NENA block captain. "If I can help out in any kind of
way, I'm willing to do that," she explained. Members of her extended
family second-guessed her decision: "'Why you wanna go back to
the Ninth Ward?'" She rolled her eyes as she recalled the questions.
"'Why you wanna go back to that raggedy house?'" Her answer was
as confident as it was simple: "It's my choice," Georgia said. "I feel so
good when I'm home."

⚜ ⚜ ⚜

Though she hid it well, Tricia Jones was tired. Her strides still came
quickly, her handshake remained firm, her gaze blazed intensely as
ever, and her rapid-fire sentences retained their trademark confidence.
The fatigue showed itself in smaller ways. Creases were etching themselves around her eyes, marring an otherwise strikingly beautiful vis-
age. When she allowed herself to sit, she looked as if she had carried
a fifty-pound bag of cement all day. Despite her fierce will, the effort
was taking its toll.

"What is today, March the eleventh?" she asked. It was 2009. She
had been going nonstop for three and a half years. "Last night was
when my husband bought the flooring for our house. So, my kitchen
is undone. I have one bathroom working. Save for the flooring in my
kids' room, we moved into an unfinished house."

Had she considered getting volunteer help? "I still struggle with
that. I had one set of volunteers at my house. The rest of it, we did
without." Their house represented autonomy. For Tricia, as for her
father before her, home ownership was an escape from the Florida
housing projects, from a life of forced dependency and broken bureaucracy and long lines. "When you have something and you work

for it honestly, and then it's ripped from you," she explained, "to get back in line again is uncomfortable to say the least."

Many families who passed through the NENA center were even more stubborn. They would "get in their houses without water. Without lights." For them, Tricia explained, there was simply "no other way to do it." Taking what they perceived to be a "handout" was out of the question. Reticence to accept help was just one of many issues that Tricia and her caseworkers contended with every day as they labored to bring neighbors home. "Each family is different," she said. "I wish I could just mass redevelop everybody, but I can't."

Early on in NENA's work, homeowner assistance involved what Tricia described as "quick projects," like gutting. The next phase of the recovery centered on applications to the Road Home program. Like residents across New Orleans, Tricia explained, many of NENA's clients had "to fight to get the maximum they deserved from Road Home." The program's structure did not favor Lower Ninth Ward residents; it doled out payments based on prestorm property values, not on the cost of rebuilding.

Tricia would draw on her years of recovery experience, both personal and professional, to counsel families. "I'm looking at the standards and the policies, and I could tell them in ten minutes, 'You should be expecting a check of fifty thousand dollars. Is your house still structurally in place? Yes? All right. You're going to still need another twenty-five. You should be expecting them to send you a little yellow sheet of paper. . . . If they don't give you that, you come back and talk to me.'"

"Now, we're at the next stage," Tricia explained. Most residents knew for sure how much money they would receive. The next question was, "How do you take that money and rebuild?" Tricia kept an architect on staff to help residents contend with the inevitable structural and permitting issues that accompanied renovations and new construction.

The architect, Burke Rafter, was a recent graduate of North Carolina State University's College of Design. He explained that many of his projects involved helping clients overcome "stuff . . . that just makes you want to pull your hair out." One of his clients "lost one of her daughters during the storm, and inherited her two children. And then, her other daughter is on dialysis, so she's taking care of *her* two children." The woman hoped to renovate her Holy Cross house for her newly expanded family.

The renovation involved "a second-story addition on top of an existing garage and accessory building. Two little cement buildings that were attached to her home through a series of generations of additions to her house. . . . They were built without a permit; they were built by folks who weren't licensed contractors. It was pretty ad hoc." To make matters worse, her house was in a historic district, and the Historic District Landmark Commission nearly put a halt to the project. Happy that construction was finally nearing completion, Burke still found it frustrating that "it's taken two and a half years to get something built."

Profound frustration at delays, and at the fundamental injustice of her community's plight, had motivated Tricia's work for three and a half years. She saw no end in sight, especially when she reminded herself that others were profiting at the neighborhood's expense. Residents, she noted, were "pissed already that they got played like this. . . . Not just the government with the breaches, but the fact that insurance companies didn't pay people from a technicality. I mean, and they made record profits? And you're not going to pay me and I have hurricane insurance? I'm not asking you for something that I haven't been paying for for years."

With thousands of families still displaced, and the return of dozens of homeowners considered real progress, it would have been easy to spiral into bitter despair. Tricia avoided the trap, focusing mightily on problems within her control while remaining disarmingly humble about her accomplishments and work ethic. "There have been people across the country who have helped me get that next wind when there's nothing left in me," she reflected. Hundreds of Lower Ninth Ward residents could say the same about her.

# CHAPTER 16

## Laurels

Six years after the Industrial Canal levee failed, Tricia Jones presses indefatigably on. One fine fall day, asked what keeps her going, Tricia replies with a story.

> Last night . . . I left very late again, in the rain. My husband came to pick me up. And I said, "You know, Phil, I'm hungry." I didn't cook dinner. It's just that kind of night. And I said, "I want to go get some beans from Popeye's. And I'm feeling a donut. I just want a donut."
>
> So we drive down, we go to Gerald's, and we go through the drive-through. I said, "I want a cake donut." And for some reason, the cake donut is just not like it always tastes. So I go out the truck, in the rain, and I go, "I don't know what's wrong with this donut. I really love your donuts. I really need a donut tonight."
>
> We get a glazed. We turn around, and there's this person, an elderly guy, in the donut shop. And he says, "Ms. Jones! Tricia!"
>
> I said, "Hi! Mr. Butler!"
>
> He said, "I love y'all. Y'all really helped me to get home."
>
> That was last night. This elderly guy, we helped five years ago. And he said, "I can't tell you how much of a blessing it was. I talk about you guys so much. I would not be here. And I just want to say thank you."

Encounters like these get her out of bed, Tricia says, giving her "juice for the next family." Despite the difficulties of her work, she shows no signs of slowing down. Tricia and the other neighborhood leaders who remain in the game are now veterans, true experts in their field. They are eager to share their lessons.

"One is that you need to shore up leaders on the ground," she says, not missing a beat after being prompted. "Those leaders on the ground need to have the flexibility to do the work that needs to be done." The most nimble and committed of these leaders, she asserts, will be "neighborhood association leaders. They have to be in place at that time." Community leaders, she tells me, should work to set up online database systems to keep track of residents and their needs. Having such leadership and information in place before a disaster will shave months, or even years, off a recovery, accomplishing tasks that would stymie even the most powerful mayor. "I would tell the mayor not to try to assume the role that he or she is going to save the city," Tricia warns, "because you are not. You are only as good as your weakest link."

On this front, neighborhood leaders across New Orleans echo Tricia's advice, and San Francisco, in particular, has taken note. The mayor's office has set up the Neighborhood Empowerment Network, which aims to foster community leadership with a long-term eye toward increasing the city's resilience.

Tricia also calls for national disaster relief and recovery organizations to define their roles more clearly. In the Lower Ninth Ward, for example, the Red Cross and Salvation Army "didn't know when they needed to stop. There was no clear line where you do X, Y, and Z, [while] the rest somebody else needs to do simultaneously." Spelling out precise organizational roles early, Tricia maintains, would have helped neighborhood groups like hers craft their own missions more clearly. "Define what success looks like within the constraints of the resources you have," she says, and your work will become clear.

Lakeview's Martin Landrieu issues a similar call for government entities. "There's been no directive about what you're going to do and what you're not going to do. You want to help everybody and help every issue and address every problem but you can't do it." Government, he argues, should focus at first on quickly restoring public schools and infrastructure, while funding emergent local social service providers that prove nimble and effective in a disaster's wake. Imagining himself as FEMA director, he says, "Okay, we're not going to do A, B, C, or D. Volunteers and [nonprofits], you guys are better at this."

Martin's belief in an early focus on schools seems to be a nearly universal lesson that neighborhood leaders draw from the recovery. Residents with children frequently cite reopening schools as their immediate reasons to return. "We actually came back in October [of 2005]," one Broadmoor mother says, reporting that she was surprised to find herself back in the city so quickly. "That's when the [private] schools opened up." Quests to found public charter schools in Village de l'Est and Broadmoor began after it became clear that the Recovery School District would not reopen the neighborhoods' schools. Broadmoor's fate rested on the Wilson Charter School, Nancy Isaacson argues, because "where you see a successful school, you see a successful neighborhood."

By contrast, Martin's laserlike focus on infrastructure restoration is not on every neighborhood leader's mind, likely because of an uneven restoration of infrastructure across the city. In the Lower Ninth Ward, where many blocks retained impassible streets and nonexistent utility service years after the disaster, the issue sits front and center. "We need some serious infrastructure repairs," Charles Allen asserts. "If I could wave a magic wand, I would change it in a heartbeat, and I think that would then draw back people." Common Ground's Thom Pepper finds it ludicrous that it took Brad Pitt's Make It Right project to "[force] the city to address infrastructure" in the neighborhood, finally leading to the repair of sewer, water, and gas lines.

Others believe outside-the-box thinking like Pitt's to be crucial for recovery. Virginia Saussy, creator of the "Broadmoor Lives" campaign, argues that recovery often demands an imaginative spark. First citing a personal example, she recounts bringing four dozen hot donuts to the city inspector's office, with her name and address written on each box, when she needed her power restored. Three hours later, a worker arrived. At the neighborhood level, she argues, leaders need to channel a creative drive to "brand" their communities, creating resilient images that returning residents and government officials alike can buy into. Lakeview's Beacon of Hope centers, whose motto became "Leading the Way Home," branded themselves with a "neighbors helping neighbors" theme. Their ubiquitous black, white, and yellow logo featured a restored house emanating hopeful rays of light. Pam Dashiell's Center for Sustainable Engagement and Development settled on a green logo featuring the Mississippi River and the motto "Sustain the Nine!"

As Virginia sees it, the best neighborhood branding is a bit quirky. She revels in the name of Broadmoor's new dog park—"Dogmoor"— and loves that the neighborhood's reputation for self-reliance is growing citywide. An article published in New Orleans' satirical *Levee* newspaper showed a tank parked on Napoleon Avenue. "The rogue city-state of Broadmoor," the article declared, "has announced its intent to declare its independence from the city."[1]

Though not all neighborhood leaders buy into Virginia's distinctive brand of mirthful ingenuity, her belief in the importance of creative work speaks to a broader trend. Neighborhood leaders across the city aim to capture the lessons they have learned about the need for postdisaster entrepreneurial drive. Hollygrove's Kevin Brown articulates these lessons particularly clearly.

First, he asserts, "Don't wait to get started. The early bird gets the worm. The money flows to the person who hits the ground fastest." Second, he says, "Your mission can be suspended, temporarily, so that you can do the things that need to be done in your community. You know, for me, I had to stop doing youth work for a while to do what needed to be done." Third, he says, "The entrepreneur is the king. The person that can think outside the box, can think creatively, innovatively, and can find new ways to do things that have never been done before, that's the person that will be the most effective." Fourth, he says, "After disaster, political power is crap. . . . It doesn't matter who is mayor. It matters who is rowing the boat to get people off the rooftop." Fifth, "Collaboration is key. You can't do it on your own. There's just not enough resources anywhere for you to be able to do it on your own." Sixth, "The main partnerships that you'll have initially are outside of the disaster area. I had to go find all of my other partners who were not affected, because they could think clearer than I could think."

Like Kevin, neighborhood leaders across the city formed partnerships with outside groups. All too often, however, these organizations acted without taking time to reflect or ask questions. "The seminal problems we've had from Katrina from day one," Father Jerry says, "have been big outside groups showing up saying, 'This is what we're going to do for you,' or 'This is what you need.' And that's absolutely the wrong way to do it."

Cam Tran echoes Father Jerry's sentiments. "The first lesson is that you make sure that you talk to the people in the community," she says. "Don't come in and assume that you know what their needs are." When planning and carrying out neighborhood recovery work, Mai Dang adds, "the direction definitely has to be from the community, and you have to find ways to sustain the organization" the community creates.

This is not to say that postdisaster leadership must always come from behind. One of the central lessons Father Vien draws from his Katrina experience is the need for confident, visionary, and selfless leadership from within affected communities. He focuses particularly on religious leaders. "We have no right to be victims," he says. "We are the ministers." After the flood, he aimed to project a sense of "calmness" and "certainty." He reassured worried parishioners that various important Masses—landmarks of the Vietnamese Catholic religious calendar—would proceed as normal. When parishioners saw him keep his word, Father Vien's optimism spread. Parishioners would say, "He was correct that time, so he must be correct the next time."

What worries Father Vien most is an impulse he sees among his parishioners. The attitude, as he describes it, says, "We've reached where we were pre-Katrina. Okay, now, let's stop." The idea strikes him as insidious. "The issue now for me is that we can't stop," he says. "Something like Katrina could happen, and the same thing would happen again. So we need to do things to prevent that." The firm desire to preserve momentum, whether to sustain recovery or push a community to the next level, is one that most neighborhood leaders share. Broadmoor's "Better Than Before" motto, for example, captures this idea.

Unfortunately, not every city neighborhood has had the opportunity to unambiguously improve upon its prestorm condition. Lamanche Street in the Lower Ninth Ward, home to NENA's headquarters, embodies this difficulty. Trending imperceptibly downward between the river and Bayou Bienvenue, Lamanche Street hosts both the best and worst of the Lower Ninth Ward's recovery. The acclaimed newly renovated Martin Luther King Charter School, just past Claiborne Avenue, speaks to the progress that determined residents, parents, and government officials can achieve when they work together. The empty, overgrown lots on subsequent blocks speak to something else. Restoring the Lower Ninth Ward, Tricia Jones believes, will take "twenty years of strong work." These lots are a visceral reminder of just how hard the work will be.

Tricia's grit suggests one more lesson, perhaps the most powerful lesson that New Orleans neighborhood leaders can share with the world. Never underestimate the power of undaunted determination, even in the face of heartbreakingly profound destruction. Few neighborhood leaders articulate this lesson explicitly, but each of them has lived it every day. It is an unspoken credo. *Never, ever, ever give up.*

❧   ❧   ❧

RayAnn Wilder Cantrell is jumping in place, her face split by a wide grin. She is the last child left. Several St. Ursuline Academy nuns who run the Catholic institution's preschool program surround her, splayed out in their chairs, exhausted. It is time to pass the baton. They smile as LaToya enters the room.

Despite the school-day's hazards, RayAnn's plaid smock remains miraculously spotless. Her hair, however, is worse for wear. Frizzy tufts have escaped from her pigtails, and the low evening light illuminates a fuzzy halo around her head. She sees us now and veritably explodes with happy energy as she toddles in our direction. "Mommmmmy!"

LaToya swoops up her delighted three-and-a-half-year-old. This is clearly the best moment of her day. For an instant, mother and daughter enjoy the bliss of their embrace. Then, remembering previous hugs soured by bad news, LaToya casts a nervous glance towards the exhausted sisters. "How'd Ray do today?" she asks. The relief on her face is palpable as one of the nuns smiles and attests to RayAnn's good behavior.

The arrival of fall 2011 seems to have lifted spirits across the city. The oppressive August heat has dissipated, the academic year has jumped to an optimistic start, and across the city, neighborhood leaders seem buoyed by a joi de vivre and genuine sense of accomplishment. Much work remains to be done, but the load seems to be lighter, the challenges familiar and surmountable.

As RayAnn bolts onto the play equipment behind the school, LaToya is beaming. She sees the light at the end of the tunnel. "Next month, I'm off of the Broadmoor Development Corporation Board, which is great," she says. She is confident that residents on the committee can do the work without her. Next, she hopes to step down as president of the Broadmoor Improvement Association. Her mission—to "get myself out of the web" of responsibilities while ensuring that the neighborhood's gains are sustained—seems to be working. She plans to stay on the Wilson Charter School board, believing that the school's success is most critical to the neighborhood's future.

RayAnn will enroll at Wilson as soon as she is old enough for kindergarten, and LaToya knows that her firebrand will be in good hands. The school board's strategic planning process was a wild success, and by all accounts, Wilson's newly hired principal is off to a strong start. Visits to Wilson have become a joy for LaToya. "It's poppin'," she says. "People are just so happy. The energy in the building is fantastic. You can just tell—everybody can tell—that we're back on the right track. It's going to be a good year."

Across the city, people are striding optimistically on with their lives. Terry Miranda has been back in his Lakeview house for three years, and has embraced a unique brand of retired bachelorhood. "My nephew is my current project," Terry explains, devouring a po' boy sandwich at his favorite haunt. "He's gone to Catholic schools all his life, and he has no idea what this city has to offer. I brought him to the Running of the Bulls the other weekend," he says with a grin, referring to a French Quarter festival in which roller derby girls don horned helmets and chase revelers through the streets. "Luckily, I'm working with a willing subject."

True to form, Terry tempers his indulgence in the joyful excesses of New Orleans life with a unique brand of asceticism. His house remains largely bare. "That's all I need," Terry says of the single pot perched atop his stove. A self-described technophobe, Terry had a friend record the message on his answering machine. The friend took advantage of the opportunity and left an ironic greeting. "You've reached the butler at the Terrance Miranda residence," his voice crows every time the machine picks up. "Terry isn't available to take your call right now."

Elsewhere, life is quieter, but equally happy. One afternoon, Phil Harris and his wife are relaxing at home in Hollygrove with one of their many grown grandchildren, who is now a local nurse. Phil's wife, Victoria, makes good-natured fun of her husband as he recalls how many grandchildren they have. Phil has to count and starts naming them off. He settles on a round number. "We have about ten grand-children, total," he says.

The two launch into stories from their childhood. Victoria recalls growing up in the small shotgun house with lots of siblings. "Where we're sitting now in this living room used to be our side yard," she says. "When we were little bitty children, Phil would come over here and play." These two wise, kindred souls share a history in this very spot that stretches back the better part of a century. The two still revel in each other's company, draw joy from their large family, and find sly humor in the inevitable declines of age. "The old gray mare, she ain't what she used to be," Victoria says with a laugh. The look in Phil's eyes tells a different story. He still sees the girl he fell in love with seven decades ago.

Blocks away, in a tidy air-conditioned office at the New Orleans Archdiocese, Father Vien The Nguyen feels similarly reflective. In

the inevitable flow of a life dedicated to God, in service to the Holy
See, Father Vien was transferred from Mary Queen of Vietnam Parish in 2010, after seven years as pastor. He works now for the church
tribunal.

Asked to consider his legacy, Father Vien pauses. "It is a sense of
empowerment in the people," he says. He also appreciates "the fact
that young people are proud of the fact that they are from the Vietnamese community in New Orleans East." He recounts the trials and
tribulations the community has faced recently, including the devastating British Petroleum oil spill in the gulf. "When you consider that
forty percent of the fishing vessels in the gulf are owned by Vietnamese Americans," he says, the impact on his parish was tremendous.
The Mary Queen of Vietnam CDC took the lead in helping affected
families apply for compensation, and cope.

"The state sent their people to the CDC office to work there, so
we could monitor them, and bridge the [linguistic] gap," Father Vien
tells me. He is proud of how the staff performed. Though he sits on
the CDC board, he says, the staffers "are the ones in charge. . . . It's
a group of young people who are actually doing the work. They are
very enthusiastic, very energetic, and they are very proud of the work
they do."

Back on the playground, RayAnn is thrilled to be with her mom.
After running in circles around the playground equipment letting off
excess steam, she is ready to go. On the car ride home, as she chat-
ters happily with her daughter about the coming weekend, LaToya
casts glances out at the surrounding blocks. Broadmoor's stretch of
Fontainebleau Avenue looks better than ever, with fresh landscaping
and newly renovated houses. Cranes rise above the Keller Library
as a new addition takes shape. LaToya points out the progress with
obvious pride.

Because of LaToya's determination, and the determination of
thousands of other Broadmoor residents, RayAnn will have a marvelous place to grow up. This story repeats itself in neighborhood
after neighborhood across the city. The recovery has been brutally
difficult, and it is far from over, but its payoff will be tremendous and
long-lived.

With each passing day, RayAnn inherits an increasing share of
this resurrected metropolis. She and thousands of other young people
in New Orleans owe a debt to the preceding generation that they
cannot repay. Instead, they will pay this debt forward, and hope that
their own children do the same. Such is the work of sustaining a city.

## EPILOGUE

As NOVEMBER 2009 SLIPPED into December, I had effectively disappeared. Though I still lived in New Orleans, I was immersed in a new world that demanded every bit of my concentration and willpower. I was a Teach for America member drowning under lesson plans, parent phone calls, grading, performance reviews, sleep deprivation, and a looming sense of failure. People told me that my first year of teaching would be all about survival, but even by that low standard, I was barely hanging on. The life of leisurely conversations, neighborhood meetings, and writing I had led just five months before seemed a distant memory. When I heard the news, it elicited an unfamiliar mix of sadness, guilt, and nostalgia.

"Did you hear that Pam Dashiell died?" No. What? I shifted in my chair, staring wide-eyed at my interlocutor. It was a Friday afternoon, the one time in the week when I seemed able to relax. My guard was down. "She was working at her computer, and then she just fell over dead."

I had last seen Pam, in passing, during the spring. One moment, I was wandering through a weekend festival at Bayou St. John, and the next, Pam had me cornered. "Where ya been?" Immersed in writing, I had missed several meetings of a committee I joined with Pam that aimed to revive St. Claude Avenue with public art displays. Pam's gaze cut right through my shrugged shoulders and sheepish grin. Mumbled excuses and an attempt to change the subject did little to help. I naively vowed to jump back into the fray once my writing was done, not anticipating the workload that awaited me as a teacher. Her eyes let me know that she expected better, though the hint of a smile on her lips kept the exchange light-hearted.

This was Pam's brilliance. She could be at once demanding and low-key, deadly serious and irreverently funny. People talking to Pam got the immediate sense that she understood who they were and where they were coming from. In every interaction, she was unabashedly herself, and she was okay with you if you were okay with her.

Her accomplishments rested on an uncanny ability to prod, cajole, and inspire hundreds of people from vastly different walks of life to listen to their better angels. Free of pretention, Pam nonetheless had an agenda, enlisting paupers and presidents alike to kindle a shared sense of possibility and work together for a brighter future. As her friend Ariane Wiltse wrote in a beautiful obituary, "Pam convinced a former president [Jimmy Carter], a Hollywood heartthrob [Brad Pitt] and thousands of ordinary folks, including her neighbors, that not only should the Lower Ninth Ward be rebuilt, but it should be rebuilt as nothing less than the nation's first carbon-neutral neighborhood. In the great tragedy and social injustice that occurred after the levee failures, Pam saw opportunity and hope."[1]

In the days following her death, my mind fixated on the notion that Pam martyred herself. I knew how hard she worked. She often arrived in the CSED offices hours before anyone else, and worked late into the night. I had seen firsthand the strain this type of work induced, and not just in Pam. Near the end of the interviews I conducted, after neighborhood leaders told me the invariably long and harrowing stories of their post-storm work, I would ask a simple, point-blank question: "How are you doing?"

Too often, the question was met with a pause, a long stare at the floor, a hand drawn through prematurely graying hair. The answer, when it came, often emerged in a shaky voice, and went something as follows. *I'm okay, but this is really hard. I'm frustrated and I'm tired. Don't write this down, but I'm not sure how much longer I can keep it up.*

For neighborhood leaders, the worst moments seemed to come when government institutions—city, state, and federal—impeded their progress. These exercises of power often seemed inexplicably arbitrary. In Hollygrove, residents still fume about the treatment they received at the hands of their city-council-appointed planner, who off-handedly dismissed the months of planning they had already completed and insisted on starting from scratch. Residents of Village de l'Est still have not forgotten being left off early recovery planning maps, and shudder at the indignity and health ramifications of becoming Mayor Ray Nagin's trash dump. Broadmoor mobilized in fear under the Bring New Orleans Back Commission's green dot, and struggled for the city to embrace the constructive efforts that blossomed thereafter. After the Carnegie Corporation granted the neighborhood $2 million to renovate Broadmoor's library in 2007, for example, LaToya and Hal were forced, year after year after year, to explain to mystified endowment representatives why the city had not begun work on the renovation. Construction did not begin until 2011. In the Lower Ninth Ward, residents could scarcely believe the city's reticence to allow utility restoration in much of the neighborhood, which impeded reconstruction in its most devastated blocks. They made do with comparatively paltry payouts from the federally funded and state-administered Road Home program, which distributed cash based on pre-Katrina property values rather than the projected cost of repairs. They still live under the threat of an Army Corps of Engineers Industrial Canal lock expansion, which would use eminent domain to repossess and demolish dozens of homes. As for Lakeview, suffice it to say, residents tried to secede from New Orleans before the storm, and would likely try again if they believed their efforts would succeed.

A bizarre confirmation of this post-Katrina state of affairs came in early 2009, when Louisiana governor Bobby Jindal told a pointed story in the official Republican response to President Obama's first address to a joint session of congress. Jindal described the frustration that Jefferson Parish sheriff Harry Lee experienced as he attempted to coordinate volunteer boat rescues after the flood, and was told by a federal official not to proceed until he had proof of rescuers' registration and insurance. "Harry just told those boaters, ignore the bureaucrats and go start rescuing people," Jindal said. "There's a lesson in this experience: the strength of America is not found in our government. It is found in the compassionate hearts and the enterprising spirit of our citizens." He went on to suggest that those who "place their hope in the federal government" were misguided.[2]

"Enterprising" New Orleans citizens with whom I spoke— Village de l'Est Republicans, Broadmoor Democrats, Lower Ninth Ward Greens—universally fumed at Jindal's message. Regardless of their preferences for the ideal size and scope of government, they believed that government institutions could and should be a help rather than a hindrance. They were living through the consequences of government neglect, and found it disturbing that their governor seemed resigned to the inevitability of government ineffectiveness.

A Broadmoor resident with whom I spoke summed up the sentiment. Government failures stemmed not from incompetence, he argued, but simply from skewed priorities. "The federal government had the responsibility, and had the resources, but failed us," he said. "It was not the hurricane that did this to us. This community, this city survived the hurricane. . . . It was the failure of the Corps of Engineers, and levees that everyone knew was inferior." The failure stemmed from "lack of interest in securing the city the way they should have," and this lack of interest persisted in the storm's wake. "I spent twenty-six years in the Marine Corps," he explained. "I have seen, we all have seen, this government get food, water, and clothes and whatever we needed on foreign soil quicker than we did here. I have to say, it shows how important [politicians] felt this area was . . . [They] showed it continuously right up 'til now."

Frequently, the neighborhood leaders I interviewed spoke of co-operative government as if it were a fantasy, at once deeply appealing and unattainable. After years of "things happening . . . in spite of city government," as one Lakeview resident put it, the scenarios neighbor-hood leaders imagined were far from grandiose. Most cited frequent, open communication as a way that collaboration could begin between neighborhood groups and city government. "Come back here and spend some time hearing it from my perspective and drive through the neighborhoods to see what we've done and understand who we are," Kevin Brown pleaded. "The school people have never consulted with any of us that I know of. The city people, the government people have never consulted with us."

Neighborhood leaders also envisioned scenarios in which City Hall and local organizations could jointly spearhead projects. Fa-ther Vien, for example, cited a neighborhood cleanup initiative he began. Fighting a slew of overgrown public spaces that became fre-quent targets for illegal trash dumping, Father Vien purchased two hundred disposable cameras and distributed them to residents. The community would fight the dumping through a combination of Mary Queen of Vietnam CDC organized cleanups and a photo reporting system whereby residents could send pictures directly to city officials. The program was a hit, with young people in particular becoming "trash vigilantes." When the city's recovery office contacted Father Vien looking for community projects to support, Father Vien sug-gested funding and formalizing the trash watch. The office turned him down, saying any project had to be work "that the city will do for you." The rebuke, though minor compared to Mayor Nagin's garbage dump, touched a nerve. "Let us do it!" Father Vien vented. "Because people, as they invest in it, they will protect it. Very simple . . . If the people don't put any sweat equity into it, there won't be any ownership."

Indeed, the ultimate dream of neighborhood organizations applying for and receiving city money to carry out their work, seemed both the most enticing and the hardest to achieve. "I've been here ten years," Kevin Brown explained, "and the city government hasn't figured out that we're effective and can be worked with. Instead of spending the money doing things on your own, why not funnel the money through Broadmoor, through TCC . . . through organizations like us? We are good at what we do. Work with us!"

Brad Fortier, who took over as LCIA president from Al Petrie, echoed Kevin's point. He imagined a scenario in which city, state, or federal agencies helped the neighborhood association hire temporary employees to carry out some of the recovery work. "Cash would have helped considerably to alleviate a lot of pressures," he said, "to where the neighbors themselves and the citizens themselves could have led this and instilled their goals for their community without having to do *all* of the legwork themselves."

I saw these critiques in a new light after Pam's death. Hers was the most extreme of numerous breakdowns and burnouts the neighborhood-driven recovery left in its wake. The work that hundreds of residents undertook on behalf of their communities, born of a sense of desperate necessity, was simply not sustainable. Though their accomplishments were often staggering, none of the neighborhood leaders with whom I spoke believed that their predicament was ideal. Leaving communities to fend for themselves after a disaster was a travesty, they argued, not a silver bullet for recovery.

They also worried about the long-term ramifications of their efforts. "Being too self-reliant can enable government to not do what it needs to do to support communities," Village de l'Est planner Trang Tu told me. Likewise, Broadmoor leader Hal Roark believed that there was a danger that successfully organized neighborhoods could become "too cut off" from the city. He rejected the notion that New Orleans neighborhoods should "go it alone," holding out hope that strong government partnerships would ultimately emerge. "At the end of the day," he said, "we're mad at government. I want them to reform, but I believe they will reform and we will get help eventually."

That sad December afternoon, as my thoughts turned abruptly from my personal struggles to those of neighborhood leaders, I hoped that Hal was right. These remarkable individuals—people like LaToya Cantrell, Father Vien, Connie Uddo, Kevin Brown, Tricia Jones—were my heroes. It was not simply that I liked them; I placed faith in them, drawing inspiration from their courage and conviction. I knew that thousands of residents across New Orleans felt the same way. "Pam Dashiell was nothing less than the matriarch of the Lower Ninth Ward," wrote Ariane Wiltse, "a real-life hero who died a hero's death—in battle, at her computer, working to sustain her beloved Lower Nine."[3] I sincerely hoped that no other heroes would have to follow in her footsteps.

# TIMELINE

**2005**

AUGUST 23 – Katrina forms as a tropical depression over the Bahamas.

AUGUST 25 – Now a Category 1 hurricane, Katrina makes landfall just north of Miami.

AUGUST 26 – Katrina enters the Gulf of Mexico, with a projected track toward the Louisiana/Mississippi border. Louisiana governor Kathleen Blanco declares a state of emergency.

AUGUST 27 – Mandatory and voluntary evacuations begin in the parishes surrounding New Orleans. New Orleans mayor Ray Nagin encourages voluntary evacuations of low-lying areas of the city. Katrina grows in strength over the warm waters of the gulf, becoming a Category 3 hurricane.

AUGUST 28 – Mayor Nagin announces a mandatory evacuation of New Orleans and opens the Louisiana Superdome stadium as a "shelter of last resort." Katrina grows in strength to a Category 5 storm, with sustained 175 mph winds. By day's end, more than 1.2 million Louisiana residents have evacuated.

AUGUST 29 – Katrina makes landfall as a Category 3 hurricane in the early morning. Its winds and storm surge devastate the Mississippi Gulf Coast. As waters rise around New Orleans levees, breaches occur in the Industrial Canal, the 17th Street Canal, and the London Avenue Canal. The city begins to fill with water.

AUGUST 30 – Local fishermen, law enforcement agencies, and Coast Guard units begin search-and-rescue efforts by boat. Mayor Nagin opens Morial Convention Center for evacuees. More than three hundred evacuees arrive at Mary Queen of Vietnam Church in Village de l'Est.

AUGUST 31 – Efforts to plug levee breaches fail, and conditions worsen throughout the city as residents remain stranded on rooftops. Twenty thousand evacuees arrive at the Morial Convention Center with no food or water. LCIA board members contact one another by phone.

SEPTEMBER 1 – Evacuees at the Superdome and the convention center grow desperate as help fails to materialize. Patients in hospitals without power die in the tremendous heat. Boats and helicopters continue search-and-rescue efforts. Finally, in the evening, hundreds of buses and newly arrived National Guard troops begin evacuating residents stranded at the Superdome. After spending the night by the side of a highway, Village de l'Est residents are evacuated. The LCIA launches a new post-Katrina website.

SEPTEMBER 5 – Crews seal the breech to the 17th Street Canal.

SEPTEMBER 12 – FEMA chief Michael Brown resigns. Forty percent of New Orleans remains underwater—down from 80 percent—as pump crews race to drain the city.

SEPTEMBER 29 – Residents of neighborhoods that did not flood are allowed to return to the city, after a delay caused by Hurricane Rita. Previously flooded areas remained sealed off.

SEPTEMBER 30 – Mayor Nagin announces the formation of the seventeen-member Bring New Orleans Back (BNOB) commission.

OCTOBER 5 – Phased re-entry begins for residents of flooded neighborhoods, but the Lower Ninth Ward remains sealed off.

OCTOBER 9 – Mary Queen of Vietnam Church holds its first post-Katrina Mass in its partially gutted building.

OCTOBER 17 – Governor Kathleen Blanco unveils the creation of the Louisiana Recovery Authority (LRA), the state authority tasked with overseeing and distributing recovery funds.

OCTOBER 23 – Three thousand Lakeview residents return to the neighborhood to attend a Lakeview Civic Improvement Association (LCIA) meeting. With none of the neighborhood's buildings inhabitable, residents converge in a parking lot.

NOVEMBER 18 – The Urban Land Institute makes recommendations to the BNOB commission, suggesting that some flooded areas of New Orleans not be allowed to rebuild.

NOVEMBER 21 – Hundreds of Vietnamese American residents of Village de l'Est stage a protest at a BNOB commission meeting, objecting to being "left off the map" in the committee's planning.

MID-DECEMBER – The Hollygrove Neighbors association holds its first meeting. Meanwhile, Trinity Christian Community (TCC) recruits a hundred AmeriCorps volunteers to assist rebuilding efforts. Common Ground Relief cofounder Brandon Darby purchases a house in the Lower Ninth Ward, paving the way for Common Ground's operations in the neighborhood.

## 2006

JANUARY 11 – The BNOB commission releases its final report, calling for a moratorium on building in flooded areas and for four months of neighborhood planning to determine which areas to rebuild. The commission also designates six areas of New Orleans, including Broadmoor and parts of the Lower Ninth Ward, as "areas for future parkland." These areas show up as "green dots" on a map published by the *Times-Picayune*.

JANUARY 14 – Three hundred Broadmoor residents gather to protest the "green dot." The rally is the leading item on the evening news.

JANUARY 18 – The Broadmoor Improvement Association (BIA) holds a five-hundred-person meeting in a tent. Residents agree to "beat the city at its own game" by creating a plan for the neighborhood's future that proves Broadmoor's viability.

LATE JANUARY – LCIA board members begin forming the District 5 Recovery Council.

JANUARY 28 – Village de l'Est residents unveil the results of their community design meetings at their Tet New Year celebration.

EARLY FEBRUARY – Lower Ninth Ward residents begin meeting weekly in the gutted remains of the neighborhood's Sanchez Community Center.

MID-FEBRUARY – Denise Thornton opens her house as the first Beacon of Hope Resource Center.

FEBRUARY 20 – Governor Kathleen Blanco unveils the Road Home Program, which grants federal money to homeowners whose insurance proceeds do not cover the cost of rebuilding.

MID-MARCH – Lower Ninth Ward residents found the Neighborhood Empowerment Network Association (NENA).

APRIL 7 – The city council places architect Paul Lambert in charge of a planning process for flooded neighborhoods.

MID-APRIL – Lakeview's District 5 Recovery Council grows to include seventy-two resident committees.

APRIL 26 – The Holy Cross Neighborhood Association begins a three-day planning process to lay the groundwork for a "sustainable restoration" of the Lower Ninth Ward.

LATE APRIL – Dumping begins at a new landfill situated less than a mile from Village de l'Est in New Orleans East. Residents mobilize in protest.

MID-MAY – Residents of Village de l'Est found the Mary Queen of Vietnam Community Development Corporation.

JUNE – NENA receives a $100,000 grant from Portland, Oregon-based Mercy Corps.

JULY 5 – The LRA, Mayor Nagin, and the city council announce a third post-Katrina citywide planning effort called the Unified New Orleans Plan (UNOP).

JULY 17 – Residents vote to approve Broadmoor's Recovery Plan, a document of over three hundred pages that lays the groundwork for a neighborhood-driven recovery.

AUGUST 25 – Lakeview holds a ribbon cutting for six new Beacon of Hope resource centers, including a large volunteer center on the campus of St. Paul's Church.

LATE AUGUST – In a victory for residents of Village de l'Est, Mayor Nagin declines to renew the operating permit for the landfill in New Orleans East.

SEPTEMBER 16 – Lakeview Fest draws five thousand current and former residents.

DECEMBER – Holy Cross residents receive grant money from Mercy Corps to open the Center for Sustainable Engagement and Development (CSED).

DECEMBER – Broadmoor residents found the Broadmoor Development Corporation, a nonprofit dedicated to implementing the neighborhood's plan.

## 2007

JANUARY – Mayor Nagin appoints Dr. Edward Blakely as the city's executive director for recovery management. Rebuilding Together, a national housing nonprofit, begins renovation work on its first house in Hollygrove.

JANUARY 20 – The UNOP process draws to a close holding its third and final community congress.

MARCH – Broadmoor's charter school application is approved.

APRIL – With house gutting in the Lower Ninth Ward nearly complete, Common Ground Relief shifts its focus to construction projects. The Hollygrove-Carrollton Community Development Corporation (CDC) opens in Hollygrove.

JUNE – In Hollygrove, TCC coordinates dozens of volunteer groups for rebuilding projects that continue throughout the summer.

JULY – The Carnegie Corporation of New York formally announces a $2 million grant to rebuild Broadmoor's Keller Library.

SEPTEMBER 4 – Broadmoor's Andrew H. Wilson Charter School opens in an offsite location.

SEPTEMBER 12 – Broadmoor's Andrew Wilson School building is one of five schools across the city selected for renovation or rebuilding by the Recovery School District.

OCTOBER – Rebuilding Together begins work on its first house in Broadmoor.

DECEMBER – Brad Pitt announces the Make It Right foundation, whose plans for green rebuilding in the Lower Ninth Ward were influenced by Pam Dashiell and the CSED.

## 2008

JANUARY – TCC begins a transition back to programming for Hollygrove youth that continues throughout the year.

MARCH – Lakeview begins a transition of power, with the Beacons of Hope turning recovery projects over to the newly strengthened Lakeview Civic Improvement Association.

APRIL – Mary Queen of Vietnam Church, becoming increasingly multiethnic, begins adding English-language homilies and choral music. Masses are already conducted in Vietnamese and Spanish.

MAY – In the Lower Ninth Ward, NENA hires an architect to work directly with residents who are rebuilding.

JUNE – U.S. Postal Service data shows that 72 percent of New Orleans households are receiving mail, showing that the city's repopulation is well under way.

AUGUST 14 – Mary Queen of Vietnam CDC and Tulane University open a health clinic in Village de l'Est.

AUGUST 18 – Village de l'Est opens its charter school on the campus of Mary Queen of Vietnam Church.

SEPTEMBER – Carrollton-Hollygrove CDC signs a lease for the Hollygrove Farm and Market.

OCTOBER – LCIA begins threatening owners of derelict properties with liens.

NOVEMBER 5 – As Lakeview recovers and demand for recovery assistance slackens, the St. Paul's Beacon of Hope Center in Lakeview closes its doors.

NOVEMBER 20 – Lower Ninth Ward residents show up in force at an Army Corps of Engineers hearing to advocate for the restoration of Bayou Bienvenue, which abuts their neighborhood.

DECEMBER – By year's end, Rebuilding Together has renovated thirty houses in Broadmoor, thirty in Hollygrove, and nineteen in Holy Cross.

## 2009

JANUARY – The St. Paul's Homecoming Center reopens in Gentilly, quickly receiving more than two hundred requests for assistance from homeowners struggling to rebuild.

MARCH – Pressing On Basketball Ministries is founded in Hollygrove, eventually growing to become TCC's largest program.

DECEMBER 4 – Family, friends, and supporters pack All Souls Episcopal Church in the Lower Ninth Ward in a memorial service for Pam Dashiell.

## 2010

JANUARY – Broadmoor's Andrew H. Wilson Charter School moves into its newly renovated building.

JANUARY 28 – Groundbreaking ceremony held for new library on Harrison Avenue in Lakeview.

APRIL – Students at Broadmoor's Andrew H. Wilson Charter School take the state-mandated LEAP (Louisiana Educational Assessment Program) exam. Their disappointing scores lead to an "Academically Unacceptable School" designation.

MAY – Hal Roark resigns as executive director of the Broadmoor Development Corporation.

NOVEMBER 2 – Broadmoor residents approve an annual $100 parcel fee to fund the BIA. The BIA subsequently reorganizes its board to be elected directly by all residents.

NOVEMBER 22 – The *Times-Picayune* heralds the "strong comeback" of commercial life on Lakeview's Harrison Avenue.

## 2011

APRIL – The Andrew H. Wilson Charter School undertakes a strategic-planning process. Meanwhile, students vastly improve their LEAP test scores.

SEPTEMBER – Work nears completion on Broadmoor's Rosa F. Keller Library renovation.

## ACKNOWLEDGMENTS

I⊤ is humbling and exhilarating to contemplate the number of people who have contributed to this book. Above all, I owe thanks to the 122 New Orleans residents who shared their stories and insights with me in formal interviews, and to the many hundreds more whose friendship and guidance made me feel at home from my very first day in the city. After the levees broke, each one undertook a tremendously difficult struggle. That so many of these individuals have flourished in the years since testifies to the indomitable power of human will.

My journey began within Harvard's undergraduate Social Studies program. Utpal Sandesara set everything in motion. Sadhana Berry encouraged me to visit the Gulf Coast and pushed me to think critically about the powerful motivational power of place. Marshall Ganz inspired me to gain firsthand knowledge of urban neighborhoods and coached me as I researched and wrote my thesis. A Lamont Public Service Fellowship allowed me to spend a formative summer in New Orleans.

The students, staff, and faculty of Harvard's John F. Kennedy School of Government, through their shared commitment to New Orleans, laid the groundwork that made my research possible. Rebecca Hummel met with me on a cold February morning to tell me about a neighborhood called Broadmoor. Doug Ahlers took a chance on me, believing copious note taking to be a sign of enthusiasm and commitment. Dutch Leonard, Arn Howitt, Archon Fung, Henry Lee, Carolyn Wood, Arietta Chakos, Amanda Swanson, and many others helped to turn Doug's vision of neighborhood partnership into a fortuitous reality. A generous grant from the Acting in Time Program allowed me to spend another year in New Orleans, conducting more interviews and writing a full-length manuscript.

Turning a manuscript into a book is no easy feat, and I was blessed with lots of indispensible help. Rick Balkin pushed me to finish my proposal, found the manuscript a stellar home, and helped me keep my head screwed on straight during my two years of teaching. Hal Roark, Stephen Tremaine, Adelaide Villmoare, Peter Stillman, Andy

Kopplin, and Walter Isaacson lent voices of support at critical junctures. Helene Atwan embraced the project and spent a long, memorable day meeting many of the book's characters. Joanna Green revolutionized the book's structure, all the while maintaining a disarmingly light-handed touch. My mom, Jamie Devol, drew the neighborhood map.

Friends and family read drafts of the manuscript, and their feedback proved invaluable. Jack McCreless, Alice Lee, Mary Brazelton, Monica Thanawala, Victor Shnayder, Emily Kaplan, Wei-Jen Hsieh, Yinliang He, Utpal Sandesara, Kathleen Onufer, and Heather Carmichael all lent keen, critical eyes to the cause. So did my sister, Caroline Wooten, and my dad, Lee Wooten.

Thanks so much to all of you.

# NOTES

The bulk of the information in this book comes from my interviews with New Orleans residents. In most cases, I digitally recorded the conversations and transcribed them after the fact. Unless otherwise cited, every quotation in the book comes from these interviews.

## CHAPTER 1: "VERY MUCH AT HOME"

1. Gordon Russell, "Nagin Orders First-Ever Mandatory Evacuation of New Orleans," *Times-Picayune* (New Orleans), August 28, 2005.
2. National Oceanographic and Atmospheric Association, "Hurricane Katrina Forecast Issued by the New Orleans, Louisiana, Weather Forecast Office," August 28, 2005, http://celebrating200years.noaa.gov/ (accessed August 14, 2011).
3. Brian Lloyd Azcona, "The Razing Tide of the Port of New Orleans: Power, Ideology, Economic Growth and the Destruction of Community," *Social Thought and Research* 27 (2006): 69–109, KU [University of Kansas] Scholar-Works, http://kuscholarworks.ku.edu/ (accessed August 14, 2011).

## CHAPTER 2: A VULNERABLE CITY

1. Russell, "Nagin Orders First-Ever Mandatory Evacuation of New Orleans."
2. Esther Scott, *Hurricane Katrina: Preparing for the "Big One" in New Orleans,* Case Study, Harvard Kennedy School (Washington, DC: CQ Press, 2009), 35.
3. Sam Coates and Dan Eggen, "In New Orleans, a Desperate Exodus," *Washington Post,* September 1, 2005.
4. Scott, *Hurricane Katrina,* 35.
5. Brian Handwerk, "New Orleans Levees Not Built for Worst Case Events," *National Geographic,* September 2, 2005, http://news.nationalgeographic.com/ (accessed August 14, 2011).
6. CNN, "New Orleans Braces for 'the Big One,'" August 28, 2005, http://www.cnn.com/ (accessed August 14, 2011).
7. Richard Campanella, *Geographies of New Orleans: Urban Fabrics Before the Storm.* (Lafayette: Center for Louisiana Studies, 2006). Also, Richard Campanella, *Bienville's Dilemma* (Lafayette: University of Louisiana Press, 2008).

8.  Campanella, *Bienville's Dilemma*.

9.  Campanella, *Geographies of New Orleans*.

10. Ibid.

11. City of Boston,•"Boston: A City of Neighborhoods," 2011, http://www
    .cityofboston.gov/ (accessed August 14, 2011). Also, City of Chicago, "City
    of Chicago Neighborhoods," 2011, http://www.cityofchicago.org/ (ac-
    cessed August 14, 2011).

12. Greater New Orleans Community Data Center, "What Is a Neighbor-
    hood?" http://www.gnocdc.org/ (accessed August 14, 2011).

13. Scott, *Hurricane Katrina*, 31.

14. U.S. Census, "Louisiana: Population of Counties by Decennial Census,"
    1990, http://www.census.gov/ (accessed August 14, 2011).

15. Campanella, *Bienville's Dilemma*.

16. U.S. Census, "Louisiana."

17. Campanella, *Bienville's Dilemma*.

18. Bureau of Governmental Research, *The Price of Civilization: Addressing In-
    frastructure Needs in New Orleans*, Financial Issues Series (New Orleans: Bu-
    reau of Governmental Research, 2010).

19. Billy Brite, "Happy Birthday, Dear Pothole," New Orleans blog, Sep-
    tember 4, 2004, http://neworleans.livejournal.com/ (accessed August 14,
    2011).

20. See, for example, Louisiana Department of Education, "2003–2004
    Accountability Results," January 2005, http://www.louisianaschools.net/
    (accessed August 14, 2011). Also, Kathryn G. Newmark and Veronique de
    Rugy, "Hope After Katrina: Will New Orleans Become the New City of
    Choice?" *Education Next* 6, no. 4 (2006): 13–21. Finally, Federal Bureau
    of Investigation, "Federal Judge Sentences Major Orleans Parish School
    Board Probe Figure," press release, April 15, 2009, www.fbi.gov/ (accessed
    August 14, 2011).

21. Newmark and de Rugy, "Hope After Katrina"

22. The first of Scott's three superb case studies on Hurricane Katrina, in which
    she traces "how governments at the local, state, and federal levels prepared
    for the on-rushing hurricane," greatly informed my writing of this section.
    Where appropriate, I have cited her case study first and then cited her pri-
    mary and secondary sources for reference. Scott, *Hurricane Katrina*.

23. Ibid., 23.

24. Ibid., 28.

25. Department of Homeland Security, *National Response Plan*, Inter-Agency
    Plan (Washington, DC: Department of Homeland Security, 2004).

26. Scott, *Hurricane Katrina*. Also, Mark Thompson, "Why Did FEMA and
    Its Chief, Michael Brown, Fail Their Biggest Test?" *Time*, September 19,
    2005, 39. Michael Grunwald and Susan B. Glasser, "Brown's Turf Wars
    Sapped FEMA's Strength," *Washington Post*, December 23, 2005.

27. Scott, *Hurricane Katrina*. Also, Select Bipartisan Committee to Investigate

the Preparation for and Response to Hurricane Katrina, *A Failure of Initiative* (Washington, DC: U.S. House of Representatives, 2005); Joe Allbaugh, "'Can I Quit Now?' FEMA Chief Wrote as Katrina Raged," CNN, November 5, 2005, http://articles.cnn.com/ (accessed September 27, 2011).

28. United States Conference of Mayors, "Report of the Stafford Act Reform Task Force," January 2010, http://www.usmayors.org/.

29. Ken Silverstein and Josh Meyer, "Louisiana Officials Indicted Before Katrina Hit," *Los Angeles Times*, September 15, 2005.

30. BBC, "Profile: Ray Nagin," May 21, 2006, http://news.bbc.co.uk/ (accessed August 15, 2011). Also, Andrew Stevens, "Ray Nagin—Former Mayor of New Orleans," City Mayors website, May 2010, http://www.citymayors .com/ (accessed August 15, 2011).

31. Peter Burns and Matthew O. Thomas, "The Failure of the Nonregime: How Katrina Exposed New Orleans as a Regimeless City," *Urban Affairs Review* 41, no. 4 (March 2006): 517–27. Also, Clarence N. Stone, *Regime Politics: Governing Atlanta, 1946–1988* (Lawrence: University of Kansas Press, 1989).

32. John Burnett, interview by Neal Conan, "Hurricane Katrina Update," *Talk of the Nation*, National Public Radio, August 29, 2005.

33. Ibid., Pete Schneider, interview by Neal Conan.

## CHAPTER 3: "SOMEBODY ELSE'S COUCH"

1. Mike Hoss et al., "First Reports of Levee Breach at 17th Street Canal," WWL-TV, New Orleans, August 30, 2005.

2. Dan Swenson, "Flash Flood," *Times-Picayune* (New Orleans), May 14, 2006, http://www.nola.com/ (accessed September 29, 2011).

3. Wallace Roberts & Todd, LLC, "Action Plan for New Orleans: The New American City," Bring New Orleans Back Commission, Urban Planning Committee, January 11, 2006, www.npr.org/.

4. James Dao and N. R. Kleinfeld, "Conditions in New Orleans Still Dire— Pumping May Take Months," *New York Times*, September 3, 2005. Also, Jim Dwyer and Christopher Drew, "Fear Exceeds Crime's Reality in New Orleans," *New York Times*, September 29, 2005.

5. Gordon Russell and Brian Thevenot, "Reports of Anarchy at Superdome Overstated," *Seattle Times*, September 26, 2005.

6. ABC News, "Thousands Desperate for Help at New Orleans Convention Center," September 1, 2005, http://abcnews.go.com/ (accessed August 15, 2011).

7. Eric Lipton et al., "Breakdowns Marked Path from Hurricane to Anarchy," *New York Times*, September 11, 2005.

8. Clifford Levy, "Post-Katrina, Bricks and Mortals," *New York Times*, September 18, 2005.

## CHAPTER 4: "THE WHOLE WORLD WAS GRAY"

1.  Martha Carr, "Rebuilding Should Begin on Higher Ground, Group Says," *Times-Picayune* (New Orleans), November 18, 2005. Also, Peter Applebome and Mark Blumenthal, "With Storms Behind Them, Gulf Residents Begin Piecing Their Lives Together," *New York Times*, September 27, 2005.
2.  Wallace Roberts & Todd, "Commission Members," 2006, Bring New Orleans Back, http://bringneworleansback.org/ (accessed August 15, 2011).
3.  Gary Rivlin, "New Orleans Forms Panel on Renewal," *New York Times*, October 1, 2005.
4.  Ibid.
5.  Christopher Cooper, "Old Line Families Escape Worst of Flood and Plot the Future," *Wall Street Journal*, September 8, 2005.
6.  Christine Hauser, "In Reopened Neighborhood, Reunions Laced With Loss," *New York Times*, October 13, 2005.
7.  Greater New Orleans Community Data Center, "Fillmore Neighborhood: People and Household Characteristics," http://www.gnocdc.org/ (accessed October 14, 2011).
8.  Kathi and her husband, KC, are amateur folk musicians who love sea shanties and seafaring history. They demolished their bungalow and eventually built an elevated house with geothermal climate control designed to look like a late-nineteenth-century ship. It sports a mast with nautical flags and an engine room painted on the garage wall. Their homecoming party in 2009 included an official christening with a bottle of champagne.
9.  Wallace Roberts & Todd, "Action Plan for New Orleans Executive Summary," Bring New Orleans Back Commission, Urban Planning Committee, January 11, 2006.
10. Wallace Roberts & Todd, "Action Plan for New Orleans: The New American City," Bring New Orleans Back Commission, Urban Planning Committee, January 11, 2006.
11. Frank Donze and Gordon Russell, "4 Months to Decide," *Times-Picayune* (New Orleans), January 11, 2006.
12. Gary Rivlin, "Anger Meets New Orleans Renewal Plan," *New York Times*, January 12, 2006.
13. Ibid.
14. Adam Nossiter, "In New Orleans, Money Is Ready but a Plan Isn't," *New York Times*, June 18, 2006.

## CHAPTER 5: VILLAGE DE L'EST: "BACK ON THE MAP"

1.  Martha Carr, "Rebuilding Should Begin on Higher Ground, Group Says," *Times-Picayune* (New Orleans).
2.  *A Village Called Versailles*, S. Leo Chiang, dir., Walking Iris Films, 2010.

3.  Andrew Martin, "Katrina's Garbage Rates a Category 5," *Chicago Tribune*, January 4, 2006.
4.  Ibid.

## CHAPTER 6: HOLLYGROVE:
## "TO RE-CREATE A NEIGHBORHOOD"

1.  David Winkler-Schmidt, "Neighborhood Watch: While Politicians Argue Over Who's in Charge of the City's Planning Process, Individuals and Neighborhoods Are Taking Charge of Their Own Fates," *Gambit* (New Orleans), June 27, 2006.
2.  Ibid.
3.  Alan Gutierrez, "The Professionals Are Coming," Alan Gutierrez blog, May 26, 2006, http://blogometer.com/ (accessed October 14, 2011).

## CHAPTER 7: LAKEVIEW: "DON'T GET IN OUR WAY"

1.  Manuel Roig-Franzia, "Backlash on Storm Recovery Plan, New Orleans Panel Supports 4-Month Building Moratorium," *Washington Post*, January 12, 2006.
2.  Leslie Eaton, "Louisiana Sets Deadline for Storm Damage Claims," *New York Times*, May 31, 2007.

## CHAPTER 9: THE LOWER NINTH WARD:
## "ALWAYS A QUESTION, AND THEN A DEAD SILENCE"

1.  Michael Luo and Sewell Chan, "Water Lifts Its Awful Veil on Landscape of Destruction," *New York Times*, September 16, 2005.
2.  "Trouble and Desire: Rebuilding the Ninth Ward," *Talk of the Nation*, National Public Radio, October 4, 2005, npr.org.
3.  Gary Rivlin, "A Mogul Who Would Rebuild New Orleans," *New York Times*, September 29, 2005.
4.  Ibid.
5.  Dan Sadowsky, "It Takes a Neighborhood," *Mercy Corps*, February 18, 2006, http://www.mercycorps.org/ (accessed October 1, 2011).

## CHAPTER 10: NEIGHBORHOODS AND CITYWIDE PLANNING:
## "PROMISES ARE MADE, AND THEY ARE NOT KEPT"

1.  Sally Saulny, "New Orleans Sets a Way to Plan Its Rebuilding," *New York Times*, July 6, 2006.
2.  "Not Ready for Prime Time: An Analysis of the UNOP Citywide Plan," Bureau of Governmental Research, New Orleans, 2007, www.bgr.org/.
3.  Ibid.
4.  Ibid.

5. Adam Nossiter, "Big Plans Are Slow to Bear Fruit in New Orleans," *New York Times*, April 1, 2008.

6. Ibid.

7. Ibid. Also, Adam Nossiter, "New Orleans Prepares to Invest in 17 Areas," *New York Times*, March 30, 2007.

8. Nossiter, "Big Plans Are Slow to Bear Fruit in New Orleans."

## CHAPTER 12: VILLAGE DE L'EST:
## "EVERYBODY'S CONNECTED"

1. John E. Salvaggio, "The Beginnings of Charity Hospital," Medical Center of Louisiana at New Orleans website, from Salvaggio, *New Orleans' Charity Hospital: A Story of Physicians, Politics, and Poverty* (Baton Rouge: Louisiana State University Press, 1992), http://www.mclno.org/.

2. Karen DeSalvo, "Delivering High-Quality, Accessible Health Care: The Rise of Community Centers," in Amy Liu et al., eds., *Resilience and Opportunity: Lessons from the U.S. Gulf Coast after Katrina and Rita* (Washington, DC: Brookings Institution Press, 2011), 47.

## CHAPTER 14: LAKEVIEW:
## "A WHOLE DIFFERENT BALLGAME"

1. Glenn Stoudt, "Letter from LCIA President," *Lakeviews* 23, no. 1 (January/February 2011), http://www.lakeviewcivic.org/.

2. Katy Reckdahl, "Lessons in Renewal," *Times-Picayune* (New Orleans), July 6, 2007. Gary Rivlin, "A Mogul Who Would Rebuild New Orleans," *New York Times*, September 29, 2005.

3. Michelle Krupa and Frank Donze, "Blight-Blaster Rita Legrand Nominated for Seat on Neighborhood Conservation District Committee," *Times-Picayune* (New Orleans), August 6, 2011.

## CHAPTER 15: THE LOWER NINTH WARD:
## "I FEEL SO GOOD WHEN I'M HOME"

1. Ariane Wiltse, "Pam Dashiell: 'You Have to Do Right and Live Right to Get Right and Be Right,'" Help Holy Cross, December 4, 2009, http://www.helpholycross.org/ (accessed September 16, 2011).

2. Douglas Brinkley, "Brad Pitt Talks About Hurricane Katrina, His Make It Right Work and His Love for New Orleans," *Times-Picayune* (New Orleans), August 25, 2010.

3. Wiltse, "Pam Dashiell."

4. The band Truckstop Honeymoon describes its origins as follows: "Katie learned whore-house piano and bucket bass in the streets of the French Quarter. There she met Mike, a banjo-slinging grifter who sold CDs he claimed cured hangovers and small-mindedness. After a courthouse wed-

ding, the pair hit the road. They spent their wedding night in a truck stop somewhere between Lafayette and the Atchafalya Swamp. And so Truck-stop Honeymoon was born." In Katie Euliss and Mike West, "Bio," 2011, http://www.truckstophoneymoon.com/ (accessed August 23, 2011).

5. Katie Euliss and Mike West, "Georgia and Blue," *Great Big Family*, comps. Katie Euliss and Mike West, 2008.

## CHAPTER 16: LAURELS

1. David Smylin, "Broadmoor's Next Battle," *New Orleans Levee*, August 2008, http://www.nolevee.com/ (accessed August 17, 2011).

## EPILOGUE

1. Wiltse, "Pam Dashiell."

2. Obama's address, while identical in form to a State of the Union, was tech-nically not a State of the Union. George W. Bush would have been able to make an official State of the Union address in January before his term ex-pired, but like Ronald Reagan, George H. W. Bush, and Bill Clinton before him, he opted not to make such a speech. Bobby Jindal, "The Republican Response by Gov. Bobby Jindal," *New York Times*, February 24, 2009, http://www.nytimes.com/ (accessed September 17, 2011).

3. Wiltse, "Pam Dashiell."